THEY DARE TO WIN!

In a world torn by strife, they battle for the hearts and minds of millions.

"Tree jumping" into embattled jungles, rescuing hostages from a plane in a Middle East desert, infiltrating Northern Ireland under outrageous disguise, the men of England's Special Air Service Regiment are portrayed here, for the first time, in vivid detail.

As a unit, they make up one of the globe's crack fighting forces. As individuals, they blaze records of unbelievable daring.

THE WORLD
IS THEIR BATTLEGROUND

D0012288

INSIDE THE SAS

Tony Geraghty

BALLANTINE BOOKS • NEW YORK

First published in Great Britain in 1980 by Arms and Armour Press, Lionel Leventhal Limited

ISBN 0-345-29749-0

This edition published by arrangement with
Arms and Armour Press

Manufactured in the United States of America

First Ballantine Books Edition: March 1982

Photos courtesy of SAS Regiment

Acknowledgments
Thanks are due to the many friends, including some companions in sport parachuting, who gave unstintingly of their time and energy in helping the writing of this book. In large measure, it is their sweat that I have "recycled."

I must also thank all those mentioned in the Bibliography, but I am especially grateful to the following authors and their publishers for permission to quote brief passages: *The Regiments Depart: The British Army, 1945-70*, by G. Blaxland, and *The Special Air Service*, by P. Warner (both published by William Kimber Ltd.); *Bunch of Five*, by F. Kitson, and *Last Post: Aden 1964-67*, by J. Paget (both published by Faber & Faber Ltd.); *The Hilton Assignment*, by P. Seale and M. McConville (published by Maurice Temple Smith Ltd.); *Oman: The Making of the Modern State*, by J. Townsend (published by Croom Helm Ltd.); and *Congo Mercenary*, by M. Hoare (published by Robert Hale Ltd.).

Tony Geraghty, 1980

Contents

List of Maps

Introduction

I N HIS TEXTBOOK ON GUERRILLA WARFARE,
The War of the Flea, Robert Taber observes that if there
is anything new about such warfare, it is only in its modern
political application. He continues: "The guerrilla is a political insurgent, the conscious agent of revolution: his military rôle, while vital, is only incidental to his political
mission . . . the overthrow of the government and the destruction of the existing . . . system." There are echoes
here of Clausewitz's dictum that war is the continuation of
"political intercourse" by other means. Of course, all armies are political and some are more political than others,
but the traditional view, as Clausewitz himself expressed
it, is that "the political element does not sink deep into
the details of war. Sentries are not planted, patrols do not
make their rounds from political considerations . . ." One
of the characteristics of the Special Air Service Regiment
which makes it a unique military force is that it does just
that. Like the guerrilla army, the modern SAS uses force
sparingly, as a precise cutting tool for political policy, and
then only as one weapon among many in the essential
business of shaping perceptions: the enemy's and that of
the civil population.

The effect of its success in post-war years (see the campaigns of Borneo and Oman) carries with it the danger
that it may reinforce the belief of ambitious politicians in
a favorite fantasy concerning military matters, namely
that armed conflict can be fine-tuned. Not surprisingly,
therefore, the SAS is sometimes hoist by its own success
and is pitchforked into a campaign for which it is ill-

1

prepared, such as Northern Ireland, or one which, politically, is already a lost cause, such as Aden. On such occasions, the lament may be sometimes aired in the regimental journal that this or that operation is not in keeping with the SAS rôle. Precisely what that rôle is, is also a subject of continuous speculation and controversy among commentators outside military circles, some of them highly partisan, as well as within the Bradbury Lines barracks and the Special Forces Club. The external critique ranges from the hagiographic style of 1950s Fleet Street journalism to the naïve dogmatism of the post-1960s New Left. Each of these extreme views overlooks—or is ignorant of—a second peculiarity of the Regiment: its ability to evolve to meet a given task, even if this means discarding centuries of military tradition.

The romantic beginnings of the SAS during the Second World War have naturally caught the imagination of most writers, with the result that all except the participants tend to overlook the fact that the Regiment was founded on a military heresy. The heresy lies in the deliberate rejection by Colonel David Stirling, whose pencil-written proposal from a hospital bed in Cairo started it all, of the traditional concept of military leadership. In his contribution to *The World History of Paratroopers* several years ago, he explained:

"Strategic operations demand, for the achievement of success, a total exploitation of surprise and of guile. Accordingly, a bedrock principle of the Regiment was its organization into modules or sub-units of four men. Hitherto, battalion strength formations, whether Airborne formations or Commandos, had no basic sub-unit smaller than a section or a troop consisting of an NCO plus eight or ten men and it was the NCO who had to do most of the thinking for what we disrespectfully referred to as 'the thundering herd' behind him.

"In the SAS each of the four men was trained to a high general level of proficiency in the whole range of the SAS capability and, additionally, each man was trained to have at least one special expertise according to his aptitude. In carrying out an operation—often in pitch-dark—each SAS man in each module was exercising his own individual perception and judgement at full stretch."

The number four, as Stirling has explained to the au-

thor, was deliberately chosen to avoid the emergence of a
leader in the orthodox sense. The implications of this decision have affected regimental thinking ever since. Officers
joining the SAS do so only after they have faced a barrage
of withering criticism from Other Ranks, and restructured
their own thinking about the men with whom they will
soldier. The obvious danger, that discipline within the unit
will break down, has not only been recognized: it was experienced in some terrifying episodes during the Malayan
campaign. But before and after that time, the ruthless selection of soldiers who motivate and, therefore, discipline
themselves, has virtually eliminated this risk. A further result has been to foster a unique military democracy within
the SAS in which, if he succeeds, a man exchanges his
former class and even identity for membership of a caste
as binding as any family, and expulsion from which,
therefore, becomes the only sanction he really fears.

In the paper cited above, Stirling described the Regiment's philosophy in the following way: "From the start,
the SAS Regiment has had some firmly held tenets from
which we never depart. They can be summarized as follows:

1. The unrelenting pursuit of excellence.
2. The maintaining of the highest standards of discipline
   in all aspects of the daily life of the SAS soldier . . .
   We always reckoned that a high standard of self-
   discipline in each soldier was the only effective foundation for Regimental disciplne. . . .
3. The SAS brooks no sense of class and, particularly,
   not among the wives. This might sound a bit porten-
   tous but it epitomizes the SAS philosophy.

"The traditional idea of a crack regiment was one of-
ficered by the aristocracy and, indeed, these regiments de-
servedly won great renown. . . . In the SAS we share
with the Brigade of Guards a deep respect for quality but
we have an entirely different outlook.

"We believe, as did the ancient Greeks who originated
the word 'aristocracy,' that every man with the right attitude and talents, regardless of birth and riches, has a capacity in his own lifetime of reaching that status in its true
sense; in fact, in our SAS context, an individual soldier
might prefer to go on serving as an NCO rather than . . .
leave the regiment in order to obtain an officer's commis-

sion. All ranks in the SAS are of 'one company' in which a sense of class is both alien and ludicrous."

The four-man group has another, intensely domestic, side effect. This is that two couples emerge, sharing their lives for months on end in conditions of isolation. The bond thus created is the kinship of the family. Stokes and Lane, who climbed Everest, survived a night near the summit, and massaged each other in order to survive, despite snow blindness and frostbite, were once asked if they talked much while they climbed together. "Not much," was the reply. "After all this time together we don't have much to say to each other." The same rapport translates into military action. During one furious firefight in Oman, which began, uncharacteristically, with the SAS having fallen victim to enemy ambush, a veteran of the regiment continued the domestic quarrel with which the two had started the day. He paused between bursts of gunfire to tell his companion: "Furthermore, you burnt the bloody dinner last night!"

Out of these peculiar elements—anarchy (in the dictionary sense of "a harmonious condition of society in which law is abolished as unnecessary"); élitism; meritocracy; insularity—has emerged a very special force indeed: a warrior caste borne into a century which regards military virtues as, at best, an anachronism. The caste has succeeded largely because of the use of its skill with non-violent weapons, in preference to, say, indiscriminate bombing by B-52s.

But of course, no one can live up to such standards consistently for a lifetime. Few even achieve them for long, which is why the number of operational SAS soldiers is very small. Another potent reason is the sheer danger of SAS undertakings, in which the intelligent man perceives the imminence of his own expendability. As one regimental veteran explained to the author, "The reason why few of our people become mercenaries is that after regular operations with the SAS, they've usually had enough to last a lifetime."

David Stirling, the man who started it all, was a Cambridge-educated Scots Guardsman who joined one of the first Army Commando units in 1940, having been sent down from university. Stirling, 6 feet 5 inches tall and an enthusiastic climber who had explored the Rockies, was ideal Commando material. He joined a unit later known as Layforce, after the name of its leader, Robert Laycock. Layforce was sent to the Middle East with the object of capturing Rhodes; instead, because of conflicting operational demands, it was scattered from Tobruk in Libya, to Syria. One of Stirling's brother officers in this organization was an Oxford graduate and rowing blue, Jock Lewes, of the Welsh Guards. Faced with the disbandment of Layforce, because of its need of ships and equipment which were simply not available, the two men mulled over other ways of hitting Germany's extended supply lines in the Western Desert.

In somewhat enigmatic circumstances, a consignment of 50 parachutes on its way to India fell off the back of a movement order in Alexandria, into the hands of Lewes. Soon afterwards Lewes, Stirling and two others—none of them a trained parachutist—rigged up their own static line system in an ancient Valentia aircraft, using seats in the plane as strong points. The design of the aircraft was such that as the parachute canopies deployed, some of them would certainly snag the tailplane. This is what happened to Stirling. The accident tore several gores out of the canopy and his sixteen-stone weight increased the acceleration of his descent. He crashed on to rock hard ground and injured his back so severely that both legs were paralysed for a time.

While he was in hospital, Stirling drafted a long memorandum, laboriously written in pencil, wherein he argued that strategic raids—that is, deep penetration operations behind enemy lines—did not require the ponderous naval back-up of full-blown Commando assaults. He did not dwell on the obvious alternative, penetration across the desert, because this was already being carried out with great skill, for reconnaissance and Intelligence purposes, by the Long Range Desert Group. Instead, Stirling proposed using parachutist saboteurs to inflict a level of damage on enemy airfields equivalent to that of a Commando force twenty times greater.

After two months' medical treatment, Stirling was able to move about on crutches. He decided, notwithstanding this disability, to deliver his plan in person to the Commander-in-Chief, Middle East, General Sir Claude Auchinlek. It was highly improbable that the C-in-C would grant audience to a mere subaltern; even less likely that the plan would work its way through the out-trays of the courtiers at GHQ Cairo, so Stirling decided to make an unannounced visit.

A high wire fence surrounded the headquarters area. Leaving his crutches on the outside of the fence, Stirling hauled himself painfully over, and dropped into the compound. He then walked gingerly into the main administrative block, bumping into various offices and their occupants, before discovering that Auchinlek was out. By now, the internal security staff had been alerted to his presence. Stirling found the deputy C-in-C, Lieutenant-General Neil Ritchie, just before they found him. He lurched into Ritchie's office, saluted the surprised general and said quietly: "I think you'd better look at this, sir." Ritchie scanned the paper and subsequently recalled Stirling for a discussion of the scheme with Auchinlek. Soon afterwards, in his new rank of captain, Stirling was given permission to recruit 66 men from the remnants of Layforce Commando.

One of those who ran into Stirling during those early days in Cairo was the brave, debonair Fitzroy Maclean, later to become a brigadier and an MP. As Maclean tells it, Stirling propositioned him with a persuasiveness that recurs throughout the Regiment's history. " 'Why not join the Special Air Service Brigade?' he said. I asked what it was. He explained it was not really a Brigade; it was more like a Platoon. It was only called a Brigade to confuse the enemy. But it was a good thing to be in. . . . We could operate in the desert first of all; then in southern and eastern Europe. Small parties could be dropped there by parachute and then picked up on the coast by submarine. There were endless possibilities. It sounded promising. I said I should be delighted to join."

What followed is now familiar military history, and is merely summarized here: the disaster of the first parachute operation, unwisely carried out during a vigorous sandstorm in which aircraft were lost and men swept away; followed by collaboration with the Long Range Desert Group to destroy more than 100 Luftwaffe aircraft on the ground within a few weeks, with a unit now only twenty strong. This led, by August 1942, to a re-expansion of the unit with the addition of French para-

troops and the provision of specially armed jeeps, and
formal regimental status as First SAS Regiment. Before
the Desert War was over, the SAS had destroyed nearly
400 German aircraft and great quantities of other war
material. Their success elicited a personal order from

SAS Raids, September 1942

One of the first SAS operations of the Second World War was a series of
concerted raids on Benghazi, Tobruk and Jalo. The route covered 800 miles
from Kabrit to Kufra Oasis, and another 800 to Benghazi. It was planned by
Middle East HQ against Stirling's advice. There were few survivors.

① Sand Seas
② SAS attack route

© ARMS AND ARMOUR PRESS 1985

Adolf Hitler which proclaimed: "These men are dangerous. They must be hunted down and destroyed at all costs."

Part of the price the Regiment paid for this success was
the capture of Stirling himself near Gabes, in Tunisia. After several attempts to escape, he was put into Colditz
prisoner-of-war camp for the rest of the war. There he
spent his time drafting a paper in which he proposed using British and American special forces to establish bases
in China from which to attack Japan. (After the European war, and before the atomic bomb induced Japanese
surrender, he was actively preparing for this operation in
Britain.)

By the time Stirling was captured, his brother Bill was commanding a second SAS regiment engaged in raids in Sicily and on the Italian coast. First SAS was now commanded by the former Irish rugby international, "Paddy" Mayne, one of David Stirling's original desert team, who joined forces with an Army and Royal Marine Commando force to seize the Adriatic port of Termoli in October 1943. The impact of this operation, at a time when the German Army was holding Rome and looking south, was to switch an entire enemy division away from its chosen operational area. Philip Warner, the official SAS historian, records: "Mayne was observed to have conducted a minor war single-handed. He was observed to have killed twelve Germans early in the fighting and then, when a truck-load of men—29 in all—had been killed by a German shell he went off on an expedition of his own. He gave no account of what had occurred, but it was thought that he had exacted some adequate revenge for the incident."

Another adventurous spirit was Philip Pinckney, whose capacity for converting to instant food anything which crawled, hopped, walked and grew, made him an object of speculation even in the SAS. After taking part in the Sicily operation he was parachuted on to the Brenner Pass, the railway tunnel of which he blew up. After being captured he was handed over to the Gestapo and executed.

In addition to the activity in Sicily—where the regiment prepared the way for the Allied invasion—and mainland Italy, its related Special Boat Service was engaging in intensive raiding activity throughout the Aegean, Greece and the Adriatic. Those who distinguished themselves included Anders Lassen, the Danish SAS major who won a posthumous VC while in support of a Royal Marine Commando attack on Lake Comacchio a month before the war in Europe ended. From Italy, the two regular SAS regiments were brought back to England in March 1944 and augmented by similar Free French and Belgian squadrons, plus a long-distance communications unit, the combined force becoming 1 SAS Brigade.

In Europe, the SAS resisted attempts by orthodox military planners to use them for short-term, pinprick raids, and it was agreed that they should parachute into occupied France and remain there as training and supply units for the Resistance, and to conduct a sabotage campaign on their own account. Colonel Brian Franks, one of the commanders, explained that "small reconnaissance party with wireless was dropped by parachute first—sometimes 'blind', sometimes with the aid of flares and torches provided by the French Resistance.

"If the report of the advance party was satisfactory, it was quickly reinforced first numerically and later, if the terrain suited, armored jeeps were dropped. . . . The bases were resupplied most efficiently by the RAF." (Soon after D-day there were 43 such bases spread across France from Brittany to the Vosges.)

"With the bases established, small parties, generally on Stirling's module of four, were dispatched to harass enemy communications in every way open to them. Roads were mined, railway lines blown up and convoys of soft transport were ambushed. Bombing targets were reported to the RAF.

"All SAS troops engaged in France were briefed to arm and train any formed bodies of the French Resistance. In certain areas this was carried out with success, but in others it was found impossible to train them. . . . This applied, too, to the population of many small villages close to SAS bases. The enemy reacted with utter ruthlessness, deporting or shooting the males and burning houses. This unpleasant factor had to be taken into account when planning operations."

It was not until after the war that the unpleasant fate of SAS prisoners-of-war became fully apparent. Between August and October of 1944, a total of 26 of the Regiment were taken prisoner in the Vosges mountains and were last heard of alive in a prison camp about fifty miles from Strasbourg. They were not there when the camp was taken by Allied forces. With the end of the war, in May of the following year, a team of British army investigators made efforts to discover what had happened to them. The team concluded that "the evidence of torture before death by shooting is conclusive concerning nine of them, and points to most of the others having been treated with the same brutality. . . . One man found dead had been beaten by the Germans until the bones of his back showed. Another was found hanging over a bonfire, and had been burned to death."

The military impact of the SAS in France was, if anything, even more formidable than it had been in the Western Desert and Italy. One considered judgement is that the disorganization of German resistance in depth after General Patton's break out of Normandy, and the swift seizure of Paris by the Third Army which followed this, was largely attributable to the combined work of the SAS and the French Maquisards.

The direct SAS assaults were damaging enough in themselves—for example, in the destruction of a train carrying 100,000 gallons of petrol—but it seems plausible to conclude that the pin-pointing of targets on behalf of the RAF bomber force was strategically decisive. As one study of the Normandy invasion recalls, during the months before the landings, "the strategic bomber forces imperceptibly shifted their attacks from targets deep in occupied Europe to objectives related more closely to the landings. Their intent was to isolate the 'Overlord' (invasion plan) lodgement area and to make it difficult, if not impossible, for the Germans to send reinforcements to the landing area; to this end, they destroyed bridges across the Seine, railway yards and other transportation facilities. They also struck coastal defences and other important installations useful to the Germans." The SAS operated mainly in Central France, concentrating on the transport system, with similar effect.

On 8 September 1944, General F. A. M. Browning, ADC to Montgomery, told the Regiment: "The operations you have carried out have had more effect in hastening the disintegration of the German Seventh and Fifth Armies than any other single effort in the army. . . . You have done a job of work which . . . no other troops in the world could have done."

In the Low Countries, Germany and Italy, the SAS regiments were in action until the end of the European war. Mayne won a third bar to his DSO in Schleswig-Holstein only weeks before hostilities ended; returned home to his law practice in Northern Ireland and died in a motor accident in 1955. After a brief operation in Norway to disarm thousands of Wehrmacht soldiers, the wartime regiments were disbanded in October 1945.

This book is concerned with the post-war SAS Regiment, from its inauspicious beginnings in Malaya until the present day. If there is a consistent theme here, it is that the Regiment is a success, though the reader will reach his own judgement about that. The measurement of success in such a context is largely a matter of educated guesswork, rendered difficult by the increasing secrecy surrounding SAS operations during the last fifteen years or so; ameliorated somewhat by the Regiment's characteristic self-criticism.

Some of the achievements are so obvious as to seem trite. First, the Regiment has survived as a permanent corps of the British Army, and the smallest. It is the only one of its kind to have done so. The rest—the Long Range Desert Group, Popski's Private Army, the Army Commando—were all consigned to the history books long ago. Second, it has evolved as a uniquely effective arm of counter-revolutionary warfare in an increasingly sensitive political climate, internationally and domestically. In an age when great powers avoid direct conflict, preferring to fight their wars by proxy in "low intensity" campaigns, it has exercised its strategic option in a new way by choosing as its battleground the British equivalent of Vietnam —in Malaya, Borneo and Oman—but with a vastly different outcome, proving that one dedicated soldier can achieve results beyond the reach of squadrons of B-52 bombers. In doing so, it has suffered minimal casualties and inflicted on its enemies only sufficient damage to achieve a given result.

Its successes have also profoundly influenced the evolution of post-war British strategy. The pioneering use of the SAS for a few critical months in an obscure campaign in Northern Oman in 1958/59 arrested the idea that nuclear weapons were the answer to all Britain's defense problems, and almost certainly inspired the strategically mobile "fire brigades" which would influence defense policy for ten years. The full importance of SAS intervention in the Omani Dhofar war in 1970 did not become apparent to the outside world until the Soviet invasion of Afghanistan in 1979.

With the encouragement of successive British governments the Regiment has also perpetuated the rule of undemocratic régimes in various parts of the world, a fact which makes it a natural target for vilification by the political Left in Britain. But then, the Left demonstrates great selectiveness in the exercise of its moral conscience: vigorous criticism, for example, of the British in Aden, followed by silence concerning the imposition on that country of a Marxist military dictatorship after the British had departed.

Interestingly, there seem to be no cases in which the Regiment's highly articulate and intelligent critics have been able to prove that the SAS soldier takes life wantonly. The smears tend to be general in nature, and probably are no more unhelpful to the Regiment than the uncritical praise occasionally handed out by right-wingers. If there are numerous war crimes in the SAS cupboard, no doubt some of them will come to light in the fullness of time, though casual brutality is entirely contrary to the Regiment's post-war tradition of winning friends and influencing people. A description of what happened when British mercenaries went to Angola, published in this work and others, is an interesting counterpoint to SAS techniques, and a gruesome illustration of how not to win a war.

Certainly, this author has revealed what he knows about the SAS, with the deliberate exclusion of some data concerning the SAS rôle in counter-terrorist campaigns in Britain (where it provides an anti-terrorist unit on three-minute standby) and elsewhere. Some light on these matters has been shed by the participation of Major Alastair Morrison and Sergeant Barry Davies in the rescue of 87 West German hostages from a hijacked airliner at Mogadishu in 1977. They were more than advisers: they led the assault team, to blind and deafen the terrorists with a "percussion" grenade devised by the SAS. Morrison was not permitted to receive a German decoration, but he was awarded the OBE. It is also known that in 1972, when it was thought that a saboteur's bomb had been planted aboard the liner *Queen Elizabeth II,* the team that parachuted to join her in mid-Atlantic included an SAS soldier; and that on occasions when aircraft hijackings have taken place in Britain, the assistance of the Regiment has been enlisted, as it was by the Metropolitan Police during the IRA siege at Balcombe Street, London, in 1975.

In May 1980, the secretly formed SAS siege-breaking, anti-terrorist Counter Revolutionary Warfare Team went into action in Britain for the first time, in an operation which was as fragile politically as it was difficult in military terms. Seven years' thought, analysis and rehearsal were tested in eleven scorching minutes at the Iranian Embassy in London. A festering international crisis was resolved, and the SAS, after being political pariahs for years, became heroes overnight.

In this context, it is interesting to note that as recently as 1969 the Defence Ministry's *Land Operations Manual,* in its discussion of counter-revolutionary warfare, still placed the SAS firmly in a colonial and probably rural environment. It remarked: "SAS squadrons are particularly suited, trained and equipped for counter-revolutionary operations. Small parties may be infiltrated or dropped by parachute, including free fall, to avoid a long approach through enemy-dominated areas, in order to carry out any of the following tasks:

a. The collection of information on the location and movement of insurgent forces.
b. The ambush and harassment of insurgents.
c. Infiltration of sabotage, assassination and demolition parties into insurgent held areas.
d. Border surveillance.
e. Limited community relations.
f. Liaison with, and organization, training and control of friendly guerrilla forces operating against the common enemy."

While the manual also acknowledges the value of the SAS as a collector of military Intelligence, it is not the case, as is popularly believed, that the Regiment is an arm of the Secret Intelligence Service. Informal links exist for a variety of reasons, notably the training which SIS men sometimes require from their military friends. But most SAS men, for whom the comradeship of the four-man patrol or sixteen-man troop is one of the fundamental parameters of life itself, are not suited to the silent, lonely, dissembling life of the espionage agent.

There is another sense in which this short history of the SAS is deficient. This is that it does not seek to be an exhaustive and complete account of the SAS campaigns it describes, still less the sometimes enigmatic "team jobs" performed by SAS training missions around the world, which are merely touched upon. There have been actions for which gallantry awards have been made which are not described, and which must await a more definitive work than this for inclusion in the historical record. This history is essentially indicative and, to some extent, impressionistic in its approach. This is perhaps appropriate for a military unit as dynamic and secretive as the SAS. The author's first attempt to describe the Regiment's methods of selection and training encountered from someone in a position to know, the criticism—the more crushing because of the gentleness with which it was expressed—that the chapter was perfectly accurate, but ten years out of date.

To offset such deficiencies, the reader will find that the highlights of SAS history are covered, as well as much that is new and perhaps surprising: the first full account of the remarkable action at Mirbat in 1972; the detailed story of the ill-fated Edwards patrol in Aden; an account of Britain's first operational use of free-fall parachuting, of which there was no public knowledge. The reader may also discover that, despite much mythology, the SAS philosophy does not reflect the motto of the pre-war Spanish Foreign Legion, "Down with intelligence, and long live Death!"

Some of those who participated in the actions concerned may differ, in matters of detail, from the consensus accounts that appear here. The author craves their indulgence, as well as the perspective of military history attributed to the Duke of Wellington: "You might as well try to write the history of a ball as of a battle."

It is interesting to speculate about the future of such a unique instrument of government policy. Conspiracy theorists, who foresee in its counter-revolutionary rôle the sharp end of a military takeover in Britain, will be disappointed. SAS men are simply not interested in political power in that sense: rather, they are profoundly conservative with a small "c", like most British soldiers. But, more than most, they have come to appreciate the political content of military activity in an age in which a single newspaper article, television program, or (as in the Blunt affair, a single book) can overturn government policy.

The lessons of Regimental history in post-war years are that, first, the SAS hates military idleness and that if there is a conflict in which it can be legitimately involved, it will not wait to be asked, but volunteer its services and adapt its techniques to meet the case. Second, the Regiment retains—most consistently through its Territorial volunteer arms—a rôle within NATO. That rôle is still the one originally envisaged by Stirling: the offensive strategic raid in which tiny groups of men live without resupply or the usual logistical support expected by orthodox troops, while creating havoc far behind enemy lines. For many years, the West's reliance upon American nuclear superiority to offset the greater number of Warsaw Pact conventional forces tended to reduce the credibility of such a force. That situation has been profoundly changed during the last five years or so, as a result of the achievement by Soviet Russia of nuclear parity with the West. Consequently, the West has now had to rethink much of its strategy where Continental Europe, Scandinavia and the Mediterranean are concerned. The emphasis is more upon conventional warfare and, where nuclear weapons are concerned, to scale down the level of conflict through the use of more precise missiles with diminished explosive power. Implicit in the new doctrine is a belief in a limited nuclear war, a concept which, in the absence of experience, must be an act of faith.

Many things are unclear about the future shape of a European conflict, but what is abundantly plain is that the smaller the military group, the better its chances of survival as a cohesive unit in an environment where both sides possess a range of firepower of all kinds, conventional as well as nuclear, on a scale unique in human history. The SAS's four-man module is the smallest organic fighting unit since prehistoric times. Its ability to call down artillery, missile and air strikes is now potentially greater than ever before. Thus, military technology as well as strategy is moving its way. But the speed at which that technology is evolving—for example through the use of lasers, communication satellites, the microchip—means that even the SAS will have to work hard to keep up with it. The problem is one affecting all armies. The SAS, through its readiness to experiment and adapt, and its reliance on the judgment and intelligence of the individual, has a better chance than most of coming to terms with high technology. In that sense, it is the shape of things to come.

I

Malaya, 1950-59:
The Inauspicious Beginning

L IKE DON JOHN OF AUSTRIA, THE VISION-
ary leader of the last crusade against the Saracens,
the post-war Special Air Service was "risen from a doubtful seat and half-attained stall." The Regiment had been
disbanded at the end of the Second World War, together
with the Army Commando, Popski's Private Army and
other esoteric "mobs for jobs." And, when a special jungle force was raised for the long counter-terrorist campaign in Malaya, it owed more to the experience of
Wingate than to Stirling. It was through a series of accidents that it became the SAS.

During much of the Malayan campaign the new unit's
structure, style, and discipline were very different from,
and inferior to, the ultra-professional force into which
it subsequently evolved. Hard drinking, indiscipline, the
"fragging" of officers, as well as some good soldiering, all
characterized those early days and it would be a long
time before the Regiment would live down the reputation
it had acquired. (The uninitiated should know that the
word "fragging" is derived from "fragmentation grenade,"
originally the US M26 sometimes used by American conscripts against their own officers in Vietnam.) But even in
retrospect, it is surprising that the Regiment got off to
quite such a bad start, combining as it did some of the
best that British Special Forces had created during the
Second World War. That this did happen was due to the
speed and ferocity at which the Malayan Emergency built
up, leaving insufficient time for selection and training, and

the fact that the war was for the hearts and minds of people, rather than for territory. Such a war, at that time, was not one for which the wartime SAS had equipped itself.

No one who knew Malaya was surprised that it contained Communists. A small Communist Party had existed in that prosperous land since the 1930s. What caused the damage was the arming of Communist guerrillas during the war against the Japanese, without thought for the possibility that these guns might be turned on the British after the war. That this had not been foreseen is neatly shown by the presentation to the Communist guerrilla supremo, Chin Peng, of an OBE in the Victory Honours, and his participation in celebrations in London after the war. The justification for arming Peng and his underground army was that until the atom bomb was used against Japan, the Far East campaign offered no short-cut to victory. To assist the guerrillas in Malaya and elsewhere, the Special Operations Executive (SOE) sent a number of adventurous spirits into the jungle, some of whom had aided the partisans of Greece and Albania. One of these was the Regimental Adjutant of the SAS, Major C. E. (Dare) Newell, OBE.

Newell and his comrades were part of a cryptically-named organization called Force 136. In January 1945, he parachuted into Johor Baharu to meet with two British members of the Underground who had remained after the fall of Singapore. When, a few months later, Japan surrendered, the Japanese commander in Malaya, General Itagaki, did not believe it. Newell and his friends were ordered to remain in hiding until a member of the Tokyo Royal Family was brought to Singapore to persuade Itagaki that the war really had ended. By now, there were at least 4,000 British and captured Japanese weapons in the hands of the guerrillas. If there was a moment when the Communists could have seized power in Malaya, this was it. The iron grip of the Japanese had been broken and the British had not yet returned in force. But the chance passed and the war ended with two gains for Chin Peng, in addition to his OBE. One was recognition of the Malayan Communist Party—withdrawn after the Emergency and whose restoration was to be a sticking point in negotiations to end the campaign against the British—and the other, a large part of the abandoned Japanese arsenal in the area.

In 1948, at a time when the gains of Mao's Communism confirmed in the minds of Chinese elsewhere their innate superiority over other races, a Communist convention was held in Calcutta. The British had left India and Burma, and had started to rule Malaya at one remove through a new Federation. The Calcutta conference seems to have inspired the Malayan Communists—most of them members of the Chinese community—with the belief that if Mao could defeat the superior Western-backed Nationalist Chinese Army in a protracted guerrilla war, they could follow his example in the jungles of Malaya itself. There were also internal stresses in the Communist movement in Malaysia following the defection of its secretary-general, which made it necessary to reunify the movement through an anti-colonial offensive.

Soon afterwards, 1,200 wartime guerrillas returned to the jungle in ten "regiments," only one of which was not exclusively Chinese. Long-hidden caches of weapons were dug up, degreased and prepared for the new offensive, and a clandestine support group among non-combatant Chinese, known as the Min Yuen, came into being to supply food, money and information. Between April and June 1948, the offensive began. Following the advice of a long-dead Chinese soldier, Sun-Zu, "Kill one, frighten a thousand," foremen and other key figures in rubber plantations on the west coast were publicly executed by groups of armed Chinese, who lectured the horrified spectators about their war against imperialism before melting back into the jungle.

At breakfast time on 16 June, it was the turn of Europeans to become ritual victims of the new order. Three young Chinese cycled into Elphil Estate in Perak and shot dead a fifty-year-old British planter, Arthur Walker. A few miles away, Ian Christian and his manager, Mr. J. Alison, were bound to chairs and similarly murdered. Only the day before, Christian had called on an old Gurkha friend, Lieutenant-Colonel J. O. Lawes, to borrow a firearm because he sensed imminent danger. Lawes later recalled: "I lent him an old Luger of my father's and said that I would try and bring some recruits out to the Estate pig-shooting the following weekend. . . . We were sitting on a volcano which was to erupt much sooner than expected."

The Emergency—limited in its scope—was declared the same day, and thenceforth the war escalated rapidly from terrorism to jungle battles against regular soldiers of the six Gurkha battalions, many of whose troops were in poor shape. Three shiploads had arrived from India without boots or shirts; they included a large number of untrained recruits, many of whom were found to have tuberculosis.

The security forces now faced a tactical dilemma. Should they merely react to events and strive to protect the towns and plantations, or try to pursue the "bandits" to their bases? Inland Malaya, as they knew from the campaign against the Japanese, was a guerrillas' paradise —mile after mile of slippery bamboo on the mountains, while in the valleys a canopy of trees rising above 200 feet obliterated the sun, reducing daylight to twilight. Below the trees, endless swamp. The first priority had to be defense of the towns, but as a gesture to offensive campaigning, an ad hoc group of veterans from Force 136 and a few volunteers from the regular army battalions was cobbled together in July 1948 into something known as the Ferret Force. Almost simultaneously, the first of 47 Dyak trackers from the Iban tribe—small, lithe tribesmen with high-pitched voices, who killed with blowpipes and removed their victims' heads as trophies—were imported from Borneo.

Ferret Force did not last long, because the services of the civilians and regular officers in it were needed elsewhere, but its exploration of the jungle revealed how great was the need for such a group. During its first offensive operation, in which it led in a battle group of Devons, Seaforths and Inniskillings from Singapore, as well as two Gurkha battalions, it had uncovered twelve permanent guerrilla camps. These were not primitive hides. They included lecture halls and accommodation for up to 200 men, and this only three months after the murder of Arthur Walker.

By March 1950, the Communists—now known as "CTs" (Communist Terrorists)—had exacted an appalling toll on Malaya. A total of 863 civilians, 323 police officers and 154 soldiers had been killed. The CT had also suffered severely (1,138 killed, 645 captured, 359 surrendered), but there was no sign of an end to the war, or even a pause in their campaign.

"WIN THE ABORIGINE"

In Hongkong at this time, a British staff officer who was an acknowledged expert on guerrilla warfare was observing events in Malaya with growing impatience. A hard-drinking, hard-fighting idealist, his name was J. M. ("Mad Mike") Calvert and he was something of a legend. A physically tough character who had won a double blue at Cambridge, he had given up a commission early in the war in order to join a Scots Guards ski battalion destined for Finland. His wartime service included three years in Burma, much of that time behind Japanese lines. Calvert then commanded the SAS brigade in northwest Europe from December 1944 until it was disbanded in November 1945.

One day in 1950, General Sir John Harding, Commander-in-Chief of Far East Land Forces, called Calvert to confer about the explosion of terrorism in Malaya. The two men talked for some time, and Harding then instructed Calvert to produce a detailed analysis of the problem, with options for its solution. During the next six months, Calvert interviewed most of those conducting the campaign, covering 1,500 miles, as he put it, "unescorted along guerrilla-infested roads and only ambushed twice." Much of his time was spent with the infantry patrols trawling through the jungle in a usually profitless hunt for an invisible enemy. This study, Calvert told the author, later formed the basis of a controversial new strategy named the "Briggs Plan" after the Director of Operations, General Sir Harold Briggs, who put it into effect.

To isolate the guerrillas from the rest of the population, Briggs decided that 410 "villages"—many of them shanty towns inhabited by Chinese squatters—should be uprooted and their occupants moved to new, fortified villages. In June 1951, Briggs followed this with an equally ambitious plan to deny food supplies to the guerrillas. Both schemes demanded a uniquely stringent control of people and food, and over the next eight years they finally destroyed the guerrilla movement.

Operations in Malaya, 1950-59

① Kota Tinggi Jungle Warfare School
② Belum Valley parachute drop, February 1952
③ Operation 'Hive', autumn 1952
④ Operation 'Termite', July to November 1954
⑤ Telok Anson swamp operation, February 1958

© ARMS AND ARMOUR PRESS 1980

Another proposal contained in Calvert's study was the creation of a special military force to live in the jungle, denying the "bandits" any sanctuary or rest. Calvert argued that British troops should be able to survive in such an environment for much longer than the seven days then regarded as the maximum for an orthodox infantry patrol. Linked with this was the suggestion that the key to winning the jungle war was the trust of its indigenous aboriginal population. Two months after submitting his report to Harding, Calvert was instructed to create the "special force" he had in mind. He called it the Malayan Scouts (SAS), with the object of converting the Army to the idea of a series of special forces raised locally whenever they were needed, with a geographical identity linked to the SAS.

Calvert now began an intensive drive to organize and recruit the new regiment. His own retrospective view is that, in spite of acknowledged shortcomings, he was creating a foundation on which others could build, and that to be too fastidious in his choice of soldiers at such a time would almost certainly mean that the unit would never be formed. He had presided over the disbandment of the wartime SAS brigade and he was determined not to lose this opportunity to resurrect the concept. Invitations were posted to units throughout the Far East for volunteers to join him and no particular criteria were laid down for selection. Some of those who responded were useful veterans of SOE, SAS, Force 136 and Ferret Force; others were men who were simply bored and whose units were happy to see them go elsewhere. One group consisted of ten deserters from the French Foreign Legion who had escaped by swimming ashore from a troopship conveying them to the war in Indo-China. Calvert, working from the premise that "the best is the enemy of the good," accepted them. The consensus within the Regiment in later years was that this approach was unwise. Another profound difference between Calvert's thinking and the consensus was Calvert's theory that any special force (such as the "Black and Tans") could be disbanded more readily than an established regiment of the line if this became expedient.

There were other pressures on Calvert at this time. Detailed administrative work was necessary at the Regi-

ment's first base in Johor. A two-month training program
had to be started in the same area. Simultaneously, rapid
results were expected from the Regiment's first operational area in Ipoh, hundreds of miles away. Such a task,
combined with the search for more recruits, required the
attention of four senior officers, but Calvert recalls that
for many crucial months he was obliged to run things unaided. Despite the circumstances, however, a surprising
amount was achieved in a short time. (Similar pressures
were felt by the Gurkhas, many of whose new recruits
were committed to the war half-trained.) The first priority, as Calvert saw it, was manpower. In search of this,
he traveled 22,000 miles in 21 days, including a trip to
Rhodesia which led to the creation of C Squadron from
1,000 volunteers in that country. From Hongkong he
brought Chinese interpreters and counter-guerrillas, who
had served with him in Burma, to join his intelligence
staff.

Another source of men was a squadron of SAS Reservists and Territorials (many of whom had served under
Stirling) which had formed up in 1947 as 21 SAS Regiment. The genesis of 21 SAS was a compromise between
those in the War Office who thought there would be a
continuing need after Hitler's defeat for clandestine special forces such as SOE, and those who did not. From the
argument there emerged a Territorial unit commanded by
regular officers, of whom Lieutenant-Colonel B. M. F.
Franks (a "Terrier" before and after the Second World
War) was the first. There is a conflict of recollection
about the circumstances in which this contribution to the
Malayan Scouts, the original B Squadron, was sent to
join Calvert's force. According to the official regimental
history by Philip Warner, the reservists were initially sent
east in order to participate in the Korean War (which
started in June 1950) and, when this scheme was abandoned, the men of 21 SAS were diverted to Malaya; but
Calvert has since told the present author that he had simply asked for a squadron from the reserve and knew
nothing of the Korean plan.

The force that now began to emerge as the modern
SAS comprised three disparate elements: Calvert's original group of 100 volunteers (A Squadron); the Reservists
from Britain (B Squadron); and the Rhodesian C Squad-

ron. Training, as devised by Calvert, was directed at real-
ism combined with domestic familiarity, with live rather
than blank ammunition. To become familiar with grenades, for example, recruits ran between monsoon drains
—narrow, concrete channels four or five feet deep—in
the base area and, on a given order, they would leap for
cover while one man threw the grenades. To learn jungle
stalking, as Warner records, "two men armed with air-
guns and wearing fencing masks would crawl towards the
center of a piece of scrub about 100 yards long. The aim
was to shoot one's opponent before being shot by him."
Rifle practice, using live ammunition on ad hoc ranges
such as the base football pitch, also took place.

Calvert's operational strategy in Ipoh, meanwhile, was
to penetrate deep into the jungle with heavily laden patrols of up to fourteen people, including Chinese liaison
officers and local police as well as the Malayan Scouts,
to establish a firm base equipped with a radio. From this,
smaller groups of three or four men would explore a large
area of jungle so thoroughly that they could set up
ambushes confident in the knowledge that they were covering guerrilla approach routes. Calvert recalls one such
patrol, led by Lieutenant Michael Sinclair Hill, which remained in the jungle for 103 days, a remarkable feat at
the time. When Sinclair Hill received a message from the
RAF asking the SAS not to invoke supportive bombing
missions on Sunday, so as to give aircrew time to rest,
Sinclair Hill responded: "Tell us when it is Sunday."

Other SAS innovations at this time, according to Calvert,
were the creation of primitive clinics from which penicillin
was distributed to cure aborigines of the skin disease,
yaws; river patrols employing inflatable craft supplied by
US special forces; and the first use of helicopters (initially
flown by the Royal Navy) for resupply of troops in the
jungle. Under Calvert, the Regiment also evolved some
startling methods of clandestine warfare. One of these resulted from the discovery that local prostitutes were demanding payment for their services in bullets and grenades,
rather than cash. This "currency" was then passed to the
enemy. Calvert's men were promptly used to pose as
clients in order to supply self-destroying ordnance including hand grenades fitted with instantaneous fuses (to
kill the users) and exploding bullets which, when fired,

served the same purpose. Jungle food stores were booby-trapped and secret dead letter boxes supplied with notes and even government money addressed to Communist organizers, some of whom were then executed by their own side. It is not known how many enemy were killed during this inaugural phase of the post-war SAS. Fatal casualties among Calvert's own men during his command totalled four: a police officer; a Chinese auxiliary; an SAS soldier who was killed while staying with an aboriginal group, and another who died in a jungle fire-fight. Three others were presumed dead after a prolonged silence about their fate. But, Calvert revealed, "they were found again living in a village on the east coast, where they had been having a bit of beano. They had a good excuse. One of them had been wounded."

By the time the first cadres of A Squadron were completing their initial operational tours in the Ipoh jungle, the other two squadrons were beginning their training in the Malayan Scouts base at Johor. The image of those first A Squadron veterans is still a subject of controversy within SAS circles. The disciplined, cohesive group from 21 SAS and the even more orthodox soldiers from Rhodesia were unfavorably impressed, to put it mildly, by what they found. Calvert himself, in an interview with the author, confirms that the London group was "shocked to the core; maybe we went too far."

There are opposing accounts of why this was. A faithful report, thirty years later, can only recount both versions. That of the newcomers was that orthodox discipline was manifestly absent; that there was too much drunkenness, and that the use of firearms in the base area was reckless. Calvert argues that such an impression is misleading and unfair, and reflects the incomprehension about jungle conditions of soldiers whose orientation was European. What the newcomers saw, he asserts, were recruits undergoing hasty battle training in realistic conditions; and the first operational veterans being deliberately encouraged to unwind therapeutically after weeks of hard living in the jungle. If anyone was shocked, Calvert believes that this was because, by the standards of jungle warfare to which he had become accustomed over the years, some of the newly arrived reservist officers were, as he puts it, "a bit soft."

The truth was probably a combination of all these things. The pioneers of A Squadron were a hard, rough bunch, including some men who were totally unsuitable for special forces as well as some who were dedicated, professional soldiers by any standard. They included a senior NCO, formerly a boxing professional and Chindit, who occasionally dispensed justice with his fists in preference to the more orthodox, if bureaucratic, procedure of putting an offender "on orders."

Differences of leadership, selection and training style were resolved through the accident of Calvert's return to England about two years after his initial discussion with Harding. Calvert was invalided home suffering from malaria, dysentry, hookworm and the cumulative stress of twelve years' intensive soldiering. By then, as he later told the author, he was a "very sick man." But, whatever the criticisms, he had the satisfaction of knowing that he had resurrected the SAS.

The unit was taken over in late 1951 by Lieutenant-Colonel John Sloane, an orthodox infantryman who had been second-in-command of the Argyll and Sutherland Highlanders in Korea. He had no special forces background and no jungle experience, but he did know about good order and discipline. By now, as a result of Calvert's intensive recruitment campaign, the SAS had four squadrons in Malaya—A, B, C and D—plus a full headquarters. Sloane persuaded various officers who had thoughts of leaving the SAS—Dare Newell, later to become Regimental Adjutant among them—to stay for a period of reorganization during which the Regiment was withdrawn from the jungle. As a result, old habits were relearned: weapons were kept clean, and basic administrative matters affecting soldiers' welfare were brought up to date. Some, though not all, of the Regiment's "cowboys" were returned to their original units. Ultimately, according to the assessment of one expert, half of those recruited in Malaya would be disposed of in this manner. The remainder were excellent soldiers.

At this time, one of Calvert's best officers, Major John Woodhouse (later to command 22 SAS), prepared to return to England to set up a selection process better suited to the Regiment's needs. A former Dorset Regiment officer, he was not much interested in drill and uniform, but where battle discipline was concerned he hated sloppiness. When a soldier accidentally opened fire with a rifle, Woodhouse removed the weapon and handed the soldier a grenade from which the safety-pin had been removed. "Carry that for a week," he said, "until you've learned how to handle a rifle." If the modern SAS had a founding father, it was he.

Outside the jungle there was important work to be done. Much of this was connected with the controversial strategy of the new Director of Operations, Lieutenant-General Sir Harold Briggs, the planning of which owed much to Calvert. But in the short run, the use of the SAS to assist the Field Police Force at jungle forts and in "jungle edge" patrols meant that Calvert's original concept of deep penetration had been put into cold storage.

RETURN TO THE JUNGLE—BY PARACHUTE

In February 1952, shortly before Woodhouse went to England, where he was to remain for three years, the Regiment returned to the jungle by parachute. The purpose of the operation was food denial. In some areas the guerrillas were already beginning to suffer from the effects of Briggs's policies and had started to grow their own crops. To do this in the jungle, however, they had to fell trees in order to create clearings which would admit sunlight. Such clearings could be spotted from the air and were therefore vulnerable to attack. One of them was at a spot near the Thai border known as Belum Valley. While Gurkhas, Royal Marine Commandos, Malayan police and two squadrons of SAS approached the site on foot, an SAS squadron of 54 men parachuted into a confined drop zone near the area. It was assumed that some men might land in the trees, but it was hoped that their canopies would snag the branches firmly enough to belay the men safely; with this in mind, the planners gave the soldiers 100 feet of rope each and some good advice about tying knots. In fact, there were no parachuting casualties on this occasion and thereafter, "tree jumping" became an SAS specialty. Later experience would demonstrate that serious injury to someone on the drop would occur almost invariably, and the technique was abandoned at the end of the Malayan campaign.

While it lasted, such parachuting produced some good

newspaper copy. *The Straits Times* described an operation that, for most of the men involved, was their first experience of tree-jumping. "They knew that if they landed in bamboo it would splinter, and cut them deeply; rocky or boulder-strewn areas, bomb blasted areas, spiky and weakened trees could smash their necks and bones. Aboard the aircraft, they joked and laughed for a few minutes after take-off. Then there was silence. Some slept, others read; a few glanced out of the windows, fixing their eyes on the jungle. All faces were stern. Ten minutes to go. They checked each other's gear. One man munched an apple; another sucked an orange. A voice said, 'Dropping Zone, two minutes to go.' Then, 'Stand up. Action stations.' A crew member stood near the door, tapping paratroopers on the shoulder, yelling 'Right, right, right,' as each approached him in turn and prepared to jump." Major John Salmon, second-in-command of 22 SAS, explained later: "When you are in the doorway, you're scared. You have to conquer the butterflies. There's no turning back, so when you feel the tap on your shoulder you don't hesitate. Next thing you know, you are floating through the air and it's one of the most wonderful feelings in the world; then you see the trees coming. You are coming down beautifully, steering for the middle of the trees. The hot air makes you swing violently, as if a giant had caught hold of you. You let the air spill out of the 'chute and look for a good, healthy tree. Sometimes you make that spot; often you don't. It's hard to tell until you are a few feet away. When you hit a tree you don't know whether you will stay there or not. Often the branch snaps, you hurtle down, smashing into branches on the way, until you finally come to a halt. If it holds you, then you know you are safe."

The first man out on that operation, acting as "drifter" to discover which way the wind was blowing, was Sergeant Ken Kidd, a veteran of more than 300 descents, but still wary of tree-jumping, nervous of the odds-on chance that he would "find himself dangling in a tree top with his spine or ankle broken." Kidd "spun into a tree and he was lucky. His feet and body smashed into the branches and the chute caught. He was 150 ft above the ground and all he could see through the branches and leaves was the thick undergrowth of the jungle. Above him, the Valletta aircraft kept circling. Now it began the first run in over the dropping zone. Inside the plane the green light flashed again above the door and the first stick of three steel-helmeted paratroopers was ready. Each seemed to half run, taking what looked like a hop, step and jump, and disappeared. The 'chutes opened 750 ft above the ground; 30 seconds later they were engulfed by trees, looking like jellyfish feeling their way into the depths of the sea." On the ground, Kidd grinned with contentment. "You need a lot of luck," he said, "but I would rather jump into trees than fly a plane. It's like anything else: you get used to it after a while." Not everyone was so comfortable. Swinging from the top of one tree was Leon Harris, a 33-year-old Australian who had just completed his first tree-jump. "He shook so much 150 ft above the ground that it took him some time to get a cigarette into his mouth. At the foot of the tree, members of a ground party yelled, 'Come on, Aussie' and Harris, securing his abseil mountaineering pack, called, 'Advance, Australia fair. I made it. Here I come. Sydney or the bush'."

On another, similiar operation, an SAS officer found himself dangling from a tree below which prowled an armed guerrilla. The officer was unable to reach the valise he had carried down, which held his rifles, and could only pray that the guerrilla would not look up. The episode led to a popular demand among some SAS soldiers for a supply of automatic pistols to cover that risk in future.

One of the first parachuting casualties was the man who succeeded John Sloane as Commanding Officer in 1953. Lieutenant-Colonel Oliver Brooke suffered a complicated leg fracture which required months of hospital treatment in England. Like Sloane, Brooke was a good regimental officer with no experience of special forces but, in contrast to the methodical Sloane, Brooke was a rumbustious, extrovert bachelor, quick to lose his temper, equally ready to bury the hatchet. His command of the SAS began eventfully.

In the officers' mess the night before Brooke formally assumed command, he and Newell were standing in a group, drinks in hand, in animated conversation. It was late. A number of NCOs and men from B Squadron who

had celebrated too enthusiastically in the nearest town
were returned to the camp by the Royal Military Police.
At about the same time, some of the sergeants decided to
"frag" the reception going on in honour of the new Commanding Officer. They did so by setting off an explosive
charge which blew down one wall of the mess. The table,
around which Brooke, Sloane and Newell were standing,
took off and landed some distance away. To Newell's surprise, Brooke did not appear to notice what had happened, but continued talking in an even, measured way.
Next morning, having assumed command, Brooke took
the unusual step of holding a disciplinary hearing on a
Sunday, and ordered the return to their units of origin of
a Senior NCO and sixteen other soldiers. They were out
of the Regiment, and out of the camp, before lunch. (Surprisingly, the rejected men were among those who had
formed the original, disciplined cadre from B Squadron,
now diluted by newcomers.) This exemplary reaction had
its effect, and discipline started to improve.

The effect of Briggs's policies for food denial and political isolation was to drive the CT deeper into the jungle.
The security forces were therefore obliged to pursue the
enemy there, which gave the SAS its second chance to
prove its value. Armed with shotguns and the new
Patchett carbine—an early version of the Stirling
submachine-gun—they formed the spearhead of deep
jungle operations in Pahang and Kelantan, entering by
helicopter and parachute. Within the theatre as a whole,
the SAS now constituted one of seven major units from
the UK. There were also seven Gurkha battalions, one
African and one Fijian, as well as eight indigenous Malay
battalions.

While more orthodox units concentrated on harrying
the Johore rebel committee, the SAS was making its first
serious contact with the aboriginal tribes of the interior.
Gregory Blaxland's masterly history of the post-war British Army explains that "The protection of the jungle-
dwelling aborigines of the Seman and Sakai tribes" was the
task. "These scrawny little people had been completely at
the mercy of the rebels and had been forced deeper into
their service as the policy of food denial developed.

"Now the Special Air Service arrived by helicopter in

groups of 15 and began to win over these nomad tribesmen, staying with them 13 weeks before relief.

"They built landing strips to enable them to market their supplies and brought them medical and engineering aid. Villages were turned into fortresses, in which police posts and even artillery were established. Much depended on the few lone persons who stayed to sell them the idea of self-defence. It was all part of the battle for hearts and minds."

Resupply by helicopter, after its introduction in this rôle in 1954, presented peculiar problems. The noise generated by these machines was not conducive to security, so the SAS decided at one stage to try moving its bulk supplies into the jungle by elephant. On paper it looked like a good idea: the beasts were quieter than helicopters and not necessarily out of place in certain types of jungle. However, a thicket of bureaucracy had to be penetrated in order to arrange insurance for the animals. Only when this had been accomplished was it discovered that they would not enter the selected jungle anyway. It is one of the few recorded cases where even the SAS had to admit defeat.

HEARTS, MINDS AND HEAD-HUNTERS

For several months, the phrase "hearts and minds" had reverberated around Malaya. Its author was the new, energetic, Military High Commissioner, General Sir Gerald Templar. Asked in June 1952, whether he had sufficient troops, he had replied, "The answer lies not in pouring more soldiers into the jungle, but rests in the hearts and minds of the Malayan people." In fact, this was an admirable summary of the essence of SAS philosophy at the time, and has been so ever since. As one of the Regiment's planners of the successful Dhofar operation was to put it years later, "It was not our numbers but our ideas which made a big difference." It was also the concept which Calvert had dreamed of when forming the Malayan Scouts.

Such politico-military operations were not so popular with more orthodox troops. For two months during the autumn of 1952, for instance, two battalions of 2/7th Gurkha Rifles, D Company of the 1st Fijian Infantry Regiment and two SAS squadrons were enmeshed in Op-

eration "Hive" around Seremban in Negri Sembilan. The
history of 2/7th summarizes what happened:

"Op 'Hive' was designed to saturate a selected area
with troops so that the terrorists' mode of life would be
completely disrupted. A concentrated programme of police checks on roads and New Villages was planned in detail with the aim of driving the bandits back on to their
jungle food dumps where they would be forced to eat up
valuable reserves. Then the military units would move in
to specific areas where it was hoped, by intensive ambushes and patrols, to force out the terrorists once more
into the open or into the many 'stop' (ambush) positions, established on recorded and likely tracks in the
jungle surrounding Seremban. . . .

"A lot of men were required to close the chinks in the
jungle, many more than were available . . . to search for
about 100 bandits, hiding in an area exceeding 600
square miles. . . . Only 16 of the enemy were killed and
in the opinion of one or two officers, not all this total was
directly attributable to 'Hive' . . . General Sir Gerald
Templar visited the Seremban Operations Room during
'Hive' at a time when he was under considerable pressure from other districts to end the Operation so that
troops could return to their normal duties. He was suitably
impressed by the food denial aspect of the Operation and,
with a typically terse 'Stick to it,' he allowed the Operation to follow its planned course."

The impatience of the troops was understandable. But
what they were learning was that there were no soft targets in the deep jungle. According to one estimate, 1,800
man-hours were expended on patrol for every contact
made with the enemy: the man-hour/kill ratio was even
more daunting. In spite of this, there was competition
among all units for a high body count, the greatest score
being that of 1/10th Gurkhas with 300. The SAS, a late
starter, "scored" 108 during a nine-year period, which
was the sort of return most infantry battalions achieved in
one third of the time. The SAS, however, was learning its
fundamental rôle in life, a dual one of Intelligence gathering and perception shaping. Its real achievements, then
and later, were much harder to quantify, and not dramatic
enough to win medals: it was 1953 before the Regiment
achieved its first Mention in Dispatches, and late in 1957

before the first Military Cross and Military Medal were
awarded to it. What is of more significance, perhaps, is
that between 1951 and 1953, when the SAS started to
penetrate hearts and minds in the jungle, casualties
among the British forces dropped sharply.

From 1953 onwards, the SAS was living more and
more in the jungle during a series of long operations. Simultaneously, it was deeply involved in training Iban
trackers in the fundamentals of modern soldiering. The
head-hunters were now formally recognized as a locally-
raised unit of the British Army, the Sarawak Rangers.
(So, at this stage, was 22 SAS: unlike the Territorial SAS,
it was not yet part of the permanent Order of Battle.) The
Rangers were issued with rifles which they sometimes used
with more enthusiasm than effect.

Typical of the operations from 1954 onward, when the
enemy was becoming concentrated in certain identifiable
areas of wilderness, was Operation "Termite." It lasted
from July to November, and began with heavy bombing
of the jungle by RAF Lincolns—an indiscriminate use of
air power which was as likely to kill aborigines as Communist guerrillas, and one which the SAS regarded as
counter-productive. (The mistake was not subsequently
repeated in Borneo.) Two SAS squadrons, a total of 177
men, then parachuted into jungle clearings created by the
bombs. That clearings had to be made in this way attests
to the number of casualties suffered by the Regiment in its
attempts to perfect "tree-jumping." Even then, the drop
generated four casualties. Such casualties were occurring
not just as a result of the unpredictable behaviour of parachutes as they were "bounced" by the thermal effect of air
above the trees: the technique of abseiling out of the trees
was also proving defective. In theory, the soldier detached
himself from his parachute, lashed a long webbing strap
to a branch, and descended safely to the ground. The
webbing bulged at intervals, where it had been stitched,
and therefore snagged at high speed as it travelled
through D rings on the soldier's harness. As a result, three
men were killed and one seriously injured taking part in
Operation "Sword" in January 1954, one of the deaths
occurring after a soldier in great pain had cut away from
the harness and fallen 150 feet.

In addition to the SAS, four infantry battalions took

part in Operation "Termite." It resulted in the death, capture or surrender of only fifteen rebels, but, as Blaxland records, "the gain was in the conversion of the aborigines to allies."

Between 1955 and 1956, there were critically important changes in SAS organization which at last set the Regiment on a winning course. The formidable John Woodhouse returned to active campaigning as a squadron commander under a new commanding officer, Lieutenant-Colonel (later Lieutenant-General) George Lea. Lea wasted no time in weeding out officers who were not good enough for the SAS, and several were sent back to their original units. He was a large, tough character—6ft 4in tall and weighing 224 pounds—and had no time for the quaint customs of earlier days. (He was horrified, for instance, to learn that a sergeant who had hit the medical officer escaped with a reprimand and an order to shake hands with the officer he had struck.) Lea acquired good officers and promoted the best of those whom he inherited, such as John Cooper, who had started his career with Stirling in the desert. The new intake included Captain Peter de la Billière and Major Harry Thompson, red haired and, like Lea, a big man, from the Royal Highland Fusiliers. Thompson would go on to become second-in-command of the Regiment in Borneo, where he died in a helicopter crash. This team was the core of the Regiment during its three most hectic years in Malaya.

Another decisive change was the replacement of the Rhodesian C Squadron with an equivalent group from New Zealand. The Rhodesians were tough, hard and willing; their leader, Peter Walls, would ultimately command all Rhodesia's armed forces after UDI; but some were also color-conscious to a degree that was not helpful in the task of seducing aboriginal sympathies from the Communists. They were also peculiarly vulnerable to jungle diseases. The New Zealanders, by contrast, included a fair sprinkling of adaptable Maoris who made excellent trackers. Their presence in the SAS also encouraged the first Fijians serving in Malaya to transfer to the SAS. Most important of all, however, was the recognition that SAS soldiers could not be selected and trained in haste. The New Zealanders were hand-picked and given a thorough grounding in jungle warfare in Malaya's Jungle Warfare School before they went operational. (For a detailed account of the New Zealanders' exploits and additional insight into the Malayan campaign, see pages 228-233.)

In the same year, 1955/56, the SAS in Malaya was further reinforced by a squadron drawn from the Parachute Regiment in England, known as the Parachute Regiment Squadron, and commanded by Major Dudley Coventry. By 1956, five squadrons totalling 560 men were operating in the jungle, and the number of people killed by the guerrillas had fallen to about half a dozen per month. From now on, the military problem was the pursuit of the estimated 2,000 CT thought to be still at large to their increasingly remote bases, which now more resembled sanctuaries than launch-pads for offensive operations. It was a time when the skills of the hunter—concealment, tracking, endurance, coolness and lethally-accurate snap shooting—were at a premium, and the time when SAS came into its own.

The soldier who personified these skills at the time was Sergeant Bob Turnbull, a gunner from Middlesborough, who combined a quick intelligence and good ear for foreign languages with the grinding determination of a human bulldozer. Turnbull befriended an Iban tracker called Anak Kayan, and achieved an eye for spoor as accurate as Kayan's own, reading the splayed toe-prints of the aborigine for what they were; the terrorist footprint, which invariably revealed cramped toes that had once known shoes; and spotting a fine human footprint imposed by the more canny walker on an elephant footmark in an attempt to blur the trace.

Turnbull once followed the tracks of four men for five days until he spotted the hut they were occupying. He then waited for an impending rainstorm to arrive, correctly guessing that the sentries would then take shelter, and drew to within five yards of the hut before killing the four guerrillas sheltering there. On another occasion, he pursued a notorious guerrilla leader called Ah Tuck, a man who always went armed with a Sten carbine, ready cocked. When the two men finally encountered one another in the bush at a range of twenty yards, Ah Tuck died still holding his unfired weapon.

According to one officer who served with him, Turnbull used a repeater shotgun with such speed and accuracy that it would "fill a man with holes like a Gruyère cheese." (The shotgun, its use perfected by the SAS for close-quarter battle, has ever since been the subject of intensive study by US as well as British forces.) One officer who went on his first jungle patrol with Turnbull was unwise enough to insist that the sergeant act as back-marker to an Iban tracker and the officer himself. When this trio encountered a guerrilla, Turnbull instantly fired over the officer's shoulder and had disabled the terrorist while the officer concerned was still reminding himself of the drill for such situations, "First, safety catch off . . ."

INTO TELOK ANSON SWAMP

One of the last major guerrilla hunts, near the Malacca Strait Coast, in Selangor, was also one of the hardest. In February 1958, 37 men of D Squadron led by Harry Thompson parachuted into the Telok Anson swamp, which covers an area measuring about eighteen miles by ten, to kill or capture two groups of terrorists led by Ah Hoi, also known as "The Baby Killer" after his murder of an informer's wife. She was pregnant. His accomplices held her down on a table while he slashed at her with a knife, before an audience of horrified villagers. Ah Hoi was now hiding in the swamp.

The drop was from a Beverley. By now, the accumulation of casualties from this type of parachuting was such that no training jumps were permitted. As one veteran of the Telok Anson operation put it, "You just got out of the aircraft and hoped to God you would land safely in the top of a tree." One man, Trooper Mulcahy, was unlucky. He hit a tall tree, but his canopy did not catch the branches. The canopy collapsed and he dropped like a stone into the tree roots, breaking his back. The Squadron's first task was to fell some trees so that a helicopter could evacuate Mulcahy. The clearance thus created was just enough to allow the aircraft's rotor blades to miss the foliage, but it was impossible to land because of the swampy terrain. Somehow, the pilot kept the machine hovering, with one wheel on a log, while the stretcher was taken aboard.

The initial search for Ah Hoi was led by de la Billière in a ten-day trek along river banks and through iron-brown water, the depth of which varied from shin- to neck-height. The parts of the body that were submerged were the prey for leeches, the more enthusiastic of which could consume half a pint of the victim's blood before being detected; those areas not submerged were the target for the malarial mosquito and other insects. Each night, the patrol slung hammocks in the trees and enjoyed temporary respite from the swamp. A stay of more than one night made it worth the effort to construct a raft as a sleeping platform.

De la Billière's troop found several camps recently vacated by the terrorists, sites littered with the shells of turtles which the "bandits" had eaten. Ah Hoi's men, it seemed, knew that they were being pursued. It is possible that the helicopter evacuation of Mulcahy had alerted them. De la Billière's route across the swamp followed the dominant feature of the place, the Tengi River. He reported his progress by radio to Thompson each evening, but made no contact with the enemy, who were now apparently heading up-river towards the center of the swamp. Simultaneously, a second troop under Sergeant Sandilands was moving on a compass bearing in that direction also, picking a cautious way through the swamp during the hours of darkness, noses alert for the smell of guerrilla cooking fires, ears straining through the cacophony of bullfrog croaks for the sound of a human voice. By day, Sandilands and his men put out sentries and slept.

Finally, at dusk on about the seventh or eighth day, soon after they had resumed the march, Sandilands' troop spotted two of the enemy about 70 yards away across a stretch of open water. Sandilands and a corporal eased themselves into the water to get closer, floating a log before them to conceal their approach. They opened fire from about 50 yards, killing one of the men. The other disappeared. Next morning, the troop cautiously followed a four-mile trail to a freshly-abandoned camp.

Thompson now tightened the cordon round the guerrillas by moving his men to a point on the River Tengi miles upstream from the point that de la Billière had reached, before the two groups started closing towards one another in a pincer movement. Simultaneously, a huge military and police cordon was thrown round the swamp perimeter and barbed wire was laid along the coast, with a notice warning anyone who crossed it that he could be shot on sight. With the need for secrecy eliminated by the Sandilands contact, helicopters now flew daily missions to replenish SAS stocks of food and clothing and to scan any open spaces of water for signs of Ah Hoi. It was now twenty days since D Squadron had dropped into the swamp, and all the men were suffering from prickly heat and other infections. Thompson's legs, ripped by thorns and mildly infected, were a mass of ulcers.

Two days after the cordon had been imposed, a diminutive, emaciated woman in an olive green uniform emerged from the jungle and approached a security forces checkpoint in a paddy-field. She was taken before a Special Branch officer and identified herself as Ah Hoi's messenger, Ah Niet. Ah Hoi had a proposition for the security forces: a payment of £3,500 by the government to each of his team and amnesty for those already in prison.

Ah Niet was told there would be no deal: Ah Hoi had a choice between surrendering within 24 hours, or death in the swamp where soldiers were already waiting for him. And if they failed, the RAF would bomb Ah Hoi out of hiding. Ah Niet, just 4 feet 6 inches tall, dissolved gnome-like, back into the jungle. Thompson, alerted by radio, flew with a troop of his men to the paddy-field and at dusk, shining torches, Ah Hoi and some of his men emerged. A contemporary account by Brian Connell reported, "He was still arrogant, still ranting that the Reds would win in the end." Given the choice of prison or exile in China, he initially chose China, then changed his mind, but was packed off to China all the same.

Ah Niet, meanwhile, led Thompson back into the swamp to make contact with another group of Ah Hoi's men who were ready to surrender. She led the way, swimming in total silence, 300 yards from a police post. It was her favorite entry-point and she had used it undetected for years. She was appalled at the amount of noise generated by the soldiers as they followed her. They did not find the remnant of the Ah Hoi band partly because Ah Niet's considerable strength now failed her. She was suffering from beri-beri, a vitamin deficiency disease. They emerged to surrender 48 hours later.

WHITEHALL JUNGLE CAMPAIGN

While the SAS was fighting on the ground to establish a reputation as a credible military force, a jungle war of a different kind was going on in Whitehall. In the long term, it was of even greater importance to the future of the SAS —if it had one—than Malaya. Argument about the rôle of special forces had been smouldering since 1945, and it had found early expression in the compromise function of 21 SAS, the volunteer Territorial regiment. Even this creation was regarded with hostility in some parts of the military establishment, which was suspicious of a "private army" whose methods and objectives it did not understand.

Efforts to ensure the SAS a permanent place in the post-war regular army also hit opposition from officers who had a chip on their shoulders about the unit, either because they had been rejected for SAS service or because someone of, say, the rank of major had been treated to that terse form of advice—usually two words, of which the second was invariably "off"—which SAS soldiers express when faced with obtuseness by higher authority. Such episodes should have no part in long-term military calculations, but armies are human organizations and some soldiers nurture grudges. It is also fair to say that some of the critics had a more substantial case, based on their contacts with the Malayan Scouts. The same men who had been company commanders in Malaya during those early days of 1950 to 1952 were staff officers in Britain by the time the political debate about the future of the SAS reached its climax between 1956 and 1957.

Another element in this domestic quarrel concerned relations between the SAS and the Parachute Regiment. The first SAS selection courses of post-war years in Britain were set up by Lieutenant-Colonel John Woodhouse in the autumn of 1952 at the Airborne Forces Depot, Aldershot. This was the home of the Parachute Regiment, an élite force for which, in those days, prior service with another unit followed by prolonged and stringent selection was required. Formal entry into the Regiment, marked by the award of parachute wings and red beret, took place only after parachute training. The SAS, by contrast, trained for parachuting after acceptance.

There were other, more profound differences. The SAS emphasized individuality while the Paras, despite their advice to "use your Airborne Initiative" to solve otherwise insoluble problems, were still much closer to orthodox traditions of infantry discipline. These differences, added to the mixed reputation of the Malayan Scouts, generated an attitude by the Paras towards SAS men that was at best patronizing and at worst downright derisive. While they awaited posting to Malaya, SAS soldiers were used exclusively for menial, fatigue duties.

In the longer term, the SAS pioneers were disturbed by a possible takeover of their fledgling unit by the Paras. According to one account, the SAS Colonel Commandant of the day, General Miles Dempsey, accompanied the SAS course organizer, Woodhouse, in an abrasive discussion with the Parachute Regiment's depot commander, Colonel Pine Coffin, during which Dempsey apparently said, "I hope it is clearly understood that there is no question of the SAS being taken over now or in the future by Airborne Forces." In spite of that, attempts to absorb the SAS into Airborne Forces continued until about 1962.

In Whitehall, the long-term problem of the Regiment's survival particularly concerned Dare Newell and the very few others who were not under pressure to survive the next 24 hours in the jungle. That the SAS did survive to fight another day during that critical decade before 1957 was the result of a committee of inquiry into the rôle of special forces, headed by a Lieutenant-General. This group soberly evaluated the impact of all the private armies of the Second World War, including the Long Range Desert Group, Lovat Scouts, Popski's Private Army, SAS, Paras, Commandos . . . even, it is jokingly suggested, the Royal Corps of Tree Climbers.

The committee found that there was a requirement in a general European war for two types of special operation behind enemy lines—in so far as mobile, modern warfare would have "lines." One was for long-term, deep penetration; the other, for short-term, shallow penetration. The first rôle, the committee found, would be most appropriately performed by the Special Air Service, the second by Royal Marine Commandos. By 1955, the range of officially-proposed SAS targets deep behind enemy lines in a general war, embraced everything from the kidnap of "important enemy personalities" to "attacks on important industrial targets invulnerable from the air."

In 1956, a new Prime Minister, Harold Macmillan, appointed Duncan Sandys as his Defense Minister to clean up some of the mess generated by the Suez operation and Britain's changing world strategy. Sandys was to "formulate policies to secure substantial reductions in expenditure and manpower" in all the armed forces. For a start, National Service conscription would be abolished gradually. This meant long-term planning for a much smaller army of professional volunteers. In the subsequent debate about which regiments should survive, the advocates of the SAS relied heavily on the findings of the earlier special forces report as a document untainted by partisan calculations. Several former Directors of Operations who liked the flexibility inherent in the SAS approach to war, backed up this argument.

On 24 July 1957, the Army Minister, John Hare, announced the cuts, and many familiar cap badges were to disappear through regimental amalgamation. The SAS survived, though only just, to become part of the permanent Order of Battle, but the regular 22 SAS Regiment was to be reduced from four squadrons to two. Implicit in this decision was the belief that the SAS would not be engaged in continuous campaigning around the Third World.

In the short run, with the end of the Malayan campaign in 1959-60, it was not difficult for the Regiment to make the required cuts. Of the four squadrons serving in Malaya, one had come from New Zealand, to which it returned. Another was a Headquarters squadron. All the original British "Sabre" (combat) squadrons—A, B and D—were well below their nominal, established strength. B Squadron was disbanded and its men absorbed by the other two. In Rhodesia, C Squadron was reduced in strength for several years. When it was raised again as the Rhodesian SAS Regiment, it continued to exist separately from the British 22 SAS both before and after the Rhodesian unilateral declaration of independence in 1964, at which point it became a "lost legion."

Although the SAS had won the first round in the battle for political survival, its existence continued to be questioned for several years. In Malaya it had justified itself, if perilously late in the day. What it now had to do was demonstrate that after nine years of jungle warfare it could function elsewhere. After all, the aboriginal Sarawak Rangers were also good in the jungle. . . . Briefly and brilliantly, in a politically sensitive environment, the SAS would make its point in Northern Oman within days of leaving Malaya.

II

Borneo, 1962-66
The Camouflaged Victory

THE JUNGLE WAR BETWEEN INDONESIA AND Britain euphemistically described by both sides as "Confrontation," lasted four years. It was fought by a mixed Allied force, never greater than 28,000 men, including Gurkhas, Australians and New Zealanders, in an environment no more tractable than that of Vietnam. The enemy was a professional army well versed in jungle warfare, which sought to de-stabilize the fledgling Federation of Malaysia, of which some Allied territory was part, through clandestine guerrilla warfare and terrorism. When that did not succeed, the Indonesian government turned to all-out invasion, including airborne attacks on the Malay Peninsula.

The conflict ended in September 1966, with the clear-cut, unequivocal defeat of the invaders. Historically, however, the victory was mistimed. It occurred during a post-imperial epoque of British history—at home, the British were mesmerized by the hedonism of Beatles, Flower Power and the Swinging Sixties—as a result of which it remained entirely uncelebrated, its architect acknowledged only through the award of a bar to his existing brace of DSOs until three years later, when he received a belated knighthood. Walker's friends attribute this enigmatic behaviour by Whitehall to the General's fierce opposition to a scheme of drastic cuts in the Gurkha force, of which he was the Brigade Major-General.

In keeping with such a low profile success, the rôle of the SAS was also discreet to the point of invisibility. The Regiment's task was a classic one of deep penetration and

Intelligence gathering across enemy lines, in which combat usually implied that something had gone wrong. This did not happen too often. To express journalistically the problem of reconstructing this campaign, there was no story because man did not bite dog: things went according to plan most of the time. Having obtained early warning from SAS patrols of Indonesian attacks, the Allies were able to hit back with mobile reserves from the roads, waterways and the air, as well as creating ambushes in the jungle.

To measure, objectively, the success of the SAS in Borneo is rendered even more difficult by the Regiment's characteristic neglect of archives and records until about 1970, and a traditional aversion to "gong-hunting." (This attitude, let it be said, is not due to excessive modesty, but more a sort of military existentialism: the important thing, in the SAS, is to be there when it happens, and then get on to the next operation.) There are, however, some historical hints about the Regiment's silent contribution to a muffled victory. The first overall commander there, General Sir Walter Walker, rated the value of a few SAS soldiers equal to a thousand infantry, not because they had equivalent firepower, but because their Intelligence gathering and ability to shape civilian perceptions could save that number in battles won without a fight. Even Whitehall was happy. It was able, perhaps uniquely, to fine-tune offensive operations to achieve a precise political outcome as a result of SAS reconnaissance.

During the three years preceding the Borneo operations, the regular SAS had been learning for the first time to live through a period when it was not involved in active operations. Since the end of the Malayan campaign in 1959 and the intensive, but brief, intervention in northern Oman in the same year, there had been much discussion in the SAS about whether its future lay in Europe, or in Britain's shrinking share of the Third World.

"THIRD WORLDERS" V. "EUROPEANS"
The Regiment was effectively divided between the "Europeans," who felt that the long-term future of the SAS, politically as well as militarily, lay in finding a deep penetration and reconnaissance function with NATO forces; and the "Third Worlders" who suspected that this course

would smother the SAS under the bureaucracy of the British Army of the Rhine. Better, they said, to forage for an immediate place in a real campaign than play games in a mock war on the North German plain. Some had joined the SAS to escape from precisely this fate.

Influential people outside the Regiment, however, were beginning to question its cost effectiveness. Some in Whitehall, thinking aloud, wondered whether it would be a good idea simply to absorb the two SAS squadrons into 16th Independent Parachute Brigade. A lack of knowledge among senior Army officers about what the SAS was supposed to be doing, and the skills it had acquired, did not discourage such thinking.

By autumn of 1962, at about the time of the Cuban missile crisis, it seemed that the "Europeans" had won the argument. The Regiment was now retraining with the United States special forces for its new rôle and the long-term, hypothetical operations that implied. Its commanding officer, Lieutenant-Colonel John Woodhouse, had been a pioneer of the Malayan days, and had made a special study of Communist philosophy. As a result of this he encouraged the process, evolved by the Chinese, of continuous self-criticism. Among the "thinking bayonets" of 22 SAS there was criticism anyway, but Woodhouse institutionalized it. The decisive moment for setting the new policy in concrete apparently came when the Director-General of Military Training, Lieutenant-General Sir Charles Richardson, visited SAS teams training in the USA. The men were learning foreign languages and advanced medical training of a kind unthinkable in Britain. Stray dogs collected for destruction were anaesthetized before being killed. Gunshot wounds were then inflicted on the animals, which SAS "bush doctors" learned to repair with basic surgery. Richardson, a pragmatic Royal Engineer, was impressed by the unique potential of 22 SAS and, within two months, Ministry of Defence clearance was given for the Regiment to be re-equipped and modernized. Even more important was the change of political climate in Whitehall. In orthodox military circles the SAS was suddenly "kosher."

But Woodhouse, the Commanding Officer, was also at that time a convert to the "domino" theory about Communist expansion in southeast Asia at a time when Viet-

The 'Confrontation' in Borneo, 1962-66
① Long Jawi incident, September 1963
② Third Division area

nam was succeeding Malaya as the principal battleground
of Asia. So he was hedging his bets and encouraging some
of his men to learn Thai—on the basis that Thailand, a
fellow member of the South East Asia Treaty Organization, might come under attack next. By doing so, Woodhouse also satisfied some of the aspirations of the "Third
Worlders."

On 8 December 1962, however, simultaneous guerrilla
attacks were launched against police stations, government
offices, a power-station and other strategically important
centers in the Sultanate of Brunei. Brunei was one of
three British dependencies in Borneo; the others were the
colonies of North Borneo (later Sabah) and Sarawak; all

were relics of nineteenth century paternalism. These territories, extensive though they were, represented only one quarter of the island. The rest belonged to Indonesia, whose head of state, President Sukarno—irreverently nicknamed "The Mad Doctor" by British troops—had been inspired by the Japanese example to dream of unifying southeast Asia under his leadership.

The Brunei revolt, although a home-grown product, had been carefully fertilized by Indonesia. In response, a hasty, shoestring military operation launched from Singapore by Gurkhas, 42 Royal Marine Commando and the Queen's Own Highlanders, freed European hostages taken by the rebels and restored order in the coastal towns within a few weeks. But it was clear that a new jungle campaign was about to begin. The only question concerned the form it would take. Another Malaya? A Kenya? A Vietnam?

Woodhouse, scenting action, called on the Director of Military Operations at the Defence Ministry in London. The commanding officer of 22 SAS wanted the Regiment to have a place in Borneo. His most persuasive argument was that in addition to the perfection of its jungle warfare skills during the painful, formative years in Malaya, the Regiment could provide for this new campaign the uniquely valuable service of reliable, long-distance morse communication on the radios with which it had now been issued. As the Gurkhas were to discover to their cost on one disastrous occasion, Borneo's jungle atmospherics could be so bad that the normal procedure of standing-to —that is, preparing for action at the main rear base— every time an outpost failed to make its daily broadcast, had to be dropped. Woodhouse, as it happened, had been studying the problem of long-distance communications in the context of the European, nuclear rôle. He was very persuasive.

Three days later, accompanied by a signaller and some of the new radios, he arrived in Brunei. Walker had gladly accepted the offer of an SAS squadron for the campaign because he was then short of helicopters and, as a Gurkha who admired SAS parachute operations into the Malayan jungle, he believed that the SAS would be just the thing for use as a mobile, reserve company of infantry. Woodhouse, with vivid memories of the casualties,

shuddered inwardly. He explained to Walker that the
SAS was not trained for orthodox infantry tactics even in
the jungle, and that a company of, say, the Parachute
Regiment would be more suitable for the task. He went
on to expound the SAS's peculiar value in Borneo. These
were men who could operate in pairs, or alone if necessary, living among the tribes, speaking Malay—of which
enough was known in Borneo to make it a lingua franca
—and, most important, providing an Intelligence and
communications network in the blank areas of Walker's
knowledge. Like any sensible commander, Walker was
worried about these blank areas. He "bought" Woodhouse's proposition and, within three days, 22 SAS was
flying to Borneo, the old hands slinging hammocks where-
ever they could find space in the aircraft, conserving their
energy for the conflict to come.

One of the first people with whom they made contact
was a British surveyor, Tom Harrisson, who had led an
underground tribal resistance movement against the Japanese during the Second World War, and who had now
raised his own aboriginal force to cut off the surviving
rebels as they fled inland from Brunei towards the sanctuary of Indonesia.

The Regiment also renewed old friendships with veterans of the Sarawak Rangers, Iban tribal trackers and
head-hunters brought to the Malay Peninsula in the
1950s as teachers and pupils of the SAS during that campaign. As pupils, the Iban had learned something about
modern soldiering and firearms from the SAS; as teachers,
they had given the Regiment a feeling for tracking an enemy in the jungle silently and invisibly. Few of these Malayan veterans were still living their old life as hunters in
the Borneo jungle—some had even taken to driving taxis
—and in most cases their jungle sense had deteriorated.
But the SAS proceeded anyway to regain its own former
expertise and self-reliance in conditions that others, even
the Gurkhas, sometimes found almost impossible.

THE 700-MILE FRONT

When the SAS arrived in Brunei in January 1963, the revolt had been extinguished, but Intelligence reports as
well as Sukarno's public speeches made it clear that Indonesia's campaign of subversion was not to be confined to

Brunei. Sabah in the north-east and Sarawak, stretching east-west across the island, were equally at risk. As Blaxland explains:

"The frontier lay open and unmarked across 970 miles of wild and mountainous country, over which raids could, and undoubtedly would be made without warning at any point, and the coastline was very much longer and just as vulnerable. The total area to be protected was slightly larger than England and Scotland, and there were only five battalions (including the Royal Marine Commando) available, controlled by a brigade headquarters at Kuching and another at Brunei, and with the need for a regular system of reliefs over an interminable period, there was no immediate prospect of any great increase."

In an effort to fill the gap, SAS teams from A Squadron, usually between two and four men, were staked out across 700 miles. Each team was responsible for a 10,000-yard front sited to block most of the obvious approaches from Kalimantan, as Indonesian Borneo was called; these generally consisted of natural faults in the mountain ridge, which lay across the center of Borneo like a quiff, and down those jungle motorways, the rivers.

It would be clearly impossible for these miniscule teams personally to watch over such an area. The trick was to arrange matters so that the jungle tribes would act as scouts for the SAS teams, who would be the reporting center for each locality. In an environment in which as little as five miles a day might be an ambitious tactical movement, a spoor even a day old was valuable information for a defense force equipped with helicopters. Basically, therefore, it was the mixture as before, in Malaya: the hearts-and-minds business to yield information; airborne assault plus familiarity with the jungle to follow it up.

But this was a very special environment. As Blaxland describes it, "the interior was a roadless confusion of jungle and rivers. . . . Innumerable village settlements or kampongs were to be found, either by the river or on a hillside, from which tribesmen of many varieties primitively tilled the land around them or went hunting for fish, deer, baboons, porcupines or the ever-pervasive snakes.

"They lived in longhouses which were made of attap wood, had foetid interiors and were apt to creak balefully on the stilts that had kept them out of the water for decades. The Iban of Sarawak . . . were small, cheerful and indolent people, who neither cut their hair nor dressed above the waist, regardless of sex, except when attired in ceremonial finery, which was worn for visiting soldiery who would be primed with rice-wine and invited to do a solo dance."

There was no question here, as in Malaya, of forcibly transplanting populations into new, fortified villages. In any case, most of the tribespeople were well-disposed towards the British. For the rest, the troops had to rely on charm, quick wits and little else—the weapons of non-violence. Styles varied. One of the Gurkha regiments, with more men than the SAS, concluded that "the old system of giving salt, tobacco, sugar and beads was wrong for Borneo. Tact, courtesy and, above all, infinite patience and human understanding were needed. . . . Bartering of a minor nature continued non-stop. . . . It was also important to uphold at all times the dignity and prestige of the local headman. One way of accomplishing this was by allowing him to take the salute at 'Retreat'." At ceremonial dances, some British officers achieved a succès d'estime by performing the Twist.

Nearer the mountainous border, the SAS approach was to move into the village, cautiously and sensitively, and to live there for five months or more. Tom Pocock, in his biography of General Walker, recounts how "at first some of the SAS men were sent up-country in civilian clothes; an unexpectedly difficult task because the shirts and jeans on sale in Borneo shops were cut for diminutive Chinese figures, not hulking British troopers." But disguise was quickly discarded as unnecessary, and the patrols wore the usual jungle green denims and soft brimmed hats with a yellow band for identification.

The first step towards penetration was to build a secret hide in the jungle within walking distance of the selected village. Having kept the place under observation long enough to ensure that neither guerrillas nor Indonesian regulars were already established, the soldiers would walk in, smile, and make contact. Sometimes conversation was possible through the medium of Malay; sometimes a basic sign-language evolved. When this failed, as one veteran wearily recalls, "they would sit and look at us, and we would sit and look at them." This entertainment was somewhat one-sided, since the soldiers were probably the first Europeans most of the villagers had seen. On a good day, the SAS patrol would be invited into the animal closeness of the collective longhouse and offered rice-wine and food, before taking their leave to sleep in their hide (basha), endeavoring to conceal the trail as they went.

The next day they would be back. Their message was that evil men from across the mountain were coming, and that the soldiers were there to protect the village. This, when finally comprehended, did not always fill head-hunting tribesmen with awe. So, to close a growing credibility gap as well as to rehearse essential reinforcement tactics, A Squadron's commander, Major Peter de la Billière, devised the "set-up" technique. For this, a full infantry company would be warned to be ready to move by helicopter to a remote forward location for a demonstration of quick deployment and firepower. On the day set for this exercise, the SAS soldiers would explain to the villagers that although the soldiers were only two in number, they had many friends, other warriors who could descend from the sky to their aid. It would be particularly helpful if the necessary space could be created for the flying soldiers to land safely. The tribesmen, who are adept at removing large trees with small, flexible axes, were fascinated by the prospect of such entertainment, and a helicopter landing zone was rapidly carved out of the jungle. The soldiers then radioed the message, "Bring in the step-up party now!" About fifteen minutes later the helicopters would appear, loaded with business-like Gurkhas armed with sharpened kukris as well as modern firearms. The show usually brought the longhouse down.

Gifts of portable radios, simple medical aid and other favors rapidly ensured that the SAS team became an institution in the community, though with one exception, its aid rarely achieved the elaboration recorded by 2/7th Gurkhas whose native protégés "made endless requests for trips to outlying kampongs (villages), movement of rice, planks, children, old people and pigs by helicopter. . . . The locals came to rely more on the soldiers and airmen than on the civil administration. . . ." One young and rich SAS troop commander expressed this hearts-and-minds offensive by flying out, at his own expense, hampers of Christmas food from Fortnum and Mason's exclusive London store to supply the nomads in his part of Borneo. Another unique contribution to village life was made by an SAS soldier of Romany origins, "Gipsy Smith." A natural improvisor, he constructed a waterpowered generator to provide the only electric light in thousands of square miles. For his next trick, he dismantled his Bergen rucksack and converted its metal frame to a still for making alcohol.

The message that accompanied these diversions was always the same: danger lay on the other side of the mountains and one day it would move closer. The villagers must help themselves by staying alert for anything unusual seen in the surrounding jungle, particularly the characteristic mark of a rubber-soled boot. Could the villagers select one of their number to be a link-man with the soldiers? They could.

By now the SAS team would have its own quarters on the edge of the village, broadcasting daily reports to Squadron Headquarters. The team might be augmented by one or two members of the local police field force. Regularly the team would make a circular tour of the area, lasting up to five days, visiting a series of villages. Like village policemen, they moved on foot. Unlike village policemen they moved unobtrusively, in single file, the lead scout of the patrol followed by the commander and his radio operator, with a gun carrier at the rear playing "tail-end Charlie."

Only towards the end of this first five-month tour did something happen to remind even the SAS that the threat about which they had been preaching was real. In the early hours of Good Friday morning, 12 April 1963, a force of thirty guerrillas surrounded the police station at the border town of Tebedu in West Sarawak. After a brisk battle, in which a police corporal was killed and two others wounded, the raiders looted the bazaar.

When the news reached the local military HQ, a troop of Royal Marine Commandos was sent to the scene. The raiders had disappeared back into the undergrowth, leaving leaflets which purported to show that the action was a manifestation of the earlier revolt in Brunei. Later evidence was to sustain the intelligent guesses made at the time that the raid was probably led by Indonesian regulars.

At a remote border kampong known as Rundum, a four-man SAS team was preparing to hand over to a relief group from D Squadron. When the Tebedu attack took place, two of the soldiers from this group had already started the 25-mile journey to the rendezvous, more than a day's march, in order to guide their successors. Meanwhile, the remaining pair had received an urgent signal from the Squadron's operations room, telling them of the Tebedu affair, instructing them to stay at their location and to dig in. This phrase, conjuring up as it did, a vision of divisions massed on the Marne, caused some merriment. The team's reaction was: "What, both of us?"

From now on, the war followed an inevitable course. More troops and helicopters were summoned to Borneo, and a search of towns in Sarawak brought to light plans by the Clandestine Communist Organization (CCO) for Malayan-style terrorism. The police began the confiscation of the 8,500 licensed shotguns circulating among the Chinese community. There were more cross-border raids from Indonesian soil, and a night curfew was imposed on Sarawak during which the security forces could open fire without prior warning.

On the long, unmarked frontier there could never be enough men to achieve total security. But the success of the SAS in creating a defensive Intelligence network among the tribesmen encouraged General Walker to create, with the help of the SAS and others, the indigenous Border Scouts. This was a controversial decision, if only because experience in Malaya had shown that, while it may be expedient to arm tribesmen and train them as guerrillas in time of crisis, they are impossible to disarm when the crisis is over, with disastrous results for long-term internal security. A more short-term consideration was the rôle the Scouts would fill.

Inevitably, perhaps, the tribesmen, trained as Border Scouts by the Gurkha Independent Parachute Company in basic weapon-handling and battle tactics within three short weeks, more closely resembled orthodox infantry than the SAS pupils, who were encouraged to think of themselves as the eyes and ears, rather than the fists of their allies. As one Gurkha regimental history acknowledges: "Although the use of the Scouts in this way in-

volved border kampongs and longhouses in the defence of
their own country and kin, their suitability for employment in defensive static positions was limited."

The unsuitability of the Scouts for this sort of warfare,
even under the overall command of such an experienced
jungle hand as Lieutenant-Colonel John Cross, became
tragically apparent in September 1963. At Long Jawi in
Central Borneo, 30 miles from the border, the Gurkhas
had established a Scout post consisting of 21 locals, 2 Police Field Force signallers and a 6-man Gurkha team
headed by a corporal. Just before dawn one day, a well-
equipped company of Indonesian regulars fell upon Long
Jawi. The signallers were killed as they tried unsuccessfully to summon aid. The raiders looted the village,
destroyed it by fire, and withdrew.

The Gurkha HQ attributed radio silence from Long
Jawi to bad atmospheric conditions until, four days later,
one Border Scout and two surviving Gurkhas reached the
headquarters, "weak and exhausted, but with weapons
spotlessly clean, and able to give a first-hand account of
the battle." Gurkha ambush parties were flown into the
area, and during the next month most of the Indonesians
were hunted down, sometimes in ones and twos, after
their escape craft had been shot to pieces by Gurkhas
waiting on the river banks. Vengeance had been extracted
but the lesson, that such warfare was a matter for professionals, was not lost on Walker and his advisers. More
SAS soldiers were needed, and urgently, in the border
area. Meanwhile, on Walker's orders the rôle of the Border Scouts was changed—no more paramilitary work, and
exclusive concentration on intelligence-gathering activities.

SQUADRONS RESTORED

As a long-term measure, Whitehall approved the restoration of the two SAS squadrons that had been axed at the
end of the Malayan Emergency four years earlier, in
1959. John Watts, one of the Regiment's most experienced soldiers, started work in England soon afterwards
to raise a new B Squadron—for which recruitment teams
toured BAOR—while the Parachute Brigade's Guards
Independent (Pathfinder) Company was sent to Borneo
to learn something like an SAS rôle on the job (as was

the 2nd Battalion, The Parachute Regiment). Later, the Guards Company would provide the nucleus of the new G Squadron.

Also from Britain, the Headquarters of 22 SAS arrived to occupy a position overlooking the palace of the Sultan of Brunei. This building was known as the Haunted House: during the Japanese occupation it had been used for interrogation by Tokyo's Gestapo, and it was popularly believed that the spirit of a young European woman, a victim of torture, lingered there.

Almost coinciding with the attack at Long Jawi, a series of political events elsewhere generated SAS reinforcements from New Zealand and Australia. Less than two weeks before the attack, Sarawak and North Borneo (Sabah) were granted independence, and they promptly joined the Malaysian Federation. (The event was celebrated in the Indonesian capital, Jakarta, with a mob attack on the British embassy, where the stone-throwers exposed themselves to a withering barrage of bagpipe music played by an SAS officer there, Major Roderic Walker, as he marched back and forth in front of the embattled building.) Since Malaysia was a member of the South East Asia Treaty Organization, the Australian and New Zealand SAS regiments each sent a squadron to Sarawak, the Australians responding to a visit by Woodhouse to their Perth headquarters early in 1964. As in Malaya in the 1950s, the New Zealanders—possibly because of the number of Maoris in their ranks—were to produce the best jungle trackers the SAS ever had.

This extra manpower enabled the next British squadron on tour in the island—D Squadron, fresh from training in West Germany and Norway—to concentrate its efforts on the shorter frontier between Indonesia and Brunei, which had chosen to remain a British protectorate rather than join the new Federation. The efforts of D Squadron as Philip Warner's official history of the Regiment records, had tangible results: "Several brisk engagements, including one in which nine out of a party of 21 rebels were captured, and the remainder fled, leaving most of their weapons and ammunition behind." But fundamentally, in the autumn of 1963, it was the mixture as before: long days in the villages, longer marches between them, for five months. An anonymous contributor to the

regimental journal, *Mars & Minerva*, described it thus:
"Four men, living as members of the longhouse itself
for months at a time, watch, listen, patrol and report . . .
Day by day, the sick come for treatment, the women
bring presents of fruit and vegetables, the men to gossip
and bring news, the children to watch, silent-eyed and the
leaders of the community to discuss their problems and to
ask, and offer advice. The patrol slips as easily into the
primitive rhythm of the day and season as the people
themselves. Soon the cycle of burning, planting, weeding
and harvesting becomes part of (the soldier's) life itself,
and customs, rites and celebrations as familiar as the Cup
Final or Bank Holidays at home. . . .

"Here a strong patrol of five or six men will train ten
or twenty times that number of tribesmen in counter-terrorist warfare. In each camp a simple longhouse houses the
Scouts; a similar, but smaller version, their instructors.
The daily programme is long and arduous, though the
syllabus is basic and directly related to the skills required
to be taught.

"The patrol embraces all responsibilities for its charges:
training, administration, discipline and morale. The language difficulty is ever present . . . pantomime is popular
and some are skilful exponents of the art. Helicopter
training without helicopters is a useful test piece. Throw-
ing live grenades presents other problems, but no pantomime is necessary. . . ."

In December 1963, this military idyll came to an
abrupt halt when 128 guerrillas struck at the prosperous
area of Tawau on the coast of Sabah, destroying a force
of the Royal Malay Regiment in its own base twenty
miles from the border. True, the raiders were all subsequently killed or taken prisoner by 1/10th Gurkhas, but
the identification of 21 of the enemy as regular Indonesian Marines confirmed that this was no longer a routine
counter-insurgency campaign.

Walker, the military supremo, himself characterized
the year 1963 as one "which began with the end of a revolution and ended with the beginning of an undeclared
war." Within a few weeks there were to be other, similar
attacks. In January 1964, the British SAS Squadron
moved back to the sensitive, unmapped mountain border
of central Sarawak, known as the Third Division.

CROSS-BORDER OPERATIONS: "THOSE BLOODY GHOSTS"

It was not long after this that the Regiment started to mount its first cross-border reconnaissance missions, which would ultimately identify the camps from which the Indonesian regulars came and the exact routes they followed to their targets in Malaysia. Such operations were —and are—ultra-sensitive politically as well as militarily, normally requiring approval from the Prime Minister in London. In this case, such operations marked the decisive turning-point of the war in Britain's favor.

The first cross-border patrols were gentle, shallow probes over the ridge into Indonesian territory by four-man groups unaccompanied by local guides. The men carried exactly the same equipment and weapons that were being used in Sarawak. If wounded and taken prisoner, the men themselves, as well as their headquarters, would attribute their presence in Indonesian territory to a simple map-reading error. In the circumstances it would be a fairly plausible cover story. As Pocock puts it: "The SAS was, as usual, a law unto itself and on reconnaissance missions would sometimes penetrate into what was certainly enemy-held territory."

Another element in almost all SAS operations in Borneo, to which particular emphasis was now given across the border, was Woodhouse's policy of "shoot-'n'-scoot" (to break contact with the enemy as soon as possible) whenever contact occurred. Woodhouse, as he admitted years later, was strenuously influenced by his own experience in a ten-man reconnaissance section during the Second World War, when only he and one other returned from a single operation. It had not been easy to find volunteers to replace the lost men.

In Borneo, conscious that he had only two operational front-line squadrons totalling about 120 men, Woodhouse was not going to allow heavy casualties to destroy the morale or the credibility of the Regiment in London at such a time. "Shoot-'n'-scoot" was not popular with the SAS, and both officers and men said so; but there was much to recommend the policy for cross-border operations. As Woodhouse explained subsequently: "There was a tendency in military circles to fear that the SAS would

suddenly take matters into their own hands and that the
first news of this to reach the top would be that 200 Indonesians had been shot up in bed. I used to emphasize that
it was more important, for that sort of reason, that we
should be seen to obey orders than anyone."

The success of the first patrols into Kalimantan led to
something more ambitious. The SAS was given the task of
finding the exact river routes used by the Indonesians to
move men and equipment up to the border. The recce
patrols counted the boats and the men in them, mapped
suitable areas from which the boats could be ambushed
on the river bank, and quietly walked back over the
mountain ridge to Sarawak. Next, the patrols were asked
to find the kampongs and bases from which the boats had
come. This was an ambitious undertaking which, if it went
wrong, could not be dismissed as a mere map-reading er--
ror. By now, the first squadron commander to take part
in the patrols had given much thought to the preparation
of his men. By temperament a man who prefers to resolve
problems before they arise, he typically organized random
urine and blood tests to ensure that they were taking their
prophylactic doses of Paludrin to avoid malaria. For these
deep penetration patrols, he took men to the airport to
weigh their Bergen rucksacks on the only available scales
before they flew by helicopter to the jungle entry-point. If
a rucksack weighed an ounce more than fifty pounds
(later reduced to thirty) something had to come out, for
the emphasis now, unlike the situation in Malaya, was not
upon how much a human being could carry, but how far
he could travel and function as a soldier carrying the minimum of equipment. As one of his officers remarked:
"You can't go head down, arse up when you are in close
proximity to the enemy."

It was also decreed that nothing be left in enemy territory to betray the presence of British troops: no casualties who might be identified; no spent cartridge cases; no
cigarette stubs; no identity discs, photographs or letters
from home; not even the heel print of a standard British
military boot. So the deep penetration patrols were equipped with the Armalite rifle, which had several advantages.
It was the perfect jungle weapon—portable and powerful
—and, although circulating in considerable quantities
around the world, not standard issue to the British Army.

Irregular footwear was preferred or, if this were impossible in the Borneo jungle, sacking or hessian was placed outside the boot to blur all marks indicating its origin.

Above all, the job was one for soldiers who were natural navigators and men who had a feel for the country, with one complete tour of Borneo duty under their belts. It was no time to get lost, since no rescue would be forthcoming. Furthermore, the only certain way to find the Indonesian bases was to follow the spoor left by the enemy's raiding parties. The reconnaissance groups had to be superlative trackers.

Having arrived at their destination, the SAS "moles" were expected to establish not just the location of the base and its approximate strength but also to draw the most detailed sketch maps of the place they could. This meant penetrating the kampongs in which the Indonesian soldiers lived, without alerting sentries or dogs, and then slipping back to the blessed cover of the deep jungle.

When they finally emerged into friendly territory after three weeks or more, their uniforms sometimes hanging in rags, their appearance often appalled Allied troops. One, recollecting the emaciated condition of these military apparitions, said afterwards: "They looked like bloody ghosts left over from the war against the Japanese. And they said nothing, nothing, except: 'Hello. Hold your fire. We're British.' "

Loss of body weight was inevitable when the men were obliged to live on dehydrated rations yielding 3,500 calories per day instead of the recommended level of 5,000. Upon their return, some men had to be debriefed (one day); allowed total rest (two days); and briefed for the next patrol (two days): a total of just five days in which to eat like hamsters and replace some of the lost weight before another trip across the border. After three of these patrols, most of the soldiers were so worn out that they needed recuperation in England. It was not surprising that Whitehall's attempts to extend SAS tours to six months or more—to reduce travel costs—were fiercely and successfully resisted by the Regiment's commanding officer.

The navigation for these operations was achieved through careful scrutiny of air photographs, cultivation of a photographic memory for such features as ridges and rivers and the compass bearings on which they ran, as well as a finely-tuned sense of distance walked to calculate a dead reckoning of mileage covered by reference to time-on-march. Tracking required the knack of seeing, as if they were motorway signposts, traces of human urine, crushed grass, muddied river crossings, bruised moss and broken bark on exposed tree roots. It required also the knowledge that fallen leaves, when brushed aside at the right spot, could reveal a perfectly shaped boot-print impressed in the soft earth beneath.

The recipe for concealment was that which General Walker had laid down for the Gurkhas when in ambush: "No chance . . . if he smoked, chewed gum, washed his hands with soap, cleaned his teeth, Brylcreemed his hair, whispered or coughed. In ambush, a man is lying in wait for a dangerous, hunted animal whose sense of smell and eyesight can be phenomenal." The nerve needed for these clandestine operations could not be taught. They involved a form of stress that scarred even the most stable SAS soldiers in some way. After they had experienced weeks of silence and near-silent communication, their comrades noticed, on their return to England, that some veterans of the Borneo patrols could not break the habit of whispering to each other, even when exchanging a joke in the men's room behind their favorite Hereford pub.

Such labors bore fruit a few months later in mid 1964 when, faced by increasingly bold attacks from the Indonesian side, General Walker sanctioned counter-strikes, first by artillery, then by "killer" groups drawn from the best infantry battalions and led by SAS guides. These were known collectively as "Claret" operations and were hardly less sensitive than the reconnaissance that preceded them.

AN OFFENSIVE WITH GOLDEN RULES

"Claret" operations were governed by what were colloquially known as the "Golden Rules" and they were graded Top Secret. The initial penetration depth permitted into Indonesia was 5,000 yards and this was increased, for specific raids, to 20,000. The objective, according to Brigadier E. D. ("Birdie") Smith of the Gurkha Rifles, was: "to pre-empt any likely build-up or attack, to harass by ambush and patrols the Indonesians, and to induce them to move their camps back and away from the border. . . . Initially, the guidelines were:

"a. All raids had to be authorized by the Director of Operations (General Walker) himself.
b. Only tried and tested troops were to be used—in other words no soldiers were to be sent across . . . during their first tour in Borneo.
c. Raids were to be made with the definite aim of deterring and thwarting aggression by the Indonesians. No attacks were to be mounted in retribution or with the sole aim of inflicting casualties on the foe.
d. Close air support could not be given except in an extreme emergency. . . ."

For a time, Smith explains, only Gurkha battalions could be used for offensive cross-border operations in addition to SAS soldiers, and no unit was to mount more than one raid at a time. Finally, "minimum force was to be the principle used rather than large-scale attacks which would have invited retaliation and risked escalation, turning the border war into something quite different, costly in lives and fraught with international problems."

The guides for these raids were usually (though not invariably) provided by the SAS, who found them almost relaxing after the nervous isolation of the earlier reconnaissance. As one SAS veteran said: "Having done your recce, and crept around and done all the sneaky bits, when you came back as part of a Gurkha company you felt as safe as houses in the middle of their perimeter: all those little brown men with GPMGs going out in all directions to set up listening posts. . . ." Safer, yes, but on windless, silent days in the jungle, no less stealthy, as the history of 2/7th Gurkha Rifles reveals: "No rifleman was allowed to eat, smoke or unscrew his water bottle without his platoon commander's permission. At night, sentries checked any man who snored or talked in his sleep. Whenever the company was on the move, a recce section led the way, their packs carried by the men behind. Because of the long approach march, each man carried six day's basic rations together with various lightweight additions and a small reserve in a belt pouch."

The effect of the raids was often devastating. At one Indonesian Army camp, the enemy were breakfasting on

roast pig when the Gurkhas arrived. In thick undergrowth, the patrol brought rocket-launchers, grenade-
throwers and machine-guns into position. Then, as the
regimental history records, "the happy camping scene by
the river was shattered as a 3.5-inch rocket flared across
the water and exploded among the breakfast party. The
hut disintegrated in a ball of flame, the men hurled in all
directions. . . .

"As two assault platoons moved in to clear the camp
they contacted a number of totally naked, panic-stricken
enemy rushing from it. These were quickly dealt with and,
covered by fierce fire from the support group, we as-
saulted the base. Resistance had ceased, but a number of
dead lay scattered about the camp and blood was everywhere."

Unaccompanied SAS units also began to attack enemy
approach routes. According to Pocock's account, once formal Government approval was received for such activities, the SAS, "instead of watching and counting," would
be given permission to begin interdiction: ambushing
tracks and rivers and setting boobytraps where it was
known that only raiders would pass. Sometimes their ambushes would be sophisticated affairs with electronically-
detonated Claymore mines catching an enemy party's
front and rear, while the SAS troopers' automatic fire
raked the center. Because the essence of SAS activity was
speed of movement and reaction, they called themselves
"The Tiptoe Boys." The ambush parties hit and vanished,
leaving the counter-attack to find nothing but apparently
empty jungle.

The impact of such operations was not always so one-
sided. On both the reconnaissance and offensive patrols
things could, and did, misfire. An Australian SAS trooper
was gored by an elephant while in Indonesian territory.
His companion bound his wounds and made him as comfortable as possible before starting a two-day trek for help
from a Gurkha camp. The wounded man had died by the
time he was found. Unusually, the body was recovered
by helicopter. Deaths on such occasions usually meant
the removal of all identification from the body and quick
burial in an unmarked grave. In another episode, a 22
SAS sergeant who had contracted the jungle disease lep-
tospirosis was lucky to survive his 20,000-yard march

home while suffering from a 105-degree temperature and other symptoms.

Inevitably, SAS reconnaissance groups were occasionally ambushed by the opposition despite all precautions. As a veteran of the Borneo patrols explained. "The man who is stationary in the jungle has the tactical advantage. We sometimes found it necessary to spend as much as twenty minutes in any half-hour period sitting and listening, and only ten minutes on the move." Only once was an SAS soldier taken prisoner. A wounded trooper, seized after an ambush, was never seen again, but the Regiment subsequently learned from local tribesmen that he had been tortured so appallingly that he died before his captors could "break" him. There were also some near-misses. Two SAS men had to be winched by helicopter out of the jungle so quickly that they were carried, still dangling from a rope, through the treetops for much of their journey. One of the men lost his rifle in the process, and a search had to be mounted to recover the weapon.

THE LILLICO PATROL

One of the best-documented cases of such an escape, recorded in the Regiment's journal *Mars & Minerva,* describes what happened to a patrol from D Squadron in February 1965.

"A small 22 SAS patrol was moving down from a ridge on a jungle track towards an old Indonesian border terrorist camp. The camp had been discovered the day before and appeared as though it had not been used for six months.

"As the leading scout, Trooper Thomson, ducked under some bamboo across the track—there was a lot of it in the area—a movement attracted his attention. He looked up and saw an Indonesian soldier six yards away to his right, just as the latter fired a burst at him. Several other enemy opened fire simultaneously.

"Thomson was hit in the left thigh, the bone being shattered, and was knocked off the track to the left. He landed in a clump of bamboo two yards away from another Indonesian soldier lying concealed there. As the latter fumbled for his rifle, Thomson picked up his own, which he had dropped as he fell, and shot him.

"The second man in the patrol, the commander, Sergeant E. Lillico, was also hit by the initial bursts and had collapsed on the track, unable to use his legs. He was still able to use his rifle, however, and this he did, returning the fire. Meanwhile the remainder of the patrol had taken cover.

"Thomson, unable to walk, hopped back to where Sergeant Lillico was sitting and joined in the fire fight. As he had seen Thomson on his feet, Lillico was under the misapprehension that he could walk and therefore sent him back up the track to bring the rest of the patrol forward, and continued to fire at the sounds of enemy movement.

"As Thomson was unable to get to his feet, he dragged himself along by his hands and, on arriving at the top of the ridge, fired several bursts in the direction of the camp ... The enemy withdrew ...

"During the remainder of the day, Thomson continued to drag himself towards where he expected to find the rest of the patrol. He had applied a tourniquet to his thigh, which he released from time to time, taken morphia, and bandaged his wound as best he could with a shell dressing."

Lillico, meanwhile, "pulled himself into the cover of a clump of bamboo, took morphia, bandaged his wound, and passed out. ..."

"The remainder of the patrol had decided that the best course of action was to move to the nearest infantry post close by and lead back a stronger party to search the area. This they did, starting back towards the scene of the contact late the same day."

The following morning, Thomson continued to crawl back towards the border, and by evening he had covered 1,000 yards, or about half the distance involved. He was found by the search party just before dusk, carried to a clearing next day and evacuated by helicopter.

On the second day, meanwhile, Lillico had dragged himself to the top of a ridge, 400 yards from the scene of the action. At about 3 pm, he fired signal shots to attract the attention of any friendly search party. Instead, the shots attracted more enemy troops, one of whom climbed a tree about 40 yards from the spot where the sergeant lay quietly in the scrub. Twice during the day, Lillico had heard a helicopter overhead, but because of the proximity of the Indonesians he did not disclose his position. In the evening, the helicopter returned for the third time that day, identified Lillico's signal, and winched him to safety about 36 hours after the action. Lillico was awarded the Military Medal and Thomson was Mentioned in Dispatches.

THE SUPERIOR SERGEANT-MAJOR

It was not only the small parties that hit trouble. From May to October 1965, Squadron Sergeant-Major L. Smith ran the SAS operations room for an area of the Sarawak border 382 miles across, the longest battalion front in Allied Borneo. Such a task, as the historians of 2/7th Gurkha Rifles point out, had not been the responsibility of any SAS rank below that of captain during post-war years. Smith, they reveal, was "entirely responsible for mounting SAS patrols, maintaining liaison with battalion commanders and for the considerable work involved in mounting and running the patrol operations. He personally led several dangerous and exacting operations when detailed preliminary reconnaissance reports were needed."

As a result of one of these patrols, a Gurkha company of 40 men set off to ambush Indonesian water traffic. Instead, it ran into an Indonesian company of 100 men marching along the same track beside the river. A confused, close-quarter battle followed in which grenades, machine-guns and Claymore mines were used. Smith had not accompanied the patrol beyond an advance base position because of a cough which might have compromised the operation. But "he had realized that something had gone wrong, so he had worked out a complete fire plan for the (artillery) gun support" and, as the first survivors straggled in, "brought down a very close-in defensive fire which helped the Gurkhas to make a clean break." As one Gurkha said later: "Without his help we would have been faced with a running battle back to the border."

Now it was discovered that some of the Gurkhas were missing. About 36 hours after the initial contact a New Zealand gunner captain who had been with the patrol, walked into the forward base with the news that he had carried or dragged a wounded Gurkha sergeant-major through 6,000 yards of dense jungle and swamp, an heroic achievement. SSM Smith now led the recovery party and, as the Gurkha history records it:

"In the jungle, SSM Smith was a tower of strength. He found a suitable winching zone, brought in the helicopter and supervised the lashing onto the stretcher of the wounded man. Had the evacuation been postponed further, the injured man would undoubtedly have lost a leg. . . . He was discharged from hospital without even a limp."

Slowly but surely, towards the end of 1965 the Indonesians were forced to abandon their front-line bases, conceding control of the border to the Allies. Nothing had been said publicly by either the British or the Indonesians about the "Claret" operations, but within Indonesia Sukarno was rapidly becoming discredited among his military commanders and the common people, who were finding the price of his dreams of glory exorbitant.

The British, meanwhile, were making plans to undermine the régime by spreading the guerrilla war to other parts of Indonesia including, if it were expedient, Sumatra and Java. Plans for these operations embraced such external Intelligence agencies as MI6 as well as the SAS, but they were overtaken by events. In March 1966, Sukarno was reduced to a figurehead by his military top brass.

THE LAST INVADER

The last Indonesian invasion, by 50 soldiers into a Sarawak border area near Brunei, ended disastrously for them. An Indonesian coffee-tin label put a Gurkha battalion on their trail. At the first contact, the invaders fragmented into small parties which were assiduously pursued for many weeks. Their leader, a charismatic figure named Lieutenant Sumbi, who had boasted that he would seize Brunei Bay and the Shell oil installations, was captured on 3 September, three weeks after Indonesia had signed a peace agreement with Malaysia.

With the end of the war, General Lea, the SAS officer who had been Allied military supremo during the final, victorious phase, was promptly knighted. Walker, meanwhile, became the only general to be made an honorary member of the SAS. As the Army's historian, Blaxland, wrote: "Thus ended what must surely rank as the British Army's neatest achievement during post-war years. What might so easily have been an interminable embroilment in the jungle, the kampongs, the villages and towns, with an ever-swelling flow of blood and hate, had been brought to a happy end in little more than three years.

"This had been achieved because the Army had won the confidence of the inhabitants and gained complete mastery over a brave and tough, if not very ably led, enemy. They had combined kindness to the defended with aggression against the attackers, two virtues not always regarded as compatible, and it had all been done with a lack of self-advertisement which must have had a deflating effect on the enemy. . . ."

The total number of British casualties was 19 killed and 44 wounded, while the Gurkhas had lost 40 killed with 83 wounded. The Indonesian dead numbered 2,000.

III

South Arabia, 1964-67:
The Lost Cause

WHAT HAPPENED TO THE BRITISH ARMY IN
Aden, a territory which is now the Soviet satellite of
South Yemen, is a well-documented example of how soldiers are obliged to continue fighting for a lost cause when
their political masters attempt the impossible feat of leaving a colony, while at the same time remaining there. The
abortive Suez operation of 1956; the emergence of Nasserism and its dissemination via the hot-gospel broadcasts
of Cairo Radio; the "shotgun marriage" of the South
Arabian Federation between 1959 and 1963, linking the
feudal, tribal sheikdoms lying between Yemen and the
coast with the urban area of Aden Colony; the establishment of Britain's Middle East Command Headquarters in
1960: all these had generated intense local opposition to
the British presence before the SAS arrived.

Most inauspicious of all, the hereditary ruler of Yemen,
the Imam, was overthrown in a Left-wing, Army-led coup
in September 1962, which was instantly consolidated by
the arrival of Egyptian troops. Recent evidence suggests
that the Soviet KGB, aided by their British agent Kim
Philby, had a hand in this. The new Republican government in Yemen promptly called on "our brothers in the
Occupied South"—Aden and the Federation—"to be ready
for a revolution and for joining the battle we shall wage
against colonialism."

What now occurred, in effect, was a war by proxy between two colonial powers: Britain on one side and
Egypt, backed by Soviet Russia, on the other. The battle-

ground was the whole of that desolate, mountainous territory lying between the Gulf of Aden and Saudi Arabia.
In Yemen itself, the deposed Imam eluded his would-be
assassins. During the next eight years or more, his Royalist guerrilla army was aided by the Saudis and stiffened
by a mercenary force largely composed of SAS veterans
using secret bases in the Aden Federation, an operation
that enjoyed discreet official backing from Whitehall.

In the Federation, meanwhile, two distinctive campaigns were fought out simultaneously. A tribal uprising
took place in the Radfan mountains adjoining Yemen,
while in Aden State the British faced their first campaign
of sustained urban terrorism. One of the paradoxes to
emerge was that in Yemen an SAS "old boys" team was
part of a guerrilla force, while a few miles south in Aden's
hinterland their successors in the regular regiment were
striving to suppress a guerrilla campaign.

But the most significant battle, as usual, was the one for
credibility. What were British intentions? Who would go
and who would remain to run the country if the British
left? There were many brave pronouncements from Westminster along the lines of "No surrender," even when in
July 1964 a Conservative Government set 1968 as the
target date for the Federation's self-government. That
promise of independence was accompanied by an arrangement that Britain would retain her bases in Aden
and not desert the tribal rulers with whom she had maintained protection treaties since the nineteenth century.
There were other reasons why Britain should keep her
bases in the area. It was a time when shrinking British
forces were still expected to maintain global commitments, particularly east of Suez. The Borneo campaign
had started, unexpectedly, only a year before. Britain had
important bases in Singapore and Hong Kong, so Aden
was a strategically important staging-post as well as a port
of regional importance (as the Russians would later demonstrate in their Ethiopian campaign of 1978). In October 1964, Mr. Harold Wilson's Labour administration
swept to power on the promise of a society transformed
by "the white heat of technology" and other instant mir-
acles. Within eighteen months, in February 1966, the
new Government announced a total evacuation deadline
of the Aden base to coincide with Independence. In

South Arabia:
Operations
in Aden and
Oman, 1964-67
① Strait of Hormuz
② Jabal Akhdar
③ Dhofar Mountains
④ Radfan Mountains
⑤ Musandam Peninsula

© ARMS AND ARMOUR PRESS 1989

March 1967, the evacuation deadline was advanced to November of that year.

These decisions destroyed the credibility of British promises in Aden, and had the lethal result of nullifying the hearts-and-minds campaign that elsewhere had proved to be a more potent peace-making force than bullets. Nor, as events turned out, did a precipitate British evacuation bring more freedom to the people of Aden, despite the promises of Cairo Radio. "Liberated" Aden became a drab military dictatorship in which those questioning the régime, such as the Chief Magistrate of the Supreme Court, simply disappeared. The Imperial British had at least doffed their caps at democracy through a limited franchise.

Britain's decision to withdraw from Aden also accelerated the guerrilla war against another of Britain's allies, the Sultan of Oman. During the final year of the Aden campaign, in 1966, Marxist rebels in a remote Adeni sultanate bordering Oman's warlike province of Dhofar, were supplying weapons to Dhofari tribesmen, effectively opening up a third front against the British. In Aden, the Irish Guards were used to attack the Dhofari bases with a spearhead provided by B Squadron of 22 SAS. This textbook infantry operation, a frontal attack, quite opposed to SAS methods, ended with the successful escape of the Dhofaris.

The ubiquitous Major John Cooper, the retired SAS officer who had served as a freelance soldier in Oman before joining the Royalist guerrillas in Yemen, took a more sophisticated interest in this extension of the war. From time to time he would appear at Aden's Intelligence center, for which he carried a permanent pass, to scrutinize photographs of known terrorist leaders. A friend of those days recalls: "At the time, John was based partly in Oman, partly in Yemen."

The British left Aden on 29 November 1967. The political beneficiaries of the war were, quaintly enough, Israel, whose secret aid to the Royalist cause in Yemen tied down 60,000 of Egypt's best troops during the 1967 Six Day War; and Soviet Russia, which took over the base facilities in Aden. It can be argued that the secret war in Yemen—more fully examined in Chapter IV—also helped to prevent an Egyptian or Marxist takeover in Oman and other Gulf states. The significance of this prophylaxis would emerge only years later, after 1978, when the Iranian revolution and the Soviet invasion of Afghanistan plunged the world into turmoil.

PUNISHING THE RADFAN

The Emergency was declared formally in December 1963, after a grenade had been hurled at the High Commissioner, Sir Kennedy Trevaskis, and several Federal Ministers as they prepared to fly to London for a constitutional conference. The ill-defined frontier with South Yemen, across which Egyptian, Yemeni and Adeni nationalists were bringing weapons (including mines left in Egypt by the British) was then closed, at least on paper. But the border tribesmen, for whom guerrilla warfare was a way of life, were still supplied with money and rifles by Yemen, and a battle now began for control of the scorching, almost waterless Radfan mountains in which there were no roads.

Yet in April 1964, when A Squadron of the SAS arrived there, the strength of opposition and the general scale of the problem was simply not comprehended by the British. One eminent officer, who had served with Aden's Federal Regular Army (FRA) as an Intelligence officer shortly before returning to the territory as officer commanding A Squadron, candidly admitted later: "We did not appreciate the intensity of the violence of the tribal reaction to our presence. I expected a few dissidents to poop off a few rounds and then go home again. . . . So often, we underrate our enemy."

Between the Emergency declaration in December and the arrival of the SAS in April, there had already been one attempt to subdue the Radfan area by a combined force of three Federal Regular Army battalions of Arabs with small numbers of British tanks, guns and engineers. Officially, this operation was described as "a demonstration in force," but as Julian Paget's analysis of the Aden affair explains: "There was no long-term plan as to what was to be done once the military task was completed; there were no plans to prevent further subversion, to finance development of the area or to initiate an intense 'hearts and minds' campaign." The real objective was punitive, and this in an area already in a rebellious mood and steeped in the tradition of "an eye for an eye." Paget records: "There were many local officials, with a profound knowledge of the Arabs, who believed strongly that any attempt to subdue the tribes by force was doomed to be a waste of time and effort."

The FRA battalions did occupy parts of the Radfan mountains for a few weeks, at a cost of five dead (one of them a British company commander) and twelve wounded. Then they withdrew to perform the even more important task of guarding the frontier. The tribesmen promptly reoccupied their former hill positions and began attacking traffic on the Dhala road linking Aden and Yemen. Meanwhile, Cairo and its puppet régime in the Yemeni capital of Sana'a announced the FRA's withdrawal from Radfan as a resounding defeat for the imperialists.

The Federal Government (a mixture of tribal rulers and Adeni merchants) now sought more substantial British military help, despite the misgivings of that government's own Ministers responsible for internal security, who believed the deployment of British troops in so hostile an area would simply make matters worse. Not for the first time, however, the lessons of colonial history were forgotten. The British had first tried to bring the Wolves of Radfan—the Qotaibi tribe—to heel in 1881. From a desk in Aden, 60 miles away, they had declared the tribe nominally subject to the Emir of Dhala, a town on the ancient trade route linking Aden and Yemen. Until then the tribesmen had regarded it as their right to extort payment from travellers using the road, a protection racket deodorized by its antiquity. For years afterwards, the British sent punitive columns trudging into the inhospitable mountains, regiments lost to memory such as the Dublin Fusiliers, Sepoys, Bombay Grenadiers and Outrams Rifles, and they never entirely subdued the hill warriors. Throughout the 1930s, control (such as it was) was left to the RAF, which bombed the rebels from time to time.

In January 1965, in a study of the Radfan tribesman's character, Mr. Harry Cockerill, a wartime SAS veteran who was already working in Aden when the Regiment arrived there, wrote: "He will never surrender in battle and will endure shocking wounds, crawling away to die on his own rather than seek aid from his enemy. His territory is such that a few men can hold up a battalion. He is fanatically independent, a local saying being "Every tribesman thinks himself a Sultan." Unless a settlement is made that will allow him his independence . . . the Qotaibi . . . will take to the hills and it will all start again."

In response to the Federal Government's request, a mixed force of brigade strength plus a squadron each of RAF Hunter ground-support aircraft, Shackleton bombers and Twin Pioneer transports, as well as about ten helicopters, was rapidly cobbled together. The vaguely-worded order to this force from the General Officer Commanding Middle East Land Forces, Major-General John Cubbon, was that it should "end the operations of dissidents in the defined area." This was subsequently refined as "to bring sufficient pressure to bear on the Radfan tribes (a) to prevent the tribal revolt from spreading; (b) to reassert our authority; (c) to stop attacks on the Dhala Road."

The troops were not deliberately to fire on areas containing women and children; villages were not to be shelled, bombed or attacked without a warning to the inhabitants by leaflet to move out. But once the troops came under fire, retaliation could include maximum force.

EXERCISE INTO REALITY

At the time this plan was being constructed, the SAS Regiment consisted of only two squadrons, A and D. A Squadron was resting and retraining after five months in Borneo, and D Squadron was in Borneo. As it happened, A Squadron had already arranged to train in Aden during May and June as a refresher in desert warfare, and its commander, who was in Aden to prepare the ground for this exercise, suggested using his men for the Radfan operation a month earlier than the proposed exercise. His offer was promptly accepted.

A top priority "flash" signal was sent to Britain to obtain the necessary permission from the Ministry of Defense. The Squadron's commander, having returned briefly to England, composed and typed the unit's manual of standard operational procedures for the forthcoming encounter—a tactical "bible"—during the flight back to Aden with the rest of the Squadron. For security reasons, families were told that the Squadron was exercising on Salisbury Plain.

The men arrived at Khormaksar, the RAF base in Aden, just two weeks before they were to spearhead the Radfan offensive. Two weeks was also the period normally allowed for acclimatization to temperatures up to 150 degrees Fahrenheit; the SAS, as usual, ignored this requirement and drove immediately to a hastily-prepared base at Thumier, sixty miles from Aden and just thirty miles from the hostile Yemeni border. The same night, the Squadron moved into the nearby Radfan mountains for a 24-hour proving patrol. In the darkness there was an exchange of fire with a group of armed men who were, in fact, British soldiers. One SAS trooper was slightly wounded. It was to avoid just such elementary failures of communication that this early patrol was mounted, but the episode was an augury of worse to come.

SAS officers discovered that Intelligence concerning the strength of the opposition was negligible. As one of them said later: "In those early days of the Radfan campaign, no one knew anything about what would be needed. They didn't know whether there was water up in the hills, or anything about the people." The improvised group that was to re-enter the Radfan now consisted of two battalions of locally-raised FRA infantry; 45 Royal Marine Commando with B Company, the Parachute Regiment, temporarily under its command; a troop of Royal Engineers; a battery of the Royal Horse Artillery armed with compact 105mm howitzers and a Royal Tank Regiment squadron equipped with Saladin armored cars.

As an opening move, it was decided that two hill objectives code-named "Cap Badge" and "Rice Bowl," should be seized from the rebels during the night of 30 April. These were key-points in the area because they dominated the camel routes from the Yemen as well as the only two fertile areas of the Radfan. The plan was that the Royal Marines should march seven miles from Thumier on the Dhala Road into hostile territory, to climb and hold "Rice Bowl," the most northerly objective. Meanwhile the Para company was to be dropped near the foot of "Cap Badge." Both groups knew that to be caught in the valley after daybreak, when the guerrilla picquets had taken up dawn positions on the heights, would be suicidal. Equally dangerous would be an attempt to land the Paras on an undefended and unmarked drop zone. The job of establishing such a DZ was traditionally that of the Paras' own independent pathfinder company, but this time the task was allocated to the SAS.

THE EDWARDS PATROL

On 29 April, as dusk approached, nine men of 3 Troop led by Captain Robin Edwards set out in armored cars, leaving the road and making their way up the steep-sided

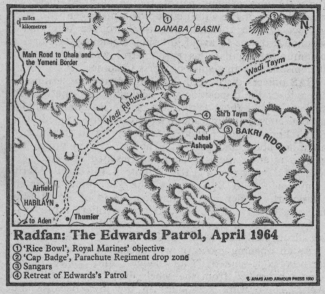

Radfan: The Edwards Patrol, April 1964

① 'Rice Bowl', Royal Marines' objective
② 'Cap Badge', Parachute Regiment drop zone
③ Sangars
④ Retreat of Edwards's Patrol

© ARMS AND ARMOUR PRESS 1990

Wadi Rabwa. Edwards, a recent recruit from the Somerset and Cornwall Light Infantry, was a brave and conscientious young officer who had contracted poliomyelitis immediately after passing the SAS selection course. His determination made him fit enough for service with the Regiment twelve months later. Since arriving in Thumier, his troop had fired on a nocturnal camel train that had refused to halt: two Arabs had been killed and a third taken prisoner. Edwards's anxiety that he might have made a mistake was relieved only when local military Intelligence identified the prisoner as a much-wanted guerrilla leader. Edwards's men were mostly veterans of Borneo and Malaya, physically hard by any standard. The exception was the troop signaller, a slightly-built young ex-sapper named Warburton, who was already suffering from severe stomach pains, about which he did not complain, when the patrol left Thumier.

The patrol had to cover roughly eight miles to reach its objective and had about twenty-four hours within which to accomplish this. Intelligence reports suggested that opposition in the hills would not be serious if the patrol moved discreetly. In the event, the opposition manifested itself from the beginning. As the armored cars nosed their way up the Wadi Rabwa, away from the Dhala Road, they came under continuous rifle and machine-gun fire. In such terrain the cars could not move at more than a snail's pace, and it became increasingly likely that the vehicles would soon be forced to halt.

Making a virtue of necessity, the patrol dismounted while the armored cars' gunners replied to the fire from the hills. By moonlight, each man hoisted his 60-pound pack on to his back and slipped quietly into the shadows. Even after nightfall here, it was like a warm summer's day in England, the heat stifling the airless, rocky bottom of the wadi.

Each soldier carried four magazines for his self-loading rifle, a total of 80 rounds, plus a bandolier of the same ammunition and 200 rounds of .303-inch for the patrol's Bren light machine-gun. The radio, and enough water for each man—a one-gallon container and four water bottles per head—were other essential items. The Squadron's commander, an old Malaya hand, preferred mobility to firepower on such occasions, and the weight carried was a compromise between two conflicting priorities. For the same reason, the Officer Commanding had stressed that ammunition was to be conserved jealously if contact with the enemy did occur. As things turned out, it was sound advice.

Despite these routine problems the Edwards patrol was in good spirits. It had ducked away from the opening battle unseen and was now tramping with quiet assurance through dunes and rocks, up Wadi Rabwa. Off to the right loomed the dark, sinister mass of the 3,900-foot Jabal Ashqab. It soon became clear, however, that young

Warburton, the signaller, was in poorer shape than his comrades. Possibly he was suffering from a mild form of food poisoning. Gradually, he fell back and the patrol waited for him. Edwards and his two sergeants, L. and Tk., decided to put Warburton in the center of the file and redistribute the loads so that the radio, weighing 44 pounds, would be carried by someone else. But after an hour or so Warburton was again struggling to keep up, and the patrol was now becoming dangerously divided.

At about 2 am, Edwards and his men paused to consider the situation. According to the original plan they should be in hiding on the objective before dawn at 5:30 am. They were then to lie concealed until dusk, when they would secure the drop zone perimeter and identify it with torches and an Aldis Lamp for the Paras' night decent. In fact, it was now clear that they would not be able to reach the proposed DZ that night at their present rate of progress. Dead reckoning suggested that they were still about three miles away. To be caught in the open after sunrise would not only make them soft targets for the ubiquitous snipers on the hill-tops, but would also compromise the entire operation.

Despite all these niggling problems, there was also cause for optimism. From the point they had now reached, Edwards and his men had a downhill journey to their objective, and there would be ample time to cover the remaining ground at dusk on the morrow. They were now almost at the top of the highest ridge on Jabal Ashqab, though short of the precipice rising to the summit. Best of all, there were two ancient stone sangars (rock-walled firing-points built by local tribesmen) in which they could hide without attracting attention. As one veteran later joked, for the SAS to have built something without local "planning permission" would instantly have attracted attention among hill people to whom every stone was familiar. The overwhelming logic of these factors was to halt in the sangars and give Warburton a chance to recover. At 2:30 am in his headquarters tent at Thumier, the Squadron commander listened carefully as Edwards explained all this by radio. Edwards was apologetic, but felt there was no alternative.

At dawn, the patrol reviewed the situation. It was, it discovered, only about 1,000 yards above the hamlet of

Shi'b Taym, a meagre collection of mud-and-stone houses. From the village, armed picquets tramped up the hill some distance from the soldiers' position to begin the long day's watch. Later, a group of children passed below, chanting "Allah yansir Nasir!" (God make Nasser victorious!). Still the patrol went undetected. All was quiet now, and it seemed as though Edwards's gamble was succeeding.

At about 11 am, however, the patrol saw a herd of goats approaching, following a small wadi only a few feet from their position. The animals were in the care of a herdsman who shouted directions to a woman coming towards the sangars from the village. Almost certainly he was asking her to watch out for strays from the herd. Edwards, without moving from concealment, softly called to the soldier who was covering the herdsman's approach: could the goat-herd be seized silently without a fuss? Out of the question, the look-out replied; the herdsman's companion would see it all. There was nothing for it now but to hope that by some miracle the herdsman would not spot them. If he did. . . . Suddenly they all heard the Arab's voice raised in alarm only a few yards away, shouting to his companion with new urgency. The game was up. As he turned to flee, a single high-velocity shot rang out from the SAS position. It was a desperate means of buying time and the only one available to the patrol.

The woman vanished, and armed tribesmen were soon on the scene. They were taking no cover as yet, apparently thinking that the shot might have been an accidental discharge, but determined to establish where it had come from. The soldiers, knowing that a battle was inevitable, decided to reduce the odds against them. As one survivor said later: "We thought we might as well put a few away while we had the advantage."

The tribesmen ducked into cover, crawling behind the boulders, still trying to locate the source of the shots echoing across the hillside. It was some time before they succeeded in this. Their solution was to observe the whole sweep of the hill from the ridge top about fifty yards away from the sangars, and twenty feet higher. Edwards had anticipated this and a crude, but effective link was created between the patrol and two pairs of RAF Hunter ground-support aircraft. Under Edwards's control, Warburton passed directions by radio to the SAS second in command, Major Mike Wingate Gray, at Thumier, where the messages were amplified by use of a civilian transistor radio. The major relayed these instructions by field telephone to the RAF Brigade Air Support Officer, Squadron Leader Roy Bowie, in another tent at Thumier. Bowie, telephone in one hand, microphone linked to the Hunters in the other, repeated the fire orders.

As the first rifle shots struck the sangars from the top of the ridge, about two hours after the herdsman's death, the first pair of Hunters roared down to deliver withering bursts of cannon fire on the enemy position. The tribesmen scuttled back down the hill to the comparative safety of the rocks and kept off the ridge for the rest of the encounter, which meant that they could not dominate the sangars. Equally, the SAS patrol had no means of escape. For the time being, it was stalemate.

The conflict that ensued was a tense, cold-blooded sniping duel in which the tribesmen fired from a range of only fifty yards at anything they could see—an elbow, a boot, the top of a skull. The Arab sharpshooters were good; even when their bullets scored no direct hits, they sent fragments of granite into the faces of their opponents whenever the British peered over the rock walls of the sangars. As a result, no member of the patrol escaped entirely unscathed. As each carefully aimed round hit their position, the men of 3 Troop called to one another: "Anyone hurt? "Anyone see where that shot came from?" —"No. They keep changing their positions."

Overhead, the Hunters wheeled and dived with one eye on the identification panels originally intended for the DZ, and now spread on the ground between two sangars. One veteran of this operation later recalled: "We developed the air link to a point where we were getting messages up to correct the aircraft's course on its run-in to strafe the guerrillas." The beleaguered troop also called down artillery support which one officer later described as "fairly continuous and intense at times."

Towards mid-afternoon, the SAS men noticed that the Hunter strikes were becoming less effective; the enemy was becoming more numerous and was creeping closer. The battle was being fought on the east side of Jabal Ashqab, which now began to cast a long shadow, first over the sangars, then over the hostile boulders below them. It was clear to both sides that by dusk the British patrol would lose its air cover completely. Until then, the guerrillas would bide their time. Their quarry was not going to escape, and there were blood-debts to collect. . . .

At about 4:30 pm, Lance-Corporal "Paddy" Baker was wounded for the first time. He was inside the larger of the two sangars, but enemy sharpshooters spotted one exposed leg and fired. Two bullets hit him in the left thigh, causing severe flesh wounds from which blood began to flood. He called to the troop commander, Edwards: "I've been hit, Boss." From outside the sangar the voice of Trooper Bill H., with a bantering third person reference to himself, added: "William's been hit as well!" Both men were lucky. Although the tribesmen were armed with accurate .303-inch rifles, their bullets were refills—old shell cases filled with a homemade charge whose velocity was insufficient to penetrate bone. Bill H. later discovered that the round that struck him had creased his back, leaving a wound like a whiplash across his shoulder blades.

The patrol "medic" threw Baker some extra field dressings. As he strapped up the wounds, Baker thanked his donor, then asked caustically: "But is this the best you can do after all the expensive medical training you've had?" Even as he made the joke, Baker was discovering that his injured leg would no longer support him. In this situation, the injury would be fatal unless he could make the leg function again by dusk. . . . As he lay there he kept testing the leg against the sangar wall. While he was doing so, a sniper's bullet grazed the inside of his uninjured right leg. His left leg recovered strength only a few minutes before the guerrillas attempted to rush the sangar. Two of the tribesmen reached the wall and attempted to push it over. This was unwise. Baker, armed with a rifle, and Sergeant Tk., with a Bren gun, rose simultaneously. The tribesmen were still looking puzzled as the sergeant killed them both with short bursts from the Bren. One even attempted a gesture of "Salaam," as if surprised that his enemy was a white man instead of an Arab soldier.

It was now almost dusk, and from the Thumier base the Squadron commander spelled out what they already knew, that air cover would have to be called off very soon. Edwards told his men, spread around him in an area of about fifteen square yards, that the original plan to mark the Paras' DZ had now "gone for a ball of chalk." They would have to break out just after dusk and make their way back to Thumier; there would be no intermediate rendezvous. By radio they requested an artillery barrage on the sangars at 7:30 pm, by which time they would have left the scene. All these plans were discussed with the Squadron commander and contact with base ended with his acknowledgement: "OK. Good night—and good luck." For the major there was now nothing to do but sweat out the longest night of his life. He tried to arrange a rescue of his beleaguered patrol by sending in another troop by helicopter, but the aircraft had been badly shot-up before it reached Edwards's position and had been forced to limp back to base.

At the sangars, Edwards's troop now smashed everything it could not carry, including the radio. From a separate morse set the soldiers extracted the vital crystals that controlled the set's operating frequencies. Each man carried only his weapon and belt equipment, consisting of water bottle, ammunition pouches and emergency rations. By this time, some of the patrol were still inside one of the larger sangars, while others had dispersed to the rocks outside. Those inside, the focus of enemy attack, were Captain Edwards; the signaller, Trooper Warburton; Lance-Corporal Baker; Sergeant Tk.; and Trooper "Darkie" B. Hiding among the rocks were Sergeant L.; the wounded Trooper Bill H.; Lance-Corporal "Taffy" B. and Trooper T. This party would give covering fire to Edwards and the rest as they stormed out, through the rocks and down the hill. Edwards's group, in turn, would then take up positions from which to cover the retreat of Sergeant L.'s party.

There was a final, absurd formality before the breakout began. Edwards, conscientious to the last, and aware of the Squadron commander's insistence on routine preventive medicine, asked all within earshot: "Has everyone taken his Paludrin?" It provoked some wry grins.

Now it was time to go, but as the party rose, ready to move, one man lay quite still in a corner of the sangar. Warburton, the signaller, was dead. He and his A41 radio set had been hit several times. "All right, we're coming out now!" shouted Edwards. As the four men clattered clumsily down the slope, they were the target of a barrage of small-arms fire from the surrounding rocks, much of it from two large boulders immediately below them. Baker, in the lead, fired back with his rifle. From somewhere behind him, Sergeant Tk. was also blasting the hostile rocks with a Bren fired from the hip. Captain Edwards was between these two and "Darkie" B. was back marker.

The leading man, Baker, lurched forward as fast as his injured leg permitted, then paused and turned to see whether the others were still with him. As he did so, a new fusillade of shots whistled past him and struck Edwards, who seemed to spin round under their impact before crumpling to the ground. The guerrillas concentrated their fire on Edwards now, and the combined force of their bullets pushed his body sideways across the slope. Baker and Sergeant Tk. continued their advance to a point fifteen yards beyond that of their covering party, and took cover themselves. Edwards lay silent and lifeless. There was nothing they could do for him.

The three survivors from the sangar—Baker, Sergeant Tk. and "Darkie" B.—now called the original covering party to follow them. They did so stealthily, gambling correctly on the chance that the guerrillas would still be watching the sanger for any survivors. As the whole group tip-toed away at an angle to the valley, they heard a firefight continuing around the sangar where, in the gloom, two concentric rings of tribesmen were now shooting at each other. The patrol was least at risk so long as it kept to the high ground. This it did, following the contours of the hill as it swung round to overlook Wadi Rabwa and the road home. They had not gone far when the prearranged artillery barrage smashed onto the sangars. But by then—as later, grisly events were to demonstrate—the tribesmen had also retired, taking the bodies of Warburton and Edwards with them.

As shock and fatigue set in, the march back to Thumier took on a nightmarish quality in which the men's judgement and perceptions were becoming distorted. The two sergeants, with Lance-Corporal "Taffy" B., "Darkie" B., the medical orderly, and Trooper T., led the way, with the two wounded men, Baker and Bill H., following some distance behind. After some time, the patrol paused while "Darkie" applied fresh dressings to Baker's still-bleeding wounds. He also cut away four old dressings which were now flopping round Baker's ankle. (Baker had been dimly aware that something was impeding him, but he was unable to comprehend what it was.)

The men resumed the march, struggling up and down the steep walls of minor gulleys near the top of the hill, which fed the main wadi below them. The moon rose, and Sergeant L. called another halt. Barring their path, he fancied he saw a group of Arab tents. If the soldiers were challenged, should they fight? Bluff it out? Or what? They decided to climb even higher to elude this latest threat. Below the "tents" lay the main wadi and a track which was the direct route home. It was an enticing prospect, but fraught with the risk of an encounter with guerrilla picquets. Only when they had skirted the mountain for some distance near the summit, always marching south-west, and had examined the "tents" from another angle, did they discover that the tents were rocks.

Farther still round the hill, the seven men struck a goat track which was going in the right direction, and they trudged slowly along it. Again, Baker and Bill H., the two wounded, fell back. Then Bill heard, or thought he heard, someone following them. Both men paused and glanced back. Some distance away a figure in white was padding quietly along the track in their wake. The two soldiers huddled behind the nearest bush, rifles slippery with sweat as they unlocked the safety catches. This time it was not a false alarm. The man in white was an Arab and there were three others following him in single file. Only the quiet tread of boots, as the rest of the SAS patrol continued on its unwitting way, broke the silence.

As the pursuing Arabs reached the bush, Baker and Bill H. rose, stepped on to the path and kept shooting until the four men went down. Baker, his rifle magazine empty, continued squeezing the trigger, bewildered—by shock, fatigue and loss of blood—that the gun no longer functioned. After some seconds of careful thought, he reloaded with a new magazine. By now, the rest of the patrol had halted, and the voice of Sergeant Tk. was inquiring: "What's going on?" Baker replied: "Hold your fire!" The two back markers, concerned that their com-

rades might inadvertently shoot them, hobbled even
higher up the hill and approached the rest of the party in
an arc. As they did so, Sergeant Tk., satisfied that
they were safe, trained his Bren back up the path and
fired three short bursts along it to discourage further pursuit. For some time they waited in ambush positions, but
there was no sound except the groans of their dying enemies.

At last the patrol moved off again, even more cautiously, every man glancing back from time to time. An
hour later, the back markers, Baker and Bill H., were
certain that they were again being followed. Again they
set up an ambush as their comrades marched on. This
time the pursuers seemed to be guerrilla picquets from the
ridge above them. These two were killed in a carbon-
copy of the previous ambush.

It was now about 2 am. The men had been under extreme pressure for 30 hours or more, but the patrol followed the same drill as before, setting a careful ambush
for any follow-up party, waiting, and then continuing the
march. The soldiers were now far enough away from the
scene of the original contact to make it reasonable to drop
down towards the main Wadi Rabwa. From there to the
camp was only a mile or so, but this, too, was fraught with
danger. If they approached on foot, as someone suddenly
recollected from the pre-operation briefing, they would
certainly be fired on by the Arab FRA sentries at
Thumier. So they walked, drunk with fatigue, down to the
wadi itself, to hide and rest until daybreak. At the bottom
of the hill they found a stream. No one had any water left,
most of the patrol having shared what they had with the
two wounded men. So, ignoring an order not to drink
from an unpurified source, the men slaked their thirst, hid
in the scrub, and waited. Baker sank into unconsciousness.

At first light the patrol moved on again, their faces cut
and bloodied by rock fragments from the sangar, the
limbs of the wounded rebelling against further movement.
After half an hour in the buzzing heat of the wadi, they
heard the sound of salvation—the rumble of a Saladin
armored car as it foraged up the slope towards them. A
radio message flashed back to the Thumier base, retailing
the good news in terse, signaller's jargon. Now the

wounded men, Baker and Bill H., were hauled into the vehicle for the last mile home. (Baker was to be awarded the Military Medal for his part in the operation.) The other five survivors marched back, grim-faced. No one spoke much. They had survived and, for the time being, that was enough. But the reverberations of the SAS skirmish at Shi'b Taym were to echo far beyond Aden.

The main operation in the hills, of which the Edwards patrol had been an essential preliminary, was restructured to seek more modest targets. Instead of a lightning strike at the 3,700-foot Al Hajaf hills in the center of the dissident area, which dominated two watered, cultivated valleys, the Paras and 45 Royal Marine Commando had to fight and climb their way in, peak by peak. Eventually, six major units required five weeks to subdue the area, after which the inhabitants were banished.

While this operation was still in its early stages, a few days after the loss of Edwards and Warburton, a strange and macabre Intelligence report about the fate of the two bodies reached the GOC in Aden, Major-General John Cubbon. Soon afterwards, on the evening of 3 May, Cubbon held a crowded press conference at which he was asked about a Radio Taiz Yemeni propaganda broadcast claim that the heads of the two dead soldiers had been put on public display "in The Yemen." The broadcast was confirmed in Aden soon afterwards by two camel-herders who had seen the display. According to *The Times,* Cubbon replied: "We have reliable information of their decapitation and the exhibition of their heads on stakes in Yemen. If this is true, I must express, on behalf of all three Services in South Arabia, our deepest sympathy with the relatives of the men and their regiments." The timing of the question and the answer were unfortunate. Not only were the next-of-kin unaware of the deaths, but, like other families of A Squadron, they had been led to believe that the men were on a routine exercise on Salisbury Plain.

At government level, meanwhile, the row was only just beginning. The Republican government in Yemen, denying its own propaganda broadcast, now denounced the decapitation story as "a British lie." In Taiz, the US Embassy, which handled British interests in the absence of UK diplomatic recognition of the Republicans, investigated and issued an ambiguously-worded statement to the effect that there was "absolutely no truth to the rumors that the heads of two British soldiers had been exhibited there." In context, "there" could mean the whole of Yemen, or merely the city of Taiz. A row in the British House of Commons followed, during which Labor's frontbench spokesman, Mr. Denis Healey, accused General Cubbon of relying on "scanty evidence" for his claim. But, as Julian Paget's study recorded, on 13 May, ten days after the press conference, "a patrol of the Federal Regular Army found two headless bodies buried in a shallow grave in the area of the SAS battle. The FRA patrol was itself fired on by some 25 rebels, but drove them off by artillery fire. The bodies were recovered and identified as those of Captain Edwards and Sapper Warburton; there was so sign of the heads."

A Squadron returned to Britain on schedule a few weeks later, the object of intense press interest. Thereafter, like the Regiment's other squadrons (D and the re-emerging B), it served in Aden for a few weeks during retraining periods between each four-month stint in the Borneo jungle. These episodes in Aden did not amount to a consistent and continuous campaign. Yet, even if accidentally, they served a number of useful technical purposes which signposted the Regiment's future evolution through the Dhofar war of Oman to counter-terrorism in Europe. In the Radfan, where the guerrilla war smoldered on until the British withdrew in 1967, SAS soldiers were regularly exposed to desert and mountain operations for the first time since the Second World War.

"KEENI-MEENI" IN ADEN

By way of contrast, in the foetid alleyways of Aden itself the Regiment had its first taste of urban terrorist warfare. Hitherto, nearly all its fighting experience since its postwar resurrection in Malaya, had been in the jungle. The urban campaign in Aden, so different from the guerrilla tactics of Radfan and beyond, was also the launching-pad for clandestine plain-clothes operations later adopted by more orthodox regiments.

True, the originality of Major (later General) Frank Kitson in Kenya's Mau Mau campaign—where 22 SAS made a brief appearance—had produced the pseudoterrorist "counter gangs," a mixture of former terrorists and loyal tribesmen led by British officers disguised as natives. It was true also that the same technique was used subsequently in Cyprus to create undercover "Q" units. Here too, British officers performed a clandestine rôle. But when the Major commanding A squadron of the SAS in Aden set up a Close Quarter Battle Course for a selected group of his soldiers, he knew that there was no hope of "turning round" Arab terrorists. Britain had announced her intention to leave the territory, and this extinguished any hope of active support even from her traditional friends in the area. So the new SAS units had to function more like the "Q" squads of the Palestine Police. These had been started by Roy Farran, a veteran of the wartime SAS, and were manned largely by others from the same source. However, it was also remotely possible that, if some terrorists could be taken alive and interrogated, some break in the total, silent security surrounding Nationalist operations might be achieved.

The basic concept in Palestine and Aden, quite simply, was to blend into the local scenery and seize on targets of opportunity. The men chosen for this undercover work were those who most closely resembled Arabs. In the matter of pigmentation the SAS Fijians had, so to speak, a head start in spite of their height. But others who had the sharp, hooked nose and high cheekbones of the Semite looked equally plausible if they were well-tanned and dressed as natives. Such undercover operations were known in Regimental jargon as "Keeni-Meeni" jobs. "Keeni-Meeni" was originally a Swahili phrase to describe the sinuous, unseen movement of a snake in the long grass. It also became a synonym in Africa—and later, via the slave trade, in the Arabian Gulf—for undercover work. British soldiers picked it up during the Mau Mau campaign in Kenya and subsequently in Aden.

The next criterion of selection for "Keeni-Meeni" work was the ability to draw the heavy, thirteen-round Browning pistol from the folds of an Arab futah, and fire it with perfect accuracy. Farran had taught his men the then-unorthodox triangular firing posture known as the "Grant-Taylor Method," and required them to be able to put six rounds through a playing-card at fifteen yards. The early SAS "CQB" Course at Aden was not very different.

Aden: The Urban Operations, 1964-67

① Rifle range, where SAS undercover 'Keeni-Meeni' marksmen were trained
② H.M. Forces married quarters (including Ballycastle House, SAS HQ)

The "Keeni-Meeni" squad of about twenty men operated from various centers in Aden, finally settling in 1966
on Ballycastle House, a block of flats formerly used as
married quarters in the military complex at Khormaksar.
From this center they slipped out in twos and threes to
make their way to the high-risk warrens around the Crater and Sheikh Othman districts.

Their main quarry was the group of skilled, Yemeni-

trained assassins who were steadily suppressing the meager
Intelligence that was reaching the British authorities by
the simple, bloody expedient of killing Special Branch
officers and their contacts. Sometimes the SAS men would
take with them a comrade dressed in Army uniform, or
European civilian clothes, for use as bait in areas where
the assassins lurked. Others copied the idea, notably Major
H. M. Tillotson of the Prince of Wales's Own Regiment
of Yorkshire, who won a British Empire Medal because of
his skill at this risky game.

Within the SAS it is felt that little of tangible value
came out of the experiment except the acquisition of new
experience and knowledge. But there were some contacts.
A pair of Fijian troopers sitting in a civilian car in Sheikh
Othman saw two Arabs approaching them with weapons
drawn, ready to fire. The Fijians leapt from the vehicle,
drew their pistols and killed the terrorists so quickly that
the latter had time only to aim, but not fire, at the soldiers.

Occasionally, the "Keeni-Meeni" patrol did arrest a
terrorist. One was seized as he was about to hurl a grenade. Such attacks became increasingly frequent during
1966 and 1967, and parties of British schoolchildren were
a favorite target for these "Cairo Grenadiers." This time,
the grenade-thrower was picked up and taken back to
SAS HQ at Ballycastle House for interrogation, but he
was unwise enough to make a break for it as they arrived, and was shot dead. Later, the man was identified as
a corporal in the Federal Regular Army, one of the growing number of terrorist converts among the local police and
armed forces.

As in Northern Ireland five years later, the popularity
of undercover patrols out-paced the elaborate training and
co-ordination required for such delicate work. After an
SAS plain-clothes patrol led by the redoubtable Fijian,
Corporal Labalaba, had opened fire on a group of armed
"Arabs" in Sheikh Othman, seriously wounding at least
two men, it was discovered, too late, that the Royal Anglian Regiment had put its newly-formed Special Branch
Squad into the same area. Through the usual channels,
the SAS had done its best to avoid exactly such a disaster,
for unlike other regiments it was not committed to any
given "parish." Against this tragedy, however, must be set

the Anglian undercover squad's success. During a single, six-month tour, a ten-man team from the Regiment's 3rd Battalion captured 105 grenades, five automatic weapons, three pistols, two rocket-launchers, an impressive collection of bombs, ammunition and explosives, and fourteen terrorists including two members of the Cairo-backed FLOSY (Front for the Liberation of Occupied South Yemen) organization.

BACK TO RADFAN

Meanwhile, those SAS soldiers who did not participate in the lethal "Keeni-Meeni" games around Aden city spent a harsher time among the baking mountains near the Yemeni border, speculating cynically about the fleshpots the luckier "urbanites" allegedly were enjoying. On a clear night, from the Bakri Ridge, one could see the lights of Aden, fifty miles away or more. . . . But in the hills there was the compensation of a more traditional hunt—a world of Hemingway rather than of Le Carré.

The presence of British soldiers in the Radfan mountains, following the initial operations of April 1964, had now ceased to be a novelty. Efforts to halt the flow of arms and guerrillas from their Yemeni bases in the north, as well as to control the war in the hills, made it inevitable and public. What still distinguished the SAS penetration was its covert nature.

The Regiment's task was somehow to create observation posts from which enemy movement could be observed silently and invisibly. It was a classic reconnaissance task aided by the terrain, but hindered by the climate. The heat in the mountains could wring, with alarming speed, the last drop of sweat from any living creature, however robust, leaving it dehydrated, exhausted and, if water were not supplied in time, dead of thirst. Medical experts fixed the minimum daily intake for British soldiers at two gallons per day, which meant laborious supply by helicopter and consequent disclosure of the OP position. The SAS overcame this problem in a variety of ways. Occasionally they would move into an overt position with an orthodox unit, remaining in concealment with extra rations for many days after the position had been ostensibly evacuated. They learned to conserve the water they carried inside their bodies by minimal movement during daylight hours, sneaking down to a local stream by night to replenish their stocks. But, even after dark, the exertion of foraging for water invoked the law of diminishing returns because much of what was collected had to be consumed on the way back. As a way of life, it was hard enough to make even the Borneo jungle seem alluring— one veteran describes the jungle as "a gracious living" when set against life in the Radfan.

From their secret eyries, the soldiers directed artillery fire on to suitable targets. Time and again, guerrilla patrols, moving discreetly along the apparently safe route of some obscure wadi, had to scatter for cover as the hiss of incoming shells told them, yet again, that they were being stalked by an invisible foe. The tribesmen's reactions combined the fatalism of Islam with superstition: the guns, they assured one another, were new weapons devised by the diabolic British, guns with eyes "which always seek you out, wherever you go."

At the same time, the tribesmen took advantage of any target they spotted. One SAS attempt to transport men by helicopter on to Bakri Ridge, overlooking the forward base at Thumier, led to a heavy exchange of fire between guerrillas on the ground and the helicopter, which had been equipped as a gunship. That patrol had to be aborted.

Not all SAS personnel up-country were perpetually in the mountains. At least one officer of the Regiment became a temporary Political Officer, advising the local tribal rulers and calculating the political implications of individual military operations. His companion, a dogged bodyguard, also drawn from the Regiment, was never seen without his rifle; as a result local tribesmen nicknamed him "Abu al-Bunduq" (Father of the Rifle). Both soldiers were fluent in Arabic.

A FRIENDLY EARLY WARNING

The nearer the projected withdrawal date came, the more essential were the SAS patrols, to give early warning of attacks on the main forward base at Thumier. The guerrillas, in their turn, now occasionally received early warning of SAS movements in the hills from Arab officers of the Federal Regular Army; they knew that, when the British left, their own lives would depend upon a record of co-operation with the rebels. On such occasions, the FRA advised the guerrillas to keep clear of any area where the SAS was operating, but they were seldom heeded.

In one of the last actions in this area, men of A Squadron were patrolling at Dhi Hirran, near the Yemeni border north of Thumier. Below them, a patrol from 1 Troop saw dissidents moving along the bottom of the wadi. The tribesmen, who were equipped with a British Land Rover, were dedicated Sha'iri supporters of the Egyptian-backed FLOSY movement. The SAS team called down an RAF Hunter strike in one of the last offensive British air operations in Radfan. Politically, the effect of this action was to force FLOSY to merge locally with the more Marxist NLF, which had now almost taken power quite openly in the regional capital of Dhala, and would soon do so in Aden itself, after a bloody internecine battle at which the British would be spectators.

By now, the only major, cohesive British unit which dared to operate at strength outside the shrinking perimeter around Thumier was 45 Royal Marine Commando. Just before dusk on 17 June, only nine days before the final British withdrawal from the Radfan, an SAS observation post spotted three armed men moving along Wadi Bilah, about fifteen miles south-west of the base. The 45 Commando historian, David Young, records:

"Within ten minutes the fully kitted stand-by Troop, Nine Troop (Lt. Phil Robinson), was embarked in Wessex helicopters prior to heading for the scene. . . . The Troop Sergeant, Sgt. John French, takes up the story:

"We leapt out of the choppers, having placed our two picquets—in case they tried to run away—and as we got out we saw the three men dashing up a low hill about 200 yds away. One stopped and fired at us. We were right out in the open and as there was such a din going on, I blew my whistle and told the lads to adopt a kneeling position for firing. This they did and two dissidents were killed outright, a great achievement as it is a most difficult position to fire from. The third ran over the crest of a hill slap into the picquet commanded by Cpl. McLaughlin and was shot at 30 yds range. Throughout the entire engagement, only 80 rounds were expended, a fantastically small amount for three kills."

"At half past five, Nine Troop re-embarked in the Wessex and by 5.32 they were back in Habilayn (Thumier) with three dead dissidents. . . . This was the last occasion on which 45 Commando was to be able to show its outward aggressiveness in the Radfan . . . For the last few days, the unit was literally fighting a rearguard action."

The handover of Radfan to the Federal Regular Army (soon renamed the South Arabian Army), on 26 June 1967, occurred immediately after Israel had crushed the Egyptian Air Force in a pre-emptive air strike of her own, and then destroyed the Egyptian Army in the field during the Six Day War. In Aden, the effect of the Egyptian defeat was to make Arab Nationalists almost mad with grief and hurt pride. Some smashed radio sets and televisions as they disseminated the bad news. For the British, what had been a long dying cause was now assuredly a lost one. It was not a situation likely to help military morale.

As Julian Paget, in his careful study of the Aden affair points out: "It was difficult to find a political or national cause that was worth dying for. But there were other causes . . . for which the soldiers were happy to fight and die, and the chief of these was their Regiment." Of no one was that more true than the politically, militarily and geographically isolated patrols of the SAS during those last days in the Radfan. Some months after Independence, in the spring of 1968, Harry Cockerill visited Thumier. There he discovered "a few Brits" assisting the operation of the airstrip by the South Arabian Army. They included, inevitably, a recently "demobilized" SAS officer.

IV

The Mercenaries, 1962-78

I N THE WORLD OF THE MERCENARY, THE SAS
Regiment suffers from the curse of the cuckold. It is
burdened by responsibility without power. In an effort to
distance itself from the problem, SAS Group Headquarters in May 1978 posted a confidential memorandum list-
ing civil security firms, some run by former SAS officers,
which were proscribed to soldiers serving with Territorial
and Reserve SAS units. Some of the proscribed firms are
merely inefficient; others are a disaster. For the Regiment,
however, all of them, proscribed or not, could generate
public embarrassment if they attract adverse publicity. Indeed, the greater the success of private enterprise in this
field, the greater the potential embarrassment.

A similar difficulty afflicts the American Green Berets,
the British Parachute Regiment and the French Foreign
Legion. The charisma of these units is such that no mercenary soldier worth his fee will disclaim a connection
with one of them—or in really ambitious cases, a permu-
tation of several of these military élites—particularly if
the fee is paid by a newspaper. For its part, the newspaper will wish to egg the pudding as succulently as possible, encouraging its sources to claim, or at least hint at,
a special forces background. Thus the process feeds upon
itself, despite the fact that most mercenaries—but by no
means all—are, at best, mediocre soldiers whose morale is
notoriously fragile if the unit they are serving with sustains serious losses.

By some mysterious law, it is also the case that such
soldiers, some of them chronic fantasists seeking to compensate for broken careers and marriages, are often in-

volved in military adventures that are doomed to failure. Their world is one of betrayal, loot and razzmatazz publicity. It is light years away from the disciplined, skilful, stealthy work of regular SAS operations, whose continued success demands as little publicity as possible.

The number of SAS soldiers who became mercenaries is a tiny fraction of the total. Some of them achieved little in the SAS before becoming freelance soldiers. In 1976, one of those who joined the mercenaries in Angola, for instance, had been obliged to leave the Regiment because of his uncontrolled violence. But soldiers of fortune are not invariably dogs of war, and there is an important distinction to be made between the "cowboys" of the mercenary trade and the professional soldiers who work for a foreign power with the same degree of skill and dedication that characterized their regular service. Most evidence suggests that the very few exclusively ex- SAS "firms" fall into the second category.

There is another reason why the word "mercenary" is a dirty one. If one accepts the neutral, dictionary definition, that of a "hired soldier in foreign service," then the mercenary's motive, by implication at least, excludes idealism as a respectable reason for soldiering. The consequent innuendo of political promiscuity inspires in the popular mind such perjorative labels as "The Whores of War" and renders the free-lance soldier the pariah of civilized society. This contemporary view of the mercenary was adopted by the International Red Cross, which in 1978 stripped from the mercenary the right to prisoner-of-war status and other benefits of lawful combat.

But, as the British government discovered when it sought to legislate against mercenary recruitment after the Angolan shambles in 1976, the pariah image of the free-lance soldier is an over-simplification. The International Brigade in the Spanish Civil War and the expatriate Americans who joined the RAF at the beginning of the Second World War are two examples of the non-mercenary "mercenary." As Anthony Mockler, in his historical study of mercenaries, points out: "So strong is this instinctive feeling that to be a mercenary is itself immoral that it is generally forgotten how recent and how illogical this sentiment is. Throughout most of European history any such moralizing attitude would have seemed ridiculous."

A WARRIOR CASTE

The reason for this ridicule, prior to the nineteenth century, was that, with a few exceptions, soldiering was an acknowledged profession, a vocation even, and by definition the concern of a minority. The involvement of entire populations in modern warfare, starting with the massive and unnecessary waste of life in the First World War, changed the popular perception not only of the soldier, but also of such concepts as "gallantry" and "patriotism." The SAS, uniquely, revived in the mid-twentieth century the characteristics of an exclusive warrior caste, fighting its wars in such a way that most of those involved were other combatants. It is not surprising that a number of its men, for whom this is a way of life, should have become mercenaries after leaving the British forces, particularly when actions fought by those forces have declined in proportion with Britain's withdrawal from the Third World. Paradoxically, it is precisely that withdrawal which has left in its wake a vacuum, which the freelance soldier has tended to fill. Personal bodyguards for heads of state; the organization of counter-coup forces; the training of indigenous government armies and professional strike forces; all have been provided, at one time or another during the past twenty years, usually with little publicity, by former SAS soldiers. On occasion, such services have resulted from links created during time spent with the regular Regiment.

One of the pioneers of the business in post-war years was the man who founded the Regiment during the Second World War, Colonel David Stirling. After the war, he worked in Rhodesia, devoting much of his time during the next twelve years to a movement known as the Capricorn Society, through which he spread a gospel blending racial equality with the ideas of meritocracy he had injected into his military thinking. In 1959 he returned to England, having won many friends in black Africa and having lost some among the more extremist whites in Rhodesia. His financial fortunes were at a low ebb, and he set about repairing them with a television program syndication company, as well as winning the franchise to run Hong Kong's television service. He became involved in military affairs again as a result of events in Arabia and his own, powerful sense of patriotism.

THE YEMEN ADVENTURE

In September 1962, the ruler of Yemen, the Imam Mohammed al Badr, was overthrown in an Egyptian-backed coup, and fled from his palace in Sana'a to the mountains in the north, near the Saudi border. As thousands of Egyptian troops poured into Yemen to stiffen the coup, the kings of Saudi Arabia and Jordan supported the Imam. An eight-year guerrilla war now began.

The British Government watched this situation with growing anxiety, for Aden, immediately to the south of Yemen, was still a British Protectorate. British intervention in the Yemen fell into the hands of a club of Scottish lairds. When the republican coup occurred, Lieutenant-Colonel N. D. I. ("Billy") McLean, DSO, was visiting Saudi Arabia. McLean was a veteran of Special Operations Executive during the Second World War, having parachuted into occupied Albania to organize partisan resistance there. Now Member of Parliament for Inverness, McLean also visited Yemen before reporting to his fellow-Scot—the Prime Minister, Sir Alec Douglas-Home—about the significance of the Imam's survival and his campaign. With Stirling, and the tacit blessing of the British government, McLean discussed the creation of an ex-SAS mercenary force to train the Royalist Yemeni troops and ensure good communications in that remote mountainous area. Stirling was excited by the idea: the British Government still needed his services, it seemed, and that was satisfying. He was also ready for another adventure for its own sake, now that his commercial fences had been mended.

Stirling invited the ex-commanding officer of the Territorial Volunteer Regiment, 21 SAS (based in London), to head the operation, and it was thus that Lieutenant-Colonel Jim Johnson took leave of absence from his job as a Lloyd's insurance broker to become a mercenary organizer. Initially, a group of six ex-SAS officers was recruited and flown to Yemen by way of British-controlled Aden. The first of these was Major John Cooper who, as a corporal, had been Stirling's driver during the brave days of Commando operations behind the German lines in the desert war of 1941–42. After the war, Cooper became commander of A Squadron of 22 SAS and fought with the Regiment throughout the Malayan campaign. He was also one of the leaders of the assault against Saudi-backed rebels on Oman's Green Mountain in 1959. After retirement from the British forces he served as an officer on private contract under the Sultan of Oman. Now, with other former SAS men who had fought in the first Oman campaign, he was sustained by his former enemy's paymaster, the Saudi Government, as the Arabian Royalists united against a common threat. With two comrades, Cooper marched into the Yemen from a safe house in Beihan, in up-country Aden, provided by the Sharif Hussein. Once over the border, the party moved by night, coming close enough to an Egyptian patrol on one occasion to see the glow and smell the smoke of their cigarettes.

Another prominent figure in the Yemen war was Colonel David Smiley, recruited under a separate contract by his old SOE friend McLean to make a series of tours of the battle zone and prepare reports for the Saudis. Later, for a while, he became the Yemeni mercenaries' commanding officer before being succeeded by two former SAS commanding officers. From 1958 to 1961, Smiley had commanded the Sultan's troops during Oman's Green Mountain campaign. On his return to England in April 1961, he was offered overall command of the three existing SAS regiments, but declined because promotion to brigadier did not go with the job. In his colorful account of the Yemeni campaign, Colonel Smiley muses over the irony that within two years of leaving Oman he would be "in the service of my former enemies, the Saudis." He comments: "Although mercenary excesses in the Congo brought discredit on our calling, I maintain that it can still be an honorable one—with the important provisos that the mercenary's own conduct is honorable, and that what he is doing is in the interests of his own country, or in defense of his own ideals. . . . I was—and am—certain that what we were trying to do in the Yemen was in the interests of Britain."

While mercenary recruitment of ex-SAS men was taking place in London, a parallel operation, with the tacit approval of the French Government, was going on in Paris. Jim Johnson's counterpart there was Roger Faulques, an enigmatic, scarred ex-Legion officer, one of the few French paras to survive a Vietminh prison-camp.

During the year before the Yemeni operation started, Faulques, with discreet backing from the French government, was leading mercenary forces in their war against UN troops in the Congo.

According to Smiley, the force that eventually emerged from these sources "at the height of the mercenary effort, when I was commanding them, never numbered more than 48, of whom 30 were French or Belgian and 18 British. They were broken down into small missions—usually one officer, one NCO wireless operator and one NCO medical orderly—and deployed according to the wishes and needs of the Royalist commanders." Although small in number, the mercenaries, through their control of tactical communications, were in a position of extraordinary power and knowledge. At their most effective, the mercenary-led Royalists set up ambush positions to destroy Egyptian columns on the country's few roads. Bob Denard, one of the most flamboyant of the French mercenaries, during a break from his Congo activities showed Smiley the remains of such an action. Smiley wrote: "The sight was indeed impressive. The Royalists had set their ambush in a valley between sand dunes and basalt rocks that looked like small volcanoes on the surface of the moon, and the grim relics of the battle littered the sand on either side of the track. There was a wrecked Russian T34 tank and the burnt-out shells of several armoured personnel carriers, and I counted—with my handkerchief to my nose —more than 50 decomposing bodies, half-buried by sand and half-eaten by jackals. I saw, also, six decapitated corpses—executed Republicans, they told me."

Smiley's advice, to concentrate on the Egyptian supply lines guerrilla fashion, and forget about frontal assaults on Republican-held towns, was ignored by the Royalists, which did not enhance their chances of a military victory. But, given the air superiority enjoyed by the regular Egyptian forces, to say nothing of their use of poison-gas bombs, there was never much hope that the Royalists would produce anything more than a military and political stalemate. This, in fact, is what happened, in the creation of what is now known as North Yemen, but not before three British mercenaries had been murdered at what they believed was a Royalist road-block. They were asked to hand over their rifles and, surprisingly, did so. They were then shot and finished off by grenades thrown by tribesmen manning the road-block. Smiley records: "All the dead men were married, with young children. One had been a good friend of mine who had served in the SAS under me in Oman. Like most of the British mercenaries he had come here to risk his life, not so much for the money, as for the adventure, and in the hope that he might be helping his own country as well; it was a tragic waste that he should lose it through trickery and murder." By now, control of the operation had passed out of Johnson's hands: he withdrew in 1967, shortly before the British left Aden. But the episode left a shadow over relations between some former members of the Regiment for reasons other than simple grief. Disputes about compensation for the families of the murdered soldiers generated the belief that their paymasters had not kept faith with the men at the sharp end.

The mercenaries' activities had an even bigger—if less direct—impact on the Middle East outside the Yemen. From August 1963, Royalist supplies of arms and ammunition were parachuted into drop zones manned by John Cooper's team and others, who guided the planes by radio. These clandestine night flights involved a number of carriers, including Rhodesian Air Services and the Iranian Air Force (then under the control of the Shah), and were negotiated by David Stirling. But, as Johnson himself subsequently revealed, US pressure on her allies, including Britain, to back Nasser's pan-Arabism rather than antique monarchies, threatened these deliveries.

According to Smiley, it had become necessary by 1965 to charter aircraft with discreet pilots "and—most delicate of all—to obtain the agreement of a Middle Eastern country to the use of its territory for mounting the operations." Which Middle Eastern country? We have Johnson's word for it that the obvious candidates—Jordan, Saudi Arabia and even France, then controlling Djibouti—had regretfully declined to act as a base for the air drops. Royalist tribesmen who asked their British advisers on the drop zones where the weapons had come from were told, "From your other enemy, Israel." Johnson uses the anecdote only to dismiss it as a cover for the true source of the flights. The fact remains that so long as the Royalist arms were flowing, so an increasing number of

Egyptian troops and aircraft became bogged down in the Yemeni desert. And, when the 1967 Six Day War occurred between Israel and Egypt, about 68,000 of Nasser's best troops and many of his MiGs were still there.

It is doubtful whether any military entrepreneur, however influential, could engineer such a risky political venture without government help. The precise involvement of Whitehall in the Yemeni war remains a matter of conjecture. But it is not without interest that in August 1967, soon after the Six Day War, the late Captain (later Major) Richard Pirie, the regular Adjutant of 21 SAS Volunteers, the London-based Territorial unit, alleged that his office had been used as a "clearing ground" for mercenaries in the Yemen and elsewhere in the Third World. According to the newspaper, *The People*, he told two of its reporters that he had passed names and military records to someone at a secret address, and that the mercenaries usually heard something in a week or two. Even more astonishing, Pirie asserted that the men's wages of £250 per month were being paid through the Foreign Office and the Ministry of Defence. Both departments promptly denied Pirie's story in identical statements.

Pirie's approach, as he explained to *The People*, was: "Why should it be so secret I don't know. The Egyptians must know that the Yemenis are being supported by the British or British Dominion troops." They did know. A letter from Johnson's second-in-command, Flight Lieutenant Anthony Boyle, ADC to the British Governor of Aden until he became a mercenary under Johnson, was taken from a Yemeni courier by Egyptian forces in December 1963. It is also the case that Western Intelligence benefited considerably from the mercenaries' operations. The former SAS men were able to obtain, for example, indisputable proof of Egypt's use of poison gas. They did so by collecting evidence for subsequent chemical analysis, including samples taken from some of the victims. The analysis suggested that the gas had been manufactured in China.

PETERS IN THE CONGO

At the beginning of the Yemeni operation, while it was still being stage-managed by the "Lairds' Club," a soldier of a very different kind was making his name in the

Congo. John Peters, a dour—and in action, cold-blooded—Yorkshireman, who was to succeed Major Mike Hoare as the commander of the English-speaking Five Commando, hated the traditional British officer class and what he described as its "lah-di-dah" ways. His attitude represents even today, if in exaggerated form, a distinctive element in SAS rank-and-file culture, that an officer merits respect only if he is as good in action as his men. Peters was an infantry sergeant in the British Army before emigrating to Rhodesia, where he served on attachment with C Squadron of the SAS. He then joined Hoare as an NCO. Hoare describes him thus:

"A professional soldier with a background in the (Rhodesian) Special Air Service. . . . A compact man of about 5 ft 8 in with the build of a welterweight boxer, which he had been in his earlier days. He had nerves of steel and a soldier's conscience which recognises only the order and the exigencies of the moment, backed up by a deadly efficiency in all weapons and every facet of soldiering.

"He was tough and untameable, as a Belgian volunteer had discovered when he made the foolish mistake of claiming Peters's camp bed for his own . . . an error which led to a knife wound for him and a severe reprimand for Peters. I hammered Peters frequently in our early days, but he always came up smiling."

The view of one Rhodesian SAS veteran who was not in the Congo was that virtually all mercenary victories were empty ones resulting from "automatic weapons versus knobkerries." This is a popular impression among those who did not participate in the series of tribal wars that wracked the Congo after Independence. In some of the campaigns, the enemy was armed only with poisoned spears and ancient Mausers, plus a belief in invincibility induced by the liberal taking of drugs. They were also very numerous. Later, however, mercenaries were to fight battles against Ugandan regulars who were armed with modern missiles, mines, Browning machine-guns, 76mm cannon and armored cars.

In 1964, four years after Independence, the United Nations force that had expelled a French mercenary group left the Congo itself, at a time when a revolt by cruel and superstitious warriors aged between ten and sixteen against central government was beginning to engulf one provincial town after another. For just over a year, the British and South African Five Commando—recruited by the Congolese Prime Minister, Moise Tshombe—performed the job that an affrighted Congolese National Army was incapable of doing, that of fighting pitched battles against the "Simbas" ("lions"), who believed that they enjoyed magical powers, including protection from enemy bullets. Thousands of European missionaries of both sexes, farmers, technicians and their families were made hostage and suffered barbaric treatment ranging from the rape of their children to slow death and cannibalism. A fraction of these hostages were rescued by Five Commando's flying columns; many were murdered only minutes before their would-be rescuers arrived.

Unlike the SAS, which prefers to operate by night, the mercenaries did not care for night attacks, for they had been ambushed with devastating effect on the road after dark. However, if the rebels' supply line from neighboring Sudan was to be cut and an enemy column overtaken before it dug into good defensive positions along the Nzoro River, a night march was essential. Hoare recalls: "I sent for John Peters. I explained the tactical position as I saw it and affirmed that I would never give the order for our column to move at night . . . but if he could find volunteers it would be a valuable night's work.

"Without so much as a second thought he decided to take the whole of Force John-John [Peters's élite fighting force of 100 men] at once. . . . Twenty minutes later the whole sky was lit up with a gigantic fireworks display. Force John-John had met the enemy column in the act of trundling on to the bridge. A lucky shot from Peters's jeep hit an ammunition truck and blew it sky high.

"The battle lasted ten minutes at the end of which Force John-John had annihilated the whole of the enemy column and captured eleven trucks and mountains of arms and ammunition. . . . Once more John Peters had risen to the occasion and by his magnificent personal example and bravery had turned the day. If the enemy had dug in on the Nzoro we would certainly have been held up for days. . . ."

Later, during a rebel counter-attack on the northern town of Niangara, "John Peters had run from the other side of town to see a solid phalanx of Simbas approaching down a narrow road. Flinging a grenade into the middle of them and shouting the only words he knew in French—'Avancez les mercenaries'—his men joined battle. After some bitter fighting the rebels were pushed back over the bridge, leaving 80 dead behind them." On another occasion, after leading a waterborne attack from Lake Tanganyika, Peters was seriously wounded but "refused morphine and continued to direct the battle until weak with loss of blood."

Hoare, an idealist who believed in prayer, and Peters, the essential warlord who fought to win, did not always find it easy to soldier together. To eliminate unnecessary civilian casualties, Hoare issued an order that anyone carrying a weapon was a rebel, but all others were to be regarded as civilians and left alone. "At the next halt to clear a road-block, I noticed John Peters's jeep was stacked full of spears. One was issued to each dead rebel, posthumously, just in case. . . ."

With the end of the Simba revolt, Hoare went home to South Africa in November 1965, and Peters succeeded him as commanding officer of Five Commando, replacing the "gentlemen" of Hoare's vintage with tough Afrikaners. Peters also wished to settle in South Africa, but his request was rejected. Mockler's history reproduces a long letter to the Pretoria government on Peters's behalf, claiming that Peters's efficiency ensured that South Africans serving with the unit—by now in the majority—or their relatives were properly compensated for death and injury.

A somewhat different picture of Five Commando under Peters is painted by Tshombe's biographer, Ian Colvin. During the year after the Simba war, Colvin asserts that "these Commandos were not of the same mettle and morale as they had been when Mike Hoare commanded them. Some of the best volunteers had perished in battle. Others had been paid off. The newly recruited replacements saw no action in 1966 and were the victims of dangerous boredom. The rot set in. They took to carrying arms off duty and that led to violence, robbery and murder. . . ."

In 1967, Peters returned to London where he worked with the now-exiled Tshombe to prepare for a new, mercenary-led Congolese coup. The scheme never materialized because Tshombe was kidnapped at gunpoint by a French agent aboard a privately-chartered British aircraft, taken to captivity and, ultimately, death in Algeria. Meanwhile Peters supplied freelance pilots to fly for the Government of General Gowon during the Nigerian civil war. He was also confident that his services would be required in the Yemen. "I'm certain I will be called in there within the next six months," he told a journalist in November, 1967. "There is nothing I'd like better than to have a go at Nasser. There is a big future for mercenaries." So there was, but not for Peters in the Yemen, where a firm with better connections had taken over the Royalist cause. Peters finally left London to live in the Far East.

PRE-PACKAGED WARFARE

If the early 1960s was a period of ad hoc, freebooting mercenary activity (mainly in Africa) by individual soldiers who made their own way to the war of their choice, the late sixties and the seventies saw the development of something more sophisticated. This was the "consumer" approach of freelance soldiering—the packaging of military services in such cities as London and Paris, far from the scene of conflict, the marketing style of which paralleled that of international corporations selling such consumer products as motor cars. There were many reasons for this. The end of the British, French, Spanish and Portuguese empires in the Third World created an indigenous demand for security. The growing cost of modern weapons meant that medium powers such as Britain and France were obliged to export war material in order to fund the modernization of their own forces. With those exports went government-sponsored military aid teams to train and advise client governments.

The British Government, fighting a festering counter-terrorist campaign in Northern Ireland from 1970 onward, refined a variety of techniques in "low intensity" warfare. Other governments, concerned for their security in face of a proliferation of "liberation" movements, were passionately interested in such techniques, creating yet another market for military expertise and hardware.

Stirling and his colleagues, alert to the trend, began meeting this demand in many parts of Africa and the Middle East. In 1967 they created the Guernsey-based

Watchguard Organization, a cadre of ex-SAS soldiers that provided bodyguards and trained the corps d'élites of countries ranging from Abu Dhabi to Zambia, by way of Sierra Leone. Some of the contracts were less prosaic and included, for example, the creation of secret regimental "command posts" to which a ruler could take his cabinet in the event of a coup d'état. It was an ironic commentary on the British withdrawal from colonialism. And, as the authors of a book dedicated to one Watchguard operation correctly point out, a process in which, most of the time, the firm's technique was to advise clients about security, but not to fight for them.

More debatably, they claim that Stirling's initiatives were "leap-frogged" by the British Government. They assert: "When President Jomo Kenyatta wanted more protection in the middle 1960s, Watchguard was nearly signed up, but lost the job to the SAS. In 1968, Stirling had quickly grasped that Sheik Zayid, the ruler of the wealthy little Persian Gulf state of Abu Dhabi, would be shopping around for protection. After the Sheik, with full retinue, had been to shoot grouse and stalk deer at the Stirling family estate in Scotland, David Stirling . . . visited Abu Dhabi to talk security.

"But the British Government considered the defence of the Sheikdom too important to leave to a private concern like Watchguard. Similarly, when Stirling offered to help the Arabian Sultan of Muscat fight off the threat from Marxist rebels in the province of Dhofar, Whitehall judged the stakes too high and again sent in the SAS. All these were situations where Stirling and his friends in Whitehall saw eye to eye about what needed to be done, but in which his little agency had been elbowed out of the picture by the official government arm."

In fact, according to those closest to Stirling, he was never "elbowed out of the picture" by the Government. His approach was always to encourage the regular SAS to take on a job which would be, in his eyes, good for his country and his regiment. Kenya was a case in point and so was Iran. Stirling himself took on contracts of which the Government approved, but which it did not wish to handle too directly. Stirling regarded the whole thing as patriotic fun even if, as sometimes happened, it were profitless.

In 1970, Watchguard proposed to King Faisal the creation of a "Task Force" to infiltrate North Yemen. According to *The Sunday Times*, the force would have carried out "destruction on a massive scale . . . using relatively sophisticated sabotage techniques." The main target was the Sana'a-Hodeida road, "with the supplementary objective of destroying gas-bomb-bearing aircraft on the ground." Stirling's proposal reminded Faisal that he had "access to the Special Air Service of the British Army" and his Director of Operations, according to a document leaked to *The Sunday Times*, was an ex-commanding officer of 22 SAS and one of the Regiment's most successful and distinguished pioneers.

For the British Government, such initiatives created political problems as well as occasionally solving them. Military intervention in the Third World was now more than a matter of fighting battles. It had to be accompanied by diplomatic adjustment in British relations with the US or at the United Nations.

THE "HILTON ASSIGNMENT"

Nothing came of the Faisal strike force, possibly because North Yemen was now ruled by a coalition government in which former Royalists were represented, but later the same year Stirling and his friends could be forgiven for thinking that a scheme to remove the new Libyan leader, Colonel Gaddafi, was politically copper-bottomed, in London at least. In September 1969, Gaddafi had seized power from the aging King Idris in a bloodless coup. A dedicated disciple of Egypt's President Nasser—and an exponent of "Nasserism" long after Nasser himself was disenchanted with revolutionary pan-Arabism—this young desert Savonarola had arbitrarily ended a multi-million-pound air defense deal with Britain and closed British and US bases in Libya. The scheme proposed to Stirling by a prominent Royalist Libyan exile was to "spring" 150 political prisoners held in Tripoli's jail as the catalyst for a general uprising to restore the monarchy.

Stirling's team, mostly former soldiers of the French SAS, would land on a beach a few miles out of town, at night, drive quietly along the desert road to the prison and blast a way in. Once the prisoners were set free, the two dozen mercenaries would withdraw to the sea, taking their dead and wounded with them. The outside world would never know that they had existed. It would be a crisp, uncomplicated operation which the Franco-Belgian team could mount with great confidence and a fair chance of success. Along the way, Stirling turned down a bribe of £2,000,000 to betray his own team and deliver those involved, including the backer, into enemy hands.

What became known as the "Hilton Assignment" (a name taken from the ironic nickname given to the Tripoli prison) has been described in a book devoted to the operation by *The Observer's* Middle East specialist, Patrick Seale, and his co-author Maureen McConville. According to their reconstruction, the planners were warned off by the British Secret Intelligence Service almost at the eleventh hour. When a further attempt was made by a former SIS man, to whom Stirling delegated the job while recovering from a motor accident, Italian security men stormed aboard one of the assault craft as it was about to leave Trieste in March 1971. To Stirling's horror, the SIS man, who used the nom-de-guerre "James Kent," later made details of the operation public. In addition to the vessel seized at Trieste, two other ships had sailed, but they were wrecked on the Algerian coast by a storm. Stirling was involved in prolonged neogiations before the men involved were set free.

According to the Seale/McConville version, both the Italians and the British were subject to pressure from the United States, which had decided that Gaddafi's Islamic fundamentalism made him sufficiently anti-Marxist to be worth protecting. That evaluation, of course, was in the innocent days before the emergence of the Ayatollah Khomeini's brand of Islam, and before Gaddafi's own demonstrated ability to reconcile Soviet aid with Islam. Whatever the truth about the "Hilton" affair, it was soon after that episode that Stirling abandoned the business of freelance soldiering. Its growing emphasis on profit rather than patriotism, he confided to a friend, disgusted him. By the increasingly cynical standards of the seventies he was, like Hoare in the Congo, too much an idealist even to wish to succeed. He withdrew from all Watchguard activity in 1972.

Ironically, it was another British company with (albeit tenuous) SAS connections that would be training Gaddafi's personal bodyguard within a few years of the "Hilton Assignment" despite Gaddafi's record of support for revolutionary groups including the IRA. The approach of this company, J. Donne Holdings, to military marketing was brash and typical of the new, apolitical, amoral style of mercenary entrepreneurs. Its glossy, six-page brochure offered courses in such techniques as "silent killing," "advanced sabotage" and "advanced lock neutralization." "In-depth instruction is given in the use of explosives including the manufacture of 'home-made' devices," it announced. Technical instruction was available using "the most sophisticated equipment available," and so too were the tools of modern interrogation.

Donne Holdings's Training Director, Mr. H. M. P. D. Harclerode, was formerly a lieutenant in the Irish Guards after which, on his return to civilian life, he became an officer in 21 SAS, the Territorial Volunteer unit based in London. In a letter to an American security expert in 1977 he claimed: "We are fortunate in that we have recruited a number of former Special Air Service Anti-Terrorist Team members who left government service only in the last two weeks. They are, therefore, completely up to date on techniques and equipment."

NEGOTIATORS AND ASSASSINS

The proliferation during the 1970s of such operations, many of which recruited former SAS soldiers, attracted much hostile publicity that inevitably damaged the image of the regular regiment. But some firms, such as Control Risks Ltd., a subsidiary of the London insurance brokers Hogg Robinson, appear to have performed a uniquely useful and merciful job, as well as a risky one, in employing former regular SAS officers to negotiate the release of kidnapped businessmen in many parts of the world. In September 1977, the *Daily Mail* revealed that two of these officers, Major Arish Turle (an SAS squadron commander who had been decorated for gallantry during the Dhofar campaign) and Captain Simon Adams-Dale, had spent eight months in Colombia, negotiating with the kidnappers of Mr. George Curtis, vice-president of Beatrice Foods of America. Curtis was released from his prison, a tiny cellar, after a ransom of £240,000 had been handed over in four suitcases. Next day, Turle and his colleague were arrested and accused of being accomplices of the kidnappers, despite their claim that they had co-operated with the local police. They were released after six weeks and returned to England.

In its annual report for 1977, Hogg Robinson stated: "Control Risks continues to expand. . . . Its kidnap and ransom service is now being used by Lloyd's underwriters as well as by many international companies both within the United Kingdom and around the world. . . ." In 1979, Control Risks successfully negotiated, on behalf of Lloyds Bank International, the release of two of the bank's British officials after they had been imprisoned by guerrillas in El Salvador.

At the other extreme was a team of a dozen former SAS troopers and NCOs recruited in 1978 to trigger off a coup in the African state of Togo, of which assassinating the head of state was an integral part. The scheme misfired after discreet but effective intervention by MI6 and the Foreign Office. The retired Canadian officer at the center of this plot appears to have had no special forces background himself, but, like others, he was attracted by the reputation of the SAS for efficiency in such matters. His team leader, a respected SAS veteran of Malaya and Borneo, twice Mentioned in Dispatches, and an ex-Watchguard employee, was recalled from Africa where, he insisted, he had been on business in Ghana.

DOUBLE AGENT AT HEATHROW

One of the most extraordinary episodes of recent years involved a former captain of 22 SAS, André ("Andy") Dennison. After serving as a troop commander with the Regiment's B Squadron in Borneo, he left the British Army. He commanded a force in the army of Botswana and then went to Northern Ireland, where he served as a regular training major in the Ulster Defence Regiment.

In May 1975, Dennison answered an advertisement placed in the *Daily Mirror* and *Daily Mail:* "Ex-Commandos, paratroopers, SAS troopers wanted for interesting work abroad. Ring Camberley 33456." The advertisement was placed by a former private soldier of the Parachute Regiment who had also served in Borneo with Dennison's original unit, the 2nd Battalion. His name was John Banks and he had been discharged prematurely from the Army. His discharge book being endorsed: "Services no longer required."

In the briefing that followed, Banks and his colleagues made it clear that the operation they were planning involved sabotage raids into Rhodesia from bases in Zambia. Banks opened his briefing with the warning: "If you have any compunction against fighting for blacks against whites, leave the room now."

At that time—and for long afterwards—the Rhodesian Special Air Service Regiment had good relations with its British side. As C Squadron of 22 SAS, it had been raised to fight in Malaya during the 1950s with Peter Walls (subsequently Rhodesia's military supremo) as its squadron commander. It took part in a "training operation" in Aden in the 1960s, and it was still, unofficially, C Squadron long after UDI. What was more, Dennison had just been accepted for service in the Rhodesian Army.

After the Banks briefing, Dennison contacted his superiors in Salisbury and told them that he was staying in London for a short while on a "private contract" that would be of interest to the Rhodesians. Dennison was selected as commander of the new mercenary force and it was as Major Dennison that he assisted in the final selection of the 200-strong Rhodesian squad at Banks's Camberley office, after the initial London briefing for volunteers. Simultaneously, Dennison was keeping the Rhodesians closely informed of the mercenaries' plans.

Late in July, a dozen of the mercenaries were assembled at the Skyline Hotel, near Heathrow Airport, prior to their departure for Africa. It was a weekend during which the mercenaries drank too much and fought among themselves, much to the delight of an attendant Press corps. Dennison, according to one of those in the party at the time, remained notably sober, guarded and withdrawn. He had reason to be. He had just been warned by one of the organizers of the operation: "We've heard from Salisbury that there is a spy in here somewhere. If he's found, we will have to 'chop' him."

Dennison's isolation ended after a weekend at the hotel during which his fellow mercenaries consumed an average of £200-worth of liquor per head, and the paymaster—never publicly identified—had decided that they frightened him more than the enemy. The operation was

aborted. Dennison went to Rhodesia where he was later
decorated for outstanding bravery while seriously
wounded. He was killed in absurd circumstances while
serving with the Rhodesian African Rifles. In July 1979
he was in the bar of the Zimbabwe Ruins Hotel near Fort
Victoria when it came under guerrilla fire: he rushed out
and was shot in error by a black Rhodesian police officer.

THE ANGOLAN DISASTER

John Banks's paper army, put together in 1975, subsequently formed the nucleus of the most disastrous freelance military force since mercenary Genoese crossbow-
men fled before English archers at Crécy only to be
butchered by their French allies. In January 1976, hundreds of thousands of dollars were funneled from the CIA
to Holden Roberto, leader of the pro-Western FNLA fac-
tion in Angola after Independence. At least two other
groups, the Marxist-oriented MPLA (and ultimate vic-
tor) and the centrist Unita group, were also in the field,
following the withdrawal of Portugal. Roberto, in his
search for mercenaries, recruited four ex-private soldiers
of the 1st Battalion, the Parachute Regiment. Of the four,
three had ended their British military service in prison and
two had been described as psychopaths at separate courts-
martial; one was said by his defending counsel to be a
potential candidate for Broadmoor hospital.

In January 1976, after a week in Zaire, where Roberto had his base, one of the four, Nicholas Mervyn
Hall, returned to London to find more recruits. He carried about £20,000 in new $100 bills whose numbers ran
in sequence, a letter of accreditation typed in French on
an English keyboard, and a photo-identification card describing him as "Major" Hall. From the Piccadilly Hotel
in London, he telephoned Peter McAleese, a former SAS
sergeant who had been among Banks's recruits the previous summer. How Hall came into possession of Mc-
Aleese's Hereford telephone number remains a mystery:
the grapevine it represented had no connection with Stirling or his friends. Through an article in *The Sunday
Times* written by the author, concerning the insurance of
mercenaries for the aborted African operation of July
1975, Hall also made contact with Banks himself, and
thus recruited most of the ill-fated advance guard of about

twenty mercenaries who left for Angola, amid considerable
publicity, about two weeks after Hall's arrival in London.
The group included Peter McAleese.

The Angolan volunteers rapidly discovered that Roberto's mercenaries were engaged in a parody of skilled
warfare which might have been funny if it were not also
releasing some murderous fantasies. For instance, the mercenaries were issued with French army rations containing an innocuous, Pernod-flavored powder contained in a
sinister capsule labelled "Boisson instantanée," an instant
drink intended to make mere water more palatable. The
mercenaries believed that the capsules contained cyanide
—"Poison instantané"—to be taken in extremis. It is
possible that the prisoners who later appeared at the Lu-
anda show trial were taken alive by their Cuban enemy
because of this misunderstanding.

In the field, the mercenaries were led by Costas Georgiou, alias "Colonel Callan," Hall's partner and former
comrade in 1 Parachute Battalion. Georgiou ensured that
his force alienated its own African support, such as it
was, through arbitary execution of FNLA soldiers, sometimes for no better reason than to test a weapon, or because the executioners felt like it. The mercenaries also
drove Land Rovers at speed over roads they had mined
themselves, with predictable results. It was not a way to
win friends and influence people.

These events culminated in the execution, on Georgiou's orders, of fourteen newly-arrived mercenary recruits from Britain, an event known subsequently as the
"Maquela Massacre." The most enthusiastic executioner
was former Parachute Regiment NCO, Sammy Copeland.

The SAS veteran, McAleese, meanwhile, was running
his own reasonably well-ordered—if unsuccessful—campaign of defense training and food distribution among local civilians in the port of Santo Antonio do Zaire, a long
way from Georgiou's grotesque reign of terror. After
Georgiou had been taken prisoner by the Cubans, Mc-
Aleese was appointed field commander of the mercenaries. With Hall, he participated in a court-martial of Copeland. In an effort to save Copeland, according to one pain-
stakingly researched book on the Angolan adventure,
McAleese proposed that another accused mercenary be
executed in Copeland's place. This appeal by McAleese to

the FNLA leader Roberto came to nothing when Hall insisted that Copeland should die as agreed by the court-martial.

Copeland's last-minute attempt to escape while the argument continued ended in a hail of bullets fired at him by other mercenaries. The coup de grace was administered by one of the original four mercenary volunteers, another ex-member of 1 Parachute Battalion. According to the study cited above: "He fired three times into the back of Copeland's head with his pistol. 'That's him finished then,' he said, returning his pistol to his holster and patting it." In such a doomed enterprise, the distinction between friend and foe had all but evaporated. Soon afterwards, all FNLA positions were overrun by Cuban and left-wing Angolan soldiers of the MPLA.

McAleese subsequently joined the Rhodesian SAS, passing its selection course although he was now in his forties, during the last months before the country acquired a new identity (Zimbabwe-Rhodesia) and a black head of state. In Rhodesia, like other former members of the British SAS Regiment there, he received the same rate of pay as indigenous troops. Such expatriate soldiers were not motivated by a desire for instant loot but by the fact that active soldiering was a way of life and Rhodesia happened to be an available war zone. The only political peculiarity of the Rhodesian SAS was that it remained an exclusively white fighting force.

In the atmosphere that followed the Angolan shambles, it was hardly surprising that other British mercenary organizations attracted excited and hostile attention from journalists, who made no distinction between one "funny firm" and another. Some of the criticism was dogmatically moralistic—"The ruthless machismo of the mercenary creed does not easily lend itself to ideas of democracy, socialism or racial equality," declared Duncan Campbell in the journal *Time Out*—and much of it was directed at the SAS. Such a value-judgment ignores the SAS tradition of meritocracy, irrespective of race, as well as Stirling's own declared commitment to racial equality.

Other enterprises which now received critical Press attention included Thor Security, which has had former SAS officers on its board, and Donne Holdings.

*   *   *

SECRETS FOR SALE

The most reasoned criticism of the activities of some of these freelance operators is that they appear to offer to their foreign clients data and techniques which are, or should be, official British secrets. Donne Holdings' material has been quoted already. Thor's sales brochure refers to new technology in safeguarding prison perimeters, and adds: "Most of this information is classified, but can be available to Thor Security Systems for suitable government or civilian design contracts." The nuance conveyed by the word "suitable" is that official clearance would be required for the sale of such information, but such a claim is sufficiently novel to justify press interest.

There is little sign yet of official anxiety about the problem of mercenaries generally, despite the inquiry which followed the Angolan affair. No one has been prosecuted for the sale of any official secret; nor is it illegal to hire soldiers for freelance military operations outside the United Kingdom. Such inactivity derives from the fact that some freelance operators can be very useful to government from time to time, and that this consideration outweighs the occasional embarrassment.

The rôle of one such organization was the subject of parliamentary questions in July and August 1978. Mr. John Tomlinson, Minister of State at the Foreign and Commonwealth Office, was asked about private security companies which the FCO had employed during the preceding five years. In Britain, the list contained such familiar names as that of Securicor. The Minister went on: "Abroad, guards have been obtained through one private firm—KMS Ltd.—to protect ambassadors at a very few particularly exposed posts. . . . The department looks for reputable firms able to provide a good and consistent standard of service."

A few days earlier, Tomlinson had been asked about "the hire of bodyguards from private firms such as KMS." He replied that "in a number of countries, the protection at our missions includes armed guards who have either been provided by the host government or recruited locally. At a very few particularly exposed posts, we have thought it advisable, with the agreement of the governments concerned, to strengthen this protection by sending out British guards from a private firm." The initials

"KMS" in this context, do not literally represent anything. Less formally, they are an insider's joke, a sidelong reference to "Keeni-Meeni Services."

It is plausible to conclude that the parliamentary questions resulted, in part at least, from an article that had appeared in *Time Out* a few days earlier, identifying KMS as a mercenary organization, linking a number of prominent, retired SAS officers including Colonel Johnson and Major Andrew Nightingale. In spite of its critical tone—the headline, "The Pedigree Dogs of War," said it all—the article did not specify what KMS did other than to recruit mercenaries and provide bodyguards.

An insight into Nightingale's rôle emerged through a parliamentary answer by Minister of Defense Frederick Mulley. Asked to state his policy on "serving officers acting for hire through private companies," Mulley replied that when Nightingale accompanied Lord Carver on his 1977 mission to Rhodesia, Nightingale was on leave at the end of his military service. "There are no regulations," the Minister added, "to prevent people in this category from taking up civilian employment in advance of their release dates."

For some time before the parliamentary questions, the Regiment itself had been disturbed about the degree to which public perceptions of its character were being distorted by the links, sometimes tenuous as in the case of Donne Holdings, with the mercenary world. On 30 May, two months before the *Time Out* article and the parliamentary questions, soldiers in the SAS Territorial and Reserve squadrons were told that their service in the Regiment was incompatible with work undertaken for eight named freelance companies. "This embargo," the Regiment announced, "covers personnel who are not directly employed by these firms, but in receipt of a retainer's fee, awaiting employment. If a person employed by one of these firms resigns or leaves that firm, a clear six months must elapse between his time of leaving and his (re)-enlistment into a unit of the SAS (Volunteers). Any individual who gains entry to the SAS (V) by knowingly making a false statement about employment with one of these firms will never be further employed by the SAS (V) again." To someone who has been accepted into the SAS family, such a sanction means everything.

There was a quaint postscript to this sonorous warning in 1980, when a team of ex-SAS soldiers, all of them good professionals, travelled to the strategically sensitive, politically non-aligned Maldive Islands in the Indian Ocean. Until 1976, the Royal Air Force had maintained a staging post on one of the islands, an atoll named Gan. Following the crisis in the Persian Gulf area resulting from the Shah's downfall, the seizure of US diplomats as hostages in Iran, and the Soviet invasion of Afghanistan, both super-powers were engaged in a search for bases in the Indian Ocean. The Maldives were perfectly located for such a base, but the neutralist government of President Gayoom politely declined to get involved in super-power war-games.

Then, with promises of £10,000 each, nine British mercenaries travelled to the Maldives to stage a coup d'état on behalf of an unknown backer. They tried, somewhat unconvincingly, to adopt a cover as "businessmen on a diving trip" but, unaccompanied by wives, they stuck out like sore thumbs among bourgeois German and Swedish holidaymakers. According to their leader's plan, they were to rely upon surprise and a few .22 pistols to seize the National Security Service headquarters and armory in the capital, Malé. But somewhere along the line, the Maldivian Government had got word of a foreign "assassination team" in the country. This was sufficient to trigger-off a security alert.

The team quit the Maldives in the nick of time, after a heavy-footed reconnaissance "holiday" which one government source described as "more Laurel and Hardy than Dogs of War." Back in England, the team disintegrated amid recriminations about unpaid fees and broken promises, in a pattern so familiar as to be a classic of its kind. But the hare-brained plan caused deep concern to 22 SAS—which abhors unauthorized freelance contracts— and the British Foreign Office. If the attempted coup had proceeded and failed—as it surely would have done—the appearance of ex-SAS soldiers at a political show-trial might have been the least serious result: at worst, the operation might have driven the non-aligned Gayoom into the arms of the Soviets.

V
Oman, 1958/59, 1970-76:
The Wild Colonial War

T HE SULTANATE OF MUSCAT AND OMAN IS A place of extremes where, according to a Persian proverb, the sinner has a foretaste of what awaits him in Hades. By day its volcanic rock acquires the heat and airlessness of an oven, generating a nocturnal summer temperature of 112 degrees Fahrenheit at sea level. On the northern mountains in winter, the temperature drops so far below freezing-point that it turns a metal water-bottle into a block of ice. Out of the valleys, the wind is incessant, and turbulence makes air travel a sickening experience. In the south, the summer monsoon brings incessant rain from which there is no shelter on the mountains of Dhofar. Everywhere, at all seasons, wounds fester with appalling speed.

The country is also a political anachronism, an absolute monarchy in a world of popular government, where political dialogue, when it exists, is traditionally violent. But, by an accident of geography, the Sultanate, through its inheritance of the Musandam Peninsula, commands the Hormuz Strait through which passes about 50 per cent of the non-Communist world's supply of crude oil. Successive British governments have concluded that the protection of this strait is vital to the British economy, and successive Sultans have found it essential to rely on British soldiers for their security. It is a delicate arrangement, in which Britain has worked with some success to make the patriarchy of Oman less barbarous while safeguarding the monarchy itself (and one that uniquely defies post-

119

war British policy of abandoning former colonies and protectorates to the wind of change).

By coincidence, a similar political interdependence has characterized the involvement of the SAS in Oman. The Regiment has fought two successful campaigns there, one lasting a few months in the winter of 1958/59; the second, a six-year war which ended with the Government's victory of 1976. On the first occasion, the Regiment had just been included in the Army's long-term Order of Battle and was under pressure to prove that it could function, as it claimed, at short notice outside its now-traditional jungle environment of Malaya. The second Oman campaign began in 1970, at a time when the SAS —never a garrison regiment—had no fighting commitments and when its raison d'être was being questioned not only in Whitehall, but also within its own ranks.

OMAN I, 1958/59: MISSION IMPOSSIBLE

The first Oman campaign had its roots in a rebellion covertly backed by American oil interests and the Royalist Saudi Government in 1954. The revolt against the Sultan at that time was rooted in fertile soil. In 1958, an official from the British Embassy in Beirut reported that in twenty years' experience of the Middle East he had never seen, until he reached Oman, "a people so poverty-stricken or so debilitated with disease capable of treatment and cure."

The rebellion was led by three men. They were Suleiman bin Hamyar; Ghalib, Imam of Oman, the "Lord of the Green Mountain"; and Talib, his ambitious younger brother, the most formidable of the trio. The "Green Mountain" (Jabal Akhdar) is an elevated, fertile plateau, twenty miles by ten in area, on average 6,500 feet above sea level, locked behind sheer cliffs of rock and shale rising to 10,000 feet above a sweltering plain. It has a climate and economy quite different from that of the surrounding countryside: it is almost an Arabian version of Conan Doyle's "Lost World." On the plateau, Talib had assembled an offensive guerrilla force of 180 sharpshooters supported by about 500 armed tribesmen. There were only twelve known easily-defended approaches to the plateau, and the rebels had ample stocks of modern weapons including .5-inch Browning machine-guns and quan-

tities of mines with which, during raids on the surrounding
plain, they blew up 150 vehicles including 18 British Ferret scout cars between March and November 1958. Although short of food and suffering from bombing attacks
by the Sultan's air force, they were still a formidable
enemy, apparently able to resist indefinitely.

By now, the conflict had already exploded one bit of
British mythology about controlling tribes in the Middle
East—that it could be achieved exclusively through the
use of air power. As Phillip Darby's account puts it: "The
myth had persisted in air force circles that the RAF's air
control method was an economical and successful way of

North Oman, 1958/9 and 1970-76
① Jabal Akhdar operations, December 1958
② Musandam Peninsula

© ARMS AND ARMOUR PRESS 1990

dealing with local tribal quarrels. Thus when the Oman
revolt broke out the RAF asserted that it could do the
job unaided and the Government, acting on this advice,
authorised rocket and cannon attacks on enemy held forts,
and certain other operations. . . .

"In his statement to the House of Commons on July 23
1957, the Foreign Secretary, Mr. Selwyn Lloyd, was cat-
egorical that there was 'no question . . . of large scale operations by British troops on the ground.' Indeed, he went
on to say that in view of the high temperatures in Oman
at that time of year, it would be an example of military
futility to seek to employ ground forces in the desert
areas."

So much for the received wisdom. The SAS was invoked in October of the following year, through a somewhat complex blend of real-politik and coincidence. In
a sensitive War Office planning post at that time was Major (later General) Frank Kitson, a pioneer of counter-
revolutionary warfare since the Mau Mau campaign in
Kenya. Kitson's plan for seizing the plateau involved the
placing of carefully chosen British officers in positions at
the foot of the mountain, with a nucleus of bodyguards
and "a substantial sum of money" with which to bribe
local informers. This, it was hoped, would bring about
the capture of guerrillas, some of whom would be turned
around to work for the government. "I visualized," wrote
Kitson later, "forming one or two teams of prisoners
augmented by some of our own soldiers in disguise." These
groups, he suggested, could then penetrate the plateau.

The Kitson plan was tentatively approved, with an
elaboration added by the Director of Military Operations, General Hamilton: why not use the SAS? In the
event, the Kitson plan was overtaken by the SAS's own,
more direct method of attack. But the notion that the
Regiment should take on a long-term Intelligence rôle,
anticipating revolution before it actually happened, was
one to which Kitson returned in later years, and which
the SAS accepted only in so far as it did not change radi-
cally its existing rôle and character. A decade later, in
Northern Ireland, some of Kitson's ideas—based, like
those of the SAS, on an economic use of small numbers
of carefully selected men—bore fruit in the creation of
the plain-clothes Military Reconnaissance Force.

In 1958, however, there were other reasons why the SAS was preferred to one of Kitson's "counter gangs." A quick military solution required climbing experts and an assault team that would operate in conditions of ultra-secrecy. Finally, there were indirect political considerations that more orthodox troops (such as Royal Marine Commandos and Parachute Regiment soldiers) would be hard put to meet—a requirement that no serious number of casualties would be suffered, to reduce the risk of adverse publicity at home, and a time-table that would ensure a conclusion before the next UN debate on the Middle East. What it all boiled down to was that the Green Mountain, unconquered since an abortive attempt by the Persians more than 900 years before, had to be taken without British casualties, in weeks rather than months.

Yet another political problem was the delicate question of relations with the Sultan and his British-officered, Arab/Baluchi army. The Sultan's new Chief of Staff, Colonel David Smiley, had been warned by his friend Julian Amery, Under Secretary for War: "We give the Sultan help; we sometimes give him advice; but we do not give him orders."

The commanding officer of 22 SAS at this time was Lieutenant-Colonel Anthony Deane-Drummond (an Arnhem veteran who had eluded captivity after that operation by hiding for three days in a cupboard in a German-occupied house). After conferring with Kitson in Oman, he returned to Malaya to gather up D Squadron, under Major John Watts, for the new operation. The Squadron was spread around a remote area of the Malayan jungle near the Thai border, still mopping-up the campaign that had kept it busy since 1950. Now it had to retrain and be on the ground in Oman within fifteen days.

The force was brought back to Kuala Lumpur within forty-eight hours, through a series of forced marches and journeys aboard improvised river rafts. It then went through a hectic retraining period lasting sixteen hours a day, during which the favorite SAS jungle weapon, the sawn-off shotgun, was exchanged for automatic rifles and rocket-launchers. When the Squadron arrived in Oman early in November 1958, its men learned that of the fifty British troops attached to Smiley's staff, 45 had been flown to hospital suffering from heat exhaustion, while two others had died of it. Furthermore, the risk of being shot on the slopes of the Green Mountain was such that virtually no Arab would act as guide. Two attempts by the British to seize the jebel in battalion strength had failed.

For the first few days, the Squadron pursued its own energetic reconnaissance program, and the dangers rapidly became apparent. One corporal—a soldier on temporary attachment from the Royal Army Medical Corps as a specialist—was riding in vehicles which were blown up on the two occasions he left the SAS base; he refused to risk his luck a third time and had to be evacuated by helicopter. Another corporal, "Duke" Swindells, an experienced SAS soldier who had won a Military Medal in Malaya a few months earlier, was shot dead by a sniper as he walked up a ridge. Given the government's insistence on casualty-avoidance, this was regarded as a very bad augury indeed.

NIGHTS ON A BARE MOUNTAIN

Swindells was killed while moving by day. The SAS response was to propose nocturnal movement only, unless the need to do otherwise was imperative. The received wisdom among the Sultan's officers was that the nature of the ground made this impossible, but the SAS went ahead with the new policy anyway, arguing that night had the additional advantage of avoiding the heat and exhaustion of daylight operations. As a result, the Squadron was able to move on the mountain with much more freedom. An early episode featured the Squadron's commander, Watts, who came striding down a precipitate path, quite alone, as an astonished patrol of the Sultan's armed forces was feeling a tentative way upwards.

The new policy produced a limited success within a few days. Guided by a very nervous local sheik, an SAS troop climbed a steep track, once used by the Persians, on the north side of Jabal Akhdar. In the darkness they reached the lip of the plateau undetected. The track they had followed was punctuated by enemy sangars which, amazingly, were unmanned. At the top, near a twin peak called "Sabrina," the guiding sheik fell on his knees and thanked Allah for salvation.

The two troops were led by Captain Roderic ("Rory")

Walker, who subsequently came to public notice as the
Piper of Jakarta during the Borneo campaign. His men
occupied sangars 3,000 yards short of a strong rebel picquet at Aqbat al Dhafar, and soon came under attack. In
one episode, 40 guerrillas armed with rifles and two
Brens moved in on a forward slope position held by Sergeant J. Hawkins and nine men. The sergeant ordered
his men to hold their fire. When the enemy was only 120
yards away, they let loose a barrage of Bren and rifle
fire, killing five men and fatally injuring another four. The
attack disintegrated.

In the same area, Walker led an exploratory raid
against Sabrina on the night of 27 December. The two
troops were detected just before they reached the top.
One of them was climbing a rope up a fault in the cliff
when the guerrillas above called, in English, "Come on,
Johnny," and opened fire. Walker hauled himself further
up the rope and lobbed a grenade over the top. One
guerrilla was killed instantly and his comrades scattered.
Walker was over the top now, his men following. In the
darkness they killed another eight of the enemy.

Meanwhile, on the south side of the mountain, a small
patrol had found a cave used by the guerrillas to guard
the main approach to Jabal Akhdar. It was also a main
store for weapons and ammunition. Two nights later, two
SAS troops moved on it. One of these, under Captain de
la Billière, made a ten-hour night march through enemy
territory in order to approach the cave from an unexpected direction. It then crept to a point 200 yards from
the cave mouth, lined up a 3.5in rocket-launcher, and
waited. The only point from which the SAS could open
fire was below the cave, and this meant that the rocket
crew had to kneel or stand to use the weapon. The same
firing-point was, faute de mieux, in a natural amphitheatre
whose upper slopes were honeycombed by many small
caves sheltering enemy snipers. At dawn, as the first of
the guerrillas emerged, stretching his sleep-laden limbs
and yawning, the soldiers poured a hail of missiles and
machine-gun fire into the main cave. Describing the action subsequently, Deane-Drummond wrote: "Even such
withering fire did not cause the rebels to panic or surrender. They quickly dropped into fire positions and returned
the best they could. Reloading and firing the 3.5in from

the standing position became interesting." What made it particularly interesting, as well as infuriating, was the failure of many of the SAS missiles to leave the launcher after being fired. They remained unfired but "active" and had to be extracted immediately and replaced with another round, regardless of the recommended safety drills.

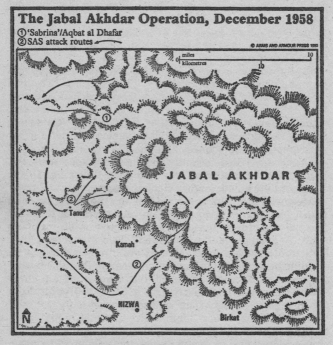

The Jabal Akhdar Operation, December 1958
① 'Sabrina'/Aqbat al Dhafar
② SAS attack routes ←
© ARMS AND ARMOUR PRESS 1990

miles
kilometres

JABAL AKHDAR

Tanuf

Kamah

NIZWA

Birkat

N

The battle instantly brought down rifle fire from the surrounding hills. Describing the encounter soon afterwards, the journalist Brian Connell wrote: "Outlying rebel pickets retreated slowly and the SAS picked them off one by one. The rebels still had a mortar firing from a crevice behind the cave, but the SAS had laid on air support. As Venom aircraft came swooping in, one of their rockets made a direct hit. Mortar and men were destroyed immediately. 'Right down the chimney!' the SAS shouted as it went up."

In fact, it was not quite so simple as that. The Venoms were "stacked" out of sight and sound, awaiting a simple radio signal for an air assault that was to last exactly fifteen minutes, during which the troop was to make an orderly, co-ordinated group withdrawal. This now became a fighting retreat, in which men moved back singly or in pairs, using every scrap of cover available. This lasted rather more than fifteen minutes, and was covered by .3-inch Browning machine-gun manned by a regimental veteran, "Tankie" Smith, from the nearest high ground held by the SAS.

As well as D Squadron, the Jabal Akhdar actions now also involved a Life Guards troop acting as infantry, two troops of local Trucial Oman Scouts, a few signallers and REMEs, a total of about 200 men. All shared the same harsh conditions. At night, the men's water-bottles froze. By day, the wind at 8,000 feet blew incessantly. It was very different from the jungle, and an environment in which soldiers' lips, and their rubber-soled boots alike, cracked open within days.

Morale, Deane-Drummond asserts, was terrific, possibly because after Malaya, in which weeks of profitless jungle patrolling were relieved by a few seconds of action, the SAS had now found an enemy who stood his ground and fought. But, in addition to the hardships of the new environment, there were also some spectacular operational muddles. In the first attempt to deliver mortar bombs to the Squadron by parachute, 12 out of 17 canopies failed to open properly and the bombs they carried exploded among the soldiers, injuring no one.

A GAME OF BLUFF

By the end of December, it was clear that the Squadron's toehold on the north side of the plateau would remain just that unless more men could be brought in to assault it. True, a total of forty rebels had been killed by now, but this had merely stiffened enemy resistance. A full squadron would be required to seize and hold the plateau, while another was essential to maintain pressure on the flanks. And time was against success. Deane-Drummond decided to bring in a second squadron from Malaya and establish a tactical headquarters to co-ordinate the two forces.

Commanded by David Stirling's wartime driver and comrade-in-arms, John Cooper, A Squadron arrived in Oman on 9 January 1959. After less than a week's joint patrolling on the north side of the plateau with an augmented "troop group" of the incumbent D Squadron, the newcomers were given the task of attacking the twin-peaked Sabrina, at whose center was the main enemy gateway. This "training-operation" as Deane-Drummond describes it, was in fact geared to bluffing the guerrillas into believing that this obvious route was indeed the main axis of the British assault; but, although a feint, it required a frontal assault up a narrow track that climbed 400 feet to a strongly-held position. A similar maneuver, launched from Tanuf, eight miles from Sabrina, would serve the same purpose. The third element of an elaborate hoax was a confidential briefing given to four local donkey-handlers, who were told that Tanuf would be the main assault route. The handlers, whose animals would carry ammunition, were threatened with death if they disclosed the secret. It was passed to the guerrillas within 24 hours.

While these bluffs were being enacted, the enlarged troop from D Squadron, which had taken part in the feint attacks, made a secret withdrawal in the darkness to join the rest of the Squadron for the main assault. It was a long march off the mountain to a pick-up point at Wadi Tanuf, from which lorries ferried the men fifteen miles to their rendezvous with the rest of the Squadron, and the beginning of another uphill climb. Planning a viable route to the plateau for the main assault on the south side of the plateau had finally become a matter of educated guesswork. The Sultan's Chief of Staff, Smiley, the commanding officer of 22 SAS, Deane-Drummond, and his squadron commanders Watts and Cooper, had all studied aerial photographs of the area. The consensus choice was a climber's route rather than a track, a fine line along a steep ridge extending like a fox's brush into low ground held by the Sultan's men near the village of Kamah. It required a nine-hour climb in darkness, up a 4,000-foot slope, for which ropes were needed on one precipitate traverse. Each soldier carried at least 60 pounds weight, most of it ammunition. Behind the SAS Squadron came a troop of Life Guards on foot, and a company of the

Sultan's Northern Frontier Regiment, hauling protesting donkeys laden with machine-guns.

This untried route was tested by de la Billière's leading troop. Almost three-quarters of the way up, the troop found just one Browning .5-inch machine-gun whose two-man crew, as Deane-Drummond put it, "could have mown down the attackers in the moonlight, but they had withdrawn to their cave secure in the knowledge of ten centuries that the jebel was impregnable." The guardians of the Browning were asleep when the SAS reconnaissance troop found them. They were left to sleep on, with an SAS guard watching over them. Guerrilla picquets on the other side of the plateau, around Sabrina, had now been increased to 100, while the remainder of their force was concentrated at Tanuf.

From this point on, it seemed to the attackers that the way was clear, but it was now almost 3 am. Watts, leading the Squadron, and the commanding officer, Deane-Drummond, therefore had a choice. They could continue to move a ponderous, but well-armed force up the hill, with the risk that it would fall into the text-book trap of mountain warfare, that of being overlooked by the enemy at sunrise. Or the SAS Squadron could cache its heavy rucksacks and make a dash for the top with only a minimum of ammunition. This plan also, had it misfired, would have been fatal—costly in British lives if even a small group of guerrillas lurked unseen at the top, and politically embarrassing. Watts decided on a quick dash. The rucksacks were dumped on a false summit short of the plateau, in what was now a race against the sun, and the main force left to catch up later. With just their rifles and what ammunition they could carry on their bodies, the SAS men slithered down the steep incline leading from the false summit they had reached, to begin climbing once more.

"In the final stages," one of those who took part recalls, "there was a race to be first on top since the Persians." The front runners included Deane-Drummond, Watts and de la Billière. They arrived on the unguarded plateau "absolutely shattered" by their climb, only to be scourged on by Deane-Drummond to advance and consolidate what was still only a tenuous hold on the guerrilla stronghold.

With the dawn came an air strike by Venoms and a parachute supply drop, which apparently convinced the few guerrillas remaining on the south side of the plateau that a full-scale airborne invasion of the area was in progress. Whatever the reason, the guerrilla leaders fled, leaving eight mortars, six heavy machine-guns, twelve Brens, quantities of mines and other ordnance, and a great deal of revealing documentation about the uprising. There was also an Aladdin's Cave, explored that morning by the SAS: a labyrinth full of boxes, which the soldiers opened by torchlight. They contained only clothes, but there were moments when the soldiers wondered if the next box might not just contain something approximating to the Crown Jewels. . . . The loot included a 6mm MAB pistol, belonging to one of the guerrilla leaders, which finally found its way to the Regimental museum.

For many of those involved, there were more orthodox rewards. Deane-Drummond was awarded a DSO and Captain Walker one of four MCs. The others went to John Watts, de la Billière and Lieutenant Anthony Jeapes. Sergeant Hawkins received a DCM and Trooper A. Cunningham, an MM. Six men, including Cooper, were Mentioned in Dispatches. The comparative lavishness of the awards reflected, not only the military achievement, but also the gratitude of Whitehall for the fact that a highly embarrassing rebellion had been snuffed out, after more than four years of failure by the security forces in Oman. It was, declared *The Times,* "a brilliant example of economy in the use of force."

It was also a risky, lucky operation and one that was to have prolonged effects on British defense policy generally. The tide of independence movements in the Third World was already beginning to run counter to the traditional, imperial idea of big overseas garrisons of British forces. Additionally, the new emphasis on nuclear weapons was having an impact on conventional forces available for low-intensity campaigns outside Europe. As Darby cogently points out: "Militarily, the Oman campaign was not much more than a skirmish, but it had important lessons for the policy-makers about the demands of British overseas commitments and the way in which they had to be supported.

"This minor operation in the arid wastes of the Persian

Gulf, in support of the feudal ruler of a country which
had not emerged into the twentieth century, powerfully
supported the hand of those ministers who argued for a
greater emphasis on conventional forces, and perhaps had
more effect on the Cabinet's thinking about defense priorities than all the carefully balanced arguments of the
preceding few months."

Even more significant was the decision of the Chiefs
of Staff in 1961 "that Britain must be increasingly prepared to intervene in Asia and Africa and that this would
be her major military role over the next decade." The
policy from now on, until the "Europeanization" embodied in the 1974 Defense Review, was strategic mobility,
the "fire brigade" approach to power projection, the first
successful experiment in which was the SAS intervention
in Oman in 1958/59.

OMAN II: DEFEAT INTO VICTORY
By the spring of 1970, the Regiment had no suitable
theatre within which to rehearse its "training operations."
The classic counter-revolutionary campaigns that had
started with Greece in 1944, and continued through to
Aden/South Yemen in 1967, were now a matter of history so far as British interests were concerned. Early in
1969, an SAS officer, disturbed by the lack of action,
analyzed British military history and concluded that since
1830 there had been only one or two years in which the
Army was not fighting a war somewhere. It seemed that
1968/69 was one of those years. True, from August 1969
onwards, violence in Ulster required the presence of
about 14,000 British troops, but they were there initially
as a peace-keeping force, UN style, rather than as
counter-insurgency forces. Apart from one brief, unpub-
licized tour of Northern Ireland as orthodox infantry in
1969, the SAS was now living from hand to mouth: testing new weapons in Britain, testing the security arrange-
ments at the country's newest prison (where they broke
out over an "unscaleable" fence in less than two minutes), training special forces and paramilitary police
forces of such allies as Iran, and even providing bodyguards for some friendly foreign heads of state. Some men
serving with the Regiment at that time heard the rumors
that afflict all special forces at such periods, that there

was no future for them and that the unit was to be disbanded.

It was in this climate that a small group of senior SAS officers decided to turn their attention to one place where their services would be of value. Twelve years after their first campaign in northern Oman, the aging Sultan Sa'id bin Taimur, the 13th hereditary monarch of Oman, now had a much more acute internal security problem in the southern mountains of Dhofar. The Regiment's interest in Oman was revived in 1969 when British Intelligence sources reported that an Iraqi-trained guerrilla training team had started work among the primitive tribesmen of the sensitive Musandam Peninsula. As a result, a squadron of SAS soldiers was landed on the peninsula by Royal Marine Special Boat Section Gemini inflatables. One suspect was shot and wounded and one SAS soldier, Trooper "Rip" Reddy, was killed during a nocturnal free-fall parachute drop into the area (probably the first operational fatality of its kind in the British Army). The drop, by a reconnaissance free-fall troop, was peculiarly hazardous —a "HALO" ("High-Altitude, Low-Opening") from 10,000 feet with equipment, into a near-vertical 120mph free-fall, to canopy deployment in a depression surrounded by 4,000-foot mountain peaks. Reddy became unstable as the heavy Bergen pack he carried shifted its position: the result was a tangled canopy deployment and instant death.

Meanwhile, at the other extremity of Oman, 625 miles away on the border with Marxist South Yemen, the Sultan's disastrous conduct of his country's affairs had provoked a Communist-led guerrilla war and brought his own régime to the brink of extinction. Even within Oman, Dhofar is a far away country of which the rest of the population knows little, a hostile mountain separated from the rest of the Sultanate by 400 miles of desert, a backwater described in the Book of Genesis as "Ophir," the easternmost edge of the known world. It lies between the sand seas and gravel deserts of the Empty Quarter and the Arabian Sea, sandwiched politically between Royalist Saudi Arabia to the north and Communist South Yemen. It is about the same size as Wales, with 4,000-foot peaks topping an escarpment that rises like a natural fortress from a narrow coastal plain. From June to September, a monsoon wind sweeps off the sea on to the hills, bringing low cloud and fine rain which runs off the hills, to be followed by months of sunshine. As a result, the narrow plain between mountain and sea luxuriates in vegetation, including frankincense. The lower slopes are cut by ravines, thousands of feet deep, through which secret paths wander beneath thick undergrowth. It is perfect guerrilla country, honeycombed by limestone caves where food and guns may be stored for months and in which men may live.

The hill people, perpetually short of water, have always had to fight for existence against their neighbors as well as nature itself, as they move with meagre herds of cattle, goats and camels from one scant grazing ground to another. According to one recent authority, "the characteristic Omani settlement is a semi-fortified village around a water source," a society in which arms are carried as a badge of masculinity and status as well as for protection. The hill man's ethnic links are with the people of what is now South Yemen, while the ruling Sultan (a client of the British since 1800) is traditionally a remote and contemptible figure, a plainsman living behind palace walls at Salalah, with an escape route to the sea guarded by foreign mercenaries.

HOW NOT TO WIN FRIENDS

In April 1969, five years after oil had been discovered in commercial quantities, a distinguished British economist, John Townsend, arrived to help Sultan Sa'id begin "a cautious move forward into the modern world." Townsend recalls: "My first meeting with the Sultan had a dreamlike unreality: I met a strange, small old man with a splendid set of Father Christmas whiskers, tended and guarded by burly young men of undoubted African origin who were known as 'slaves.' He gave me, in excellent English, careful instructions as to whom I should meet and what I might say. All the people with whom I was to work were expatriate; I was not to meet any Omanis. 'Our people are not yet ready for development,' was the explanation. . . .

"There was great poverty and disease . . . yet nothing was done because the Sultan would not permit it. No man could leave his village and seek work without the permis-

sion of the Sultan. No man could repair his house without
the permission of the Sultan. This remote old man, who
never left his palace in Salalah and ruled by radio-
telephone through expatriates, had instilled such a fear in
his people that very few of them dared defy him and undertake any initiative to improve their lot."

There were no schools, so Omanis who wished to study
were obliged to become political exiles. Some did so in
Russia and East Germany, others elsewhere in the Middle
East. There were no hospitals in Dhofar, and only one
road out of the coastal plain. Almost all foreign goods
were forbidden, and Omanis were prohibited from danc-
ing, playing music, smoking, wearing sun-glasses, taking
photographs or wearing Western clothes. As an official
British press briefing document was later to admit: "The
penalties for disobedience were either flogging or imprisonment." Such penalties were the minor ones. As one
SAS veteran was to discover, Sa'id's collective punish-
ments included the cementing over of water wells with
catastrophic results for entire communities. Sa'id, the official brief concluded, was "a medieval and somewhat
despotic ruler."

Across the border in Aden and South Yemen, left-
wing Arab Nationalists had been engaged in a terrorist
campaign against the British since 1963. It was inevitable
that Sultan Sa'id's régime should also provoke rebellion.
Dhofari tribesmen, trained in Iraq, started a sporadic
campaign of armed ambush, mine-laying and assassination in 1965, and this led to savage repression by the increasingly isolated ruler. Within a year, the Sultan was
the target of an assassination attempt by his own bodyguard, several of whom fired at him from a range of a few
feet while he was inspecting them. They missed. It is part
of the legend of Sultan Sa'id that he then drove himself
to his principal Army garrison (leaving behind a wounded
Pakistani palace guard commander) to tell its British
commander: "We seem to be having a little trouble down
at the palace. I wonder if you would be so good as to
come down?"

Not surprisingly, opposition to Sa'id prospered. Fred
Halliday, a left-wing British journalist and academic who
has studied the Oman campaign, records: "In the first
five years, up to 1970, the British were on the defensive

and merely tried to hold out with their ramshackle army
and colonial administration. The main tactics used were
traditional ones: villages were burnt to punish the populations, corpses of guerrilla fighters were hung up in the
main square in Salalah; the mountains were blockaded
and Salalah itself was ringed with a barbed-wire fence so
that no food could be taken out or weapons brought in."

In November 1967, a year after Sa'id's bodyguard had
tried to kill him, the British left neighboring Aden. Although the hinterland bordering Dhofar became a battleground for two warring factions within what was now
South Yemen, it was clear that Sa'id's opponents in the
mountains would soon have more room for maneuver:
the British were, almost literally, off their backs. It is an
axiom of guerrilla warfare that a sanctuary and a secure
source of war materials, preferably contiguous with the
war zone, must be established if the campaign is to succeed. Clearly, the rebels would soon have just this. The
war would be lost if something were not done to change
Sa'id's disastrous conduct of affairs, and this change occurred soon after the unexpected election in June 1970
of Edward Heath's Conservative Government in Britain.
Townsend has recounted how the outgoing Wilson Government of 1970 had announced that there would be a
British withdrawal from the Arabian Gulf at the end of
1971, while "the Conservative Government which followed it was less inhibited about dabbling in the affairs
of other states. Both the Foreign Office and the Ministry
of Defense were worried that an unstable situation in
Oman could well prejudice the smooth withdrawal from
the Gulf in the following year." There was another, more
pressing reason for anxiety in London: the flow of oil
through Hormuz.

On the afternoon of 23 July, less than a month after
Heath's election in Britain, Sheik Braik bin Hamud bin
Hamid al-Ghafari, an Omani aristocrat and the Wali
(Governor) of Dhofar province, entered the Salalah palace to demand the abdication of Sultan Sa'id. It was an
act of courage buttressed by Sheik Braik's knowledge that
the Sultan's son and heir, Qaboos—Sheik Braik's close
friend—as well as key British officers in the administration were part of the plot. The Sultan responded to the
Sheik's unexpected appearance by snatching a pistol from

his desk and opening fire. One round wounded the Sheik, another killed a palace servant and one or two more wounded the Sultan in the foot and stomach. (It is generally believed that the Ruler himself was the cause of all these injuries.) That night, the Sultan agreed to surrender himself to a British colonel seconded to his armed forces, and abdicate. Both Sheik Braik and the Sultan were then flown to a Gulf hospital aboard the same aircraft, separated by a curtain, and the RAF spirited Sa'id away to London where he spent the last two years of his life in seclusion.

OPERATION "STORM"

A few months before these events, after comparing notes at the Hereford Headquarters of 22 SAS, three senior officers had spent the Easter holiday weekend of 1970 examining the Dhofar problem and devising a winning strategy. By now the Regiment had come a long way from its rôle as saboteurs during the Second World War. "Low intensity" operations still involved hard, if unorthodox soldiering, but Confrontation in Borneo and the Vietnam war had shown that a winning strategy, in an age of revolutionary fish swimming in a proletarian sea, was a matter of shaping the perceptions and loyalty of the population at large. By Easter Monday, one of the three had produced a plan for what was to become Operation "Storm" in Dhofar, the basic elements of which would change the course of the war there. The plan demanded, first, a vigorous but intelligent and coherent military campaign run by soldiers, in which indiscriminate reprisals would be avoided. The other basic elements of the strategy were:
1. A medical campaign to provide aid for the 50,000 or so people living in the Dhofar mountains, most of whom were then regarded by Salalah as enemies.
2. A veterinary campaign to improve farm stock, including the provision of that most scarce commodity, fresh water, as well as skilled advice about husbandry.
3. A coherent Intelligence-gathering operation that would embrace every scrap of knowledge about the opposition (as the rebels were regarded at Hereford) aimed at isolating them and breaking their morale as well as underpinning military operations.
4. A psychological operation to persuade the rebels to

change sides, the basic ingredients of which were communication by air-dropped leaflets, offer of amnesty to tribesmen wishing to surrender and an aggressive civil-aid program that would outbid anything the opposition could afford.

Possibly because Sultan Sa'id was still ruling Oman, such a change of style did not meet with universal approval in "informed" circles. It was a risk strategy and one that required cunning co-ordination as well as greater discipline among the military leadership in Salalah. For example, the existing use of air power—then consisting of six BAC Strikemasters—was, in the view of one SAS officer, remarkably informal. "At that time," he noted, "the Sultan's Air Force operated in an ad hoc way. The pilots seemed to sit around the mess in Salalah, then someone would suggest, off the top of his head, 'Let's go and hit such-and-such a place.' Systematic air support for infantry operations did not really exist."

The removal of Sultan Sa'id, however, gave the SAS the chance for which it had been waiting. Within hours of the palace coup, a small SAS team (officially an "information team") was on its way to Salalah, led by the chief architect of the "win strategy" document. It provided an instant bodyguard for the new Sultan, Qaboos, about which there is a story (possibly apocryphal) that it stood behind a two-way mirror while Qaboos received petitions in his palace. One petitioner was a venerable, bearded figure much given to florid gestures. He did not know that each time an arm swept towards his robe, the trained hands of SAS men behind the mirror moved towards their weapons.

One of the team's first operations was to organize a leaflet drop over rebel territory. Despite some mild mockery from the British Left, which criticized the leaflets' Arabic syntax, and scepticism within the Salalah old guard, and the real objection that only a tiny percentage of the intended audience was literate anyway, the operation produced an unexpected prize. The best military brains among the guerrillas at the time included Mohammed Suhail, a former soldier in the Sultan's British-officered Trucial Oman Scouts. Suhail had been sent to Mons Officer Training School at Aldershot, sponsored by the Foreign and Commonwealth Office. He was a good soldier: best rifle and machine-gun shot on his course, and top of the FCO sponsorship list. On his return to Oman, however, he was disillusioned with the Sa'id régime and joined the opposition in the mountains. The first leaflet, with its offer of amnesty from the new ruler, Sultan Qaboos (himself a British-trained officer), brought Suhail back again to work with the SAS and the Sultan's Intelligence staff, headed by an SAS officer.

The team in Salalah consisted initially of one troop of fifteen men, plus specialists including Intelligence Corps linguists, a doctor, a veterinary surgeon, and a "psyops" expert to disseminate information among the guerrillas. As a first step to penetrating the community it started a model farm on the outskirts of Salalah, which included cattle and poultry as well as root crops. The SAS even sent a soil sample for analysis by British agronomists, via one of its officers on his way to London.

As it turned out, penetration worked both ways. First, two thoroughbred bulls flown in by the RAF by way of Dubai (where they created a commotion aboard the plane, to the alarm of the air crew) were used to serve Dhofari cows before an appreciative civilian audience. But the SAS's prize cockerels met a less happy fate: local farmers, anxious to improve their stock, smuggled hens into the roost, and these passed on fowl pest to the imported cocks, which died in action as a result soon afterwards. The experience had a deadly familiarity. No regiment suffers so much from exotic diseases as the SAS —18 out of 36 men on a subsequent Oman operation contracted hepatitis in one hill locality—but the team's vet was undismayed. Asked how he liked working in Dhofar, he replied, enigmatically, that he preferred it to caring for homosexual goats at Harwell.

Only a fortnight after the coup, the SAS team leader was on his way back to London with a long shopping list of unmilitary equipment, including drilling gear with which to dig water wells. The Dhofari hill men and their livestock had been cruelly impeded in their nomadic pursuit of water as a result of both the war and Sa'id's repressive habit of sealing off such wells as there were. Water, above all, was the currency that was to prove decisive in winning friends and influencing people. The SAS took its request to the Army's Chief Engineer, Richard

Clutterbuck, who is now a distinguished political scientist specializing in counter-revolutionary warfare. Asked to provide drilling gear to help dissident tribesmen in Oman he replied: "That's what we're here for."

At this stage, London would not sanction the use of SAS patrols into rebel territory. Political considerations as well as the need for the soldiers to familiarize themselves with the environment both played a part in the decision. And at this stage, too, a troop of fifteen men was just not sufficient. The politics of Oman as well as Britain made caution necessary. On 20 December 1970, *The Financial Times*'s Ralph Izzard reported from Bahrein that, although SAS soldiers wearing the familiar beret with its winged-dagger emblem had been spotted in Bahrein, Sharjah and Oman, their presence was officially denied at first.

"It is now explained," Izzard continued, "that this denial was meant to save embarrassment to Sultan Qaboos who ousted his father in a palace coup in July. . . . He clearly would not want it to be thought his own British-officered armed forces were incapable of dealing with Dhofar's Chinese-trained guerrillas.

"Services spokesmen maintain that the SAS have been in Dhofar purely for training purposes. They had no contact with the insurgents and no shot was fired in anger. . . . Dhofar has special attractions as a training ground because it is partly covered with thick vegetation as a result of the summer monsoon."

In Britain it was clear that the premature commitment of the SAS to action, with perhaps the risk of large numbers of casualties, would generate publicity that could have imperilled the whole strategy to retrieve Oman's security. In those early days of the campaign, then, the SAS worked at hearts-and-minds, dispensing medical aid in villages on the plain, setting up two- and three-man teams to assist the people in any way that seemed useful. In some cases the soldiers even organized an efficient postal service. Their olive green uniform was nondescript, though recognizably European garb, and cap-badges were not worn. It all helped to ensure that the incomers were accepted by the Sultan's men, expatriate British officers, as well as the locals. Because of the SAS's unique constitutional position in Dhofar, finally answerable not to the

Sultan and his military command but to the Ministry of Defence in London, it was a delicate and vital exercise in credibility before military operations could begin.

Meanwhile the amnesty campaign—much criticized by some British soldiers as a double-edged weapon that supplied much war material to the rebels—was reaping a useful harvest of "surrendered enemy personnel." The price paid by security forces was that rebel camel-trains moved unmolested in and out of the Dhofar mountains. But the defections were accelerated in September 1970, by a split within the rebel camp between the Communists and Islamic traditionalists, which led to fighting between the two. A British Army brief records that "the attempted counter-revolution was ruthlessly suppressed by the Communists and resulted in mass defections to the Government." Between September 1970 and March 1971, encouraged by promises of cash as well as amnesty, a total of 201 rebels surrendered. Some handed over their Kalashnikov AK–47s and were paid an extra bounty of £50. The most useful men were then screened with the aid of Mohammed Suhail, and recruited into irregular counter-guerrilla units known as "firqas." The training, management and leadership of the firqas was one of the most important tasks taken on by the SAS in its rôle as a British Army Training Team. As the operation got under way, SAS soldiers were sent for intensive, ten-week courses in colloquial Arabic at Beaconsfield, before being attached in three- or four-man groups to firqa units in their own tribal areas. One such team was to be involved in one of the Regiment's most desperate actions of this, or any other campaign.

THE BATTLE OF MIRBAT

On 18 July 1972, the British Army Training Team at Mirbat—a meagre group of ten SAS soldiers, despite its grandiloquent title—was looking forward to the following morning, a Wednesday. On that day, the men, drawn from the Regiment's B Squadron, would fly out of the desolate, barbed-wire enclave they had occupied for more than three months and return to England. They were glad to be going home. Even by Omani standards, Mirbat was not much of a place—a huddle of flat-topped houses and a couple of ancient, mud-walled forts flanked on two sides by the sea, 40 miles from the provincial capital, Salalah. Children and insects were numerous, but not much else. More than most wars, this one was a long, grinding spell of boredom punctuated by brief spurts of action. In Mirbat even the "action" was frustrating: the whistle of incoming mortar bombs or anti-tank missiles fired by an unseen enemy. On 28 May, six mortar bombs had hit the town. On 6 June, another six. Two days later, three 75mm shells. And that, throughout the tour, was that.

The training team—acronymously known as "Batmen" —had kept busy and alert, training local forces, repairing vehicles and dispensing rudimentary medical care to human beings and camels in the quest for goodwill, while keeping their undisciplined allies in check through a prudent control of the ration stock. Their departure date was well into the monsoon season. It was a time of incessant rain, low cloud and damp clothes, and therefore a time when visibility towards the hostile mountain three miles inland was dangerously limited. The season favored the Marxist guerrillas of the Dhofar Liberation Front, biding their time in limestone caves on the mountain, in another important way. It usually made flying all but impossible. In a tight situation, as both sides well understood, the British team might depend upon air supply for ammunition, reinforcement and casualty evacuation, as well as supportive aerial bombardment. On the eve of the team's departure it seemed that no such problems existed. As the soldiers turned into their sleeping-bags for their last night in the "Batthouse," they could hear the wind screeching in from the Indian Ocean and buffeting past them to rage against the mountain. But that night the guerrillas were also on the move, launching a silent attack on the town to begin the most ambitious frontal assault of their ten-year war against the Sultan and his British advisers. More than 250 of their best warriors had been assembled for this battle, armed with Kalashnikov AK-47 automatic rifles, light, heavy and medium machine-guns, mortars of various calibres up to 82mm, two 75mm recoilless anti-tank rifles and an 84mm Carl Gustav rocket-launcher. As well as ammunition for these weapons, each man carried a profusion of hand-grenades. The guerrilla column marched south towards the town and sea, and then broke into carefully-organized combat groups, each of about ten men, which spread out in a wide arc around the town. Another group made a circular trek east to the beach and then back again along the coast to penetrate the town from that side. Before dawn, the garrison was isolated with no way of escape.

Inside the wire, in addition to the SAS team, was a group of about 30 Askaris from northern Oman, 500 miles away, armed with accurate but slow-firing .303-inch rifles. They served the Sultan's representative, the Wali, as town gatekeepers, searching all who came and went for messages and supplies, including food, that might be going to the enemy on the hill. The Askaris occupied a fort near the water's edge, known as the Wali's Fort. Living in the town itself, armed with FN automatic rifles and light machine-guns, was the local "firqa." Nominally its strength was about 60, but at least 20 of them were somewhere on the mountain on a reconnaissance patrol. The remaining 40 were in bed with their wives. Finally, there was another force of about 25 men of the Dhofar Gendarmerie, armed with FN rifles and a single light machine-gun, in a second fort just inside the wire. In front of the fort was the dug-out position for a venerable 25-pounder artillery piece of Second World War vintage. The DG Fort dominated the town and Mirbat's only airstrip. It was a vital position. Apart from the artillery piece, the heaviest weapons available to the SAS, at their nearby Batthouse, were a single .50-inch Browning and an 81mm mortar.

About 800 yards outside the wire, on a hill to the north of the town, another eight Gendarmes were on picquet duty. Predictably, it was their position, known as Jabal Ali, that first came under attack. Completely surrounded, it was to have been suppressed in a silent attack, but, as the guerrillas crept up on the position just before 5:30 am, the Gendarmes spotted them and a single high-velocity shot rang out. In the fight that followed, four of the Gendarmes were killed; the other four escaped. It was the start of a battle as remarkable as that fought at Rorke's Drift during the Zulu War.

Guerrilla mortarmen, realizing that surprise had been lost, immediately began raining bombs on the DG Fort, the Batthouse and the town itself. Inside the house, Cap-

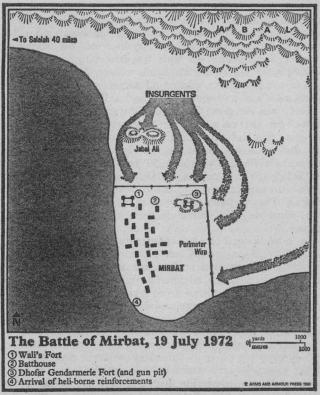

◄To Salalah 40 miles

JABAL

INSURGENTS

Jabal Ali

① ② ③

Perimeter Wire

MIRBAT

④

N

The Battle of Mirbat, 19 July 1972

0 yards 1000
0 metres 1000

① Wali's Fort
② Batthouse
③ Dhofar Gendarmerie Fort (and gun pit)
④ Arrival of heli-borne reinforcements

© ARMS AND ARMOUR PRESS 1990

tain M. J. A. ("Mike") Kealy, aged 23, rolled out of his
sleeping-bag, slipped on a pair of "flip-flop" beach san-
dals, seized his automatic rifle and ran to the rooftop to
see what was happening. What he saw was unlike any
enemy attack of the war, and Kealy thought it possible
that the firing was an appalling confusion caused by false
identification of the friendly firqa patrol on its return. In
the half-light of a grey dawn he could see groups of
armed men running across open ground in front of the
Batthouse, pausing to fire at the DG Fort away to his
right. Men were also swarming over the picquet position
on Jabal Ali: clearly it was already in enemy hands.

Kealy ordered the team's only mortar, pre-laid to fire over the picquet to cover just such a situation, to open fire with high explosive and white phosphorous smoke to obscure the enemy's vision. Another of his soldiers, Trooper W., opened up with the Browning, raking the area between the two forts, while others, firing from the roof of the Batthouse, picked off targets with careful precision with FN automatic rifles and a light machine-gun.

Kealy was by now profoundly disturbed. A frontal assault of this sort on a government garrison must mean that the guerrillas had assembled an unusually large force and that they probably knew the real fighting strength of the defenders (effectively, about 50 men). He handed control briefly to one of his NCOs, Corporal B., while he drafted an urgent signal to the provincial headquarters at Salalah. The message safely away, Kealy prepared for a long, hard day by changing from flip-flops into desert boots.

By now, a well co-ordinated assault was under way. Guerrilla combat groups moved as though presenting an infantry demonstration of fire and movement back home in Britain, one group advancing under covering fire until it could find dead ground from which to cover those who followed. From the overrun Jabal Ali, above the town, came accurate, considered bursts of heavy machine-gun fire, and mortar bombs were landing all round the DG Fort and the Batthouse. Even more sinister, stray enemy rounds were whistling in from the southern, seaward side of the town, "overs" which told Kealy and his men that they were surrounded. The battle now raging round them was a three-cornered affair in which the Askaris were firing from the Wali's Fort near the water's edge on guerrillas advancing towards the DG Fort and gun position; the SAS mortar team under Corporal B. was identifying its targets from the flash of enemy mortars; and the DG Fort was hitting back with everything including the artillery piece. The 25-pounder was manned by an Omani gunner, Walid Khamis and two Fijian SAS men, Corporal Labalaba and Trooper Ti., who had run to the fort at the start of the fight. The noise was stunning.

None of this deterred the guerrillas despite the casualties they were suffering. As one group was cut down another replaced it, until they advanced to within a few

yards of the perimeter wire. Once there they opened fire
on the DG Fort with Soviet RPG–7 rockets and the Carl
Gustav. At a range of only thirty meters the Carl Gustav's 84mm armor-piercing rounds had a devastating effect on the fort's ancient masonry: its tower crumbled in
a plume of smoke and dust. Throughout the confusion,
Corporal B. calmly indicated targets for the SAS mortar,
the Browning and light machine-guns, using lines of
tracer to emphasize his fire orders. He also picked off
leading guerrillas with his own rifle. This firepower, such
as it was, now turned on the leading group of guerrillas
at the wire, manning the Carl Gustav, as it attempted to
rush the fort less than a hundred yards away.

Kealy meanwhile was trying to maintain radio contact
with the gun crew in its pit in front of the DG Fort and
the Wali's men in their fort. Messages from the gun crew
were laconic, giving little sign of a situation that was turning from bad to desperate. On the radio, Labalaba's
voice, which had been indicating possible mortar targets
to the Batthouse crew, announced, "Enemy now very
close. I've been chinned but I'm all right." It was now
about 7 am. Within the Batthouse it was almost impossible
to hear anything but a steady roar of battle as rounds
from the Carl Gustav hissed across the roof to explode
just behind the building. Kealy had already asked for
strike aircraft at Salalah to stand by, but in these conditions, with cloud almost at ground level, it seemed a remote hope that the Air Force could do much. Now, in the
light of Labalaba's last message. Kealy summoned a helicopter to attempt a casualty evacuation.

Both sides had been firing intensively at one another
for about an hour. The guerrillas, although they had
breached the wire, had not yet taken the DG Fort. Both
sides needed to pause to see to their casualties and bring
up more ammunition. In the lull that resulted, the firing
became spasmodic—so much so that children gathered on
the roof of a building behind the Batthouse to watch the
action.

Kealy, concerned about the absence of any return fire
from the Gendarmerie Fort and its nearby gun position,
as well as continued radio silence, now took a brave decision. He would go to the fort himself. This meant crossing about four hundred yards of almost open ground

under enemy fire. It was also possible that by now the fort had been overrun. Others in the training team volunteered to share the risk, but he took just one man, his medical orderly, Trooper T. P. A. Tobin to aid the casualties. Simultaneously, Lance-Corporal C. slipped away from the Batthouse, through the town to a helicopter landing-pad near the beach, to guide the machine in as a preliminary to clearing the casualties. Kealy and his medical orderly were en route to the DG Fort when the "casevac" helicopter clattered in over the sea. On the landing site, the lance-corporal threw a green smoke grenade to indicate that all was clear. But, as the aircraft made its final approach, the guerrillas, reinforced and rearmed in dead ground around the DG Fort, started shooting with renewed ferocity. One of the first targets was the helicopter. Another was the man trying to guide it in. The lance-corporal stayed long enough to throw a red grenade to warn off the helicopter, and then dived for cover. The helicopter whined back into the cloud, its cabin pockmarked by machine-gun bullets.

When the battle erupted afresh, Kealy and his medical orderly were still 350 yards from the fort. From the Batthouse their comrades laid down a covering barrage from the Browning and light machine-guns, as the two men bobbed and weaved their way forward through the smoke, one pausing to fire while the other advanced. Luck was with them and they at least reached the gun position. As Kealy and Trooper Tobin slithered into the gun-pit and peered through the smoke, they found an appalling situation. Walid Khamis, the Oman Artillery gunner lay on his back seriously wounded. Above the gunpit on the parapet of the DG Fort, a dead soldier sprawled across his machine-gun. Another dead Gendarme was in the pit itself. Both the SAS Fijians were still fighting. One of them, Trooper Ti., was propped against the wall of the bunker, bleeding from serious head and shoulder wounds, still firing his rifle at the guerrillas. The other, Corporal Labalaba, wore a shell dressing on his face to staunch the flood from his chin wound. He was loading and firing the 25-pounder unaided. The gun itself, its shield riddled with bullet holes, had been depressed through 45 degrees to be sighted down the barrel and fired at pointblank range.

Labalaba reloaded the gun yet again as the medical orderly set to work to dress Trooper Ti.'s wounds. From the ammunition bunker, Kealy snapped a terse radio message to the Batthouse calling for an air strike. Before he had completed it, Labalaba was shot dead, and soon afterwards Trooper Tobin had his jaw shot away. (Later in the battle, the same man was to be wounded in the back and hand by a grenade.) The bunker was now being defended by two men, Kealy and the wounded Fijian Trooper Ti. By now, the guerrillas were only thirty yards away, moving on the gun-pit and ammunition bunker from left and right. Both gun position and the fort behind it were being hammered by small-arms fire and shuddering blows from the 84mm Carl Gustav. Kealy, from the right of the bunker wall, picked off first one guerrilla who was about to shoot Trooper Ti., then another who clambered out of a ditch towards their position. Trooper Ti., still propped up, fired carefully-aimed shots at enemy coming from the left. From somewhere too close for comfort, a light machine-gun fired at the two men, and Kealy felt a bullet pass through his hair. Now came the enemy grenades, which burst near, but not near enough to achieve their intention. One, lobbed right into the gun-pit itself, landed among the dead and dying, but failed to explode. From his position on the left of the bunker the obstinate, brave Trooper Ti. asked Kealy for more ammunition.

A hopeless position was retrieved at that moment by the arrival of two Strikemaster jets of the Sultan's air force, hurtling over the scene just above ground level and under a cloud base of only 150 feet. From the radio in the ammunition bunker, Kealy passed targets to the Batthouse: 500-pound bombs on a ditch where the guerrillas had gathered in force and 7.62mm machine-gun fire along the wire only 60 yards from both fort and gun-pit. As the guerrillas retreated, Kealy hastily draped an air identification panel over a body in the bunker to identify his own position to the jets. Even before the first air strike was over, Kealy was also issuing orders to his mortar position at the Batthouse, a few hundred yards away. The mortarman, Lance-Corporal H., found that the proposed targets were now so close that he could not elevate the barrel sufficiently by orthodox means. His solution was to pull the barrel up to his chest, lifting the supporting bipod off the ground, and to grip the weapon with his legs before dropping bombs down the barrel.

The battle around the bunker had now been going on for ninety minutes. From the Batthouse, Corporal B. directed the second wave of Strikemasters. One of these hit guerrilla machine-guns on Jabal Ali, overlooking the town, while the other made several attacks on the enemy hiding in dead ground near the fort and the wire perimeter. "There are hundreds of them down there!" an astonished pilot reported. One of the aircraft, seriously damaged by heavy machine-gun fire at close range, cut out of the battle and limped back to Salalah.

While the pressure was off his position, Kealy gave water to the wounded and re-dressed their injuries, then went to fetch the DG Land Rover inside the fort for use as an ambulance to the heli-pad. He found the vehicle unusable, its tires and petrol tank holed by machine-gun fire.

If the air strikes had taken the heat off the fort for the time being, it was clear that nothing less than substantial reinforcements could save the situation completely. That they were on their way was due to a fortunate coincidence. Before B Squadron (to which Kealy belonged) could leave the territory, it had to hand over to its successor in Oman. This group, from G Squadron, had arrived in Salalah the previous day. When Kealy's first messages alerted the base, the men of G Squadron were dressed and armed to check their weapons on the firing range. Instead they flew by helicopter, almost at sea level, direct to Mirbat beach. Their arrival at 9:15 am almost coincided with the second air strike around the fort. A party of 18 from the first helicopter lift advanced inland in two groups, wiping out a ridge position held by five guerrillas. The new SAS group was spotted by guerrillas near the DG Fort, who fired at it before starting to withdraw. The tide had turned at last.

From the beach, a second wave of SAS reinforcements, operating in three-man teams, engaged in brief, vicious battles with three guerrilla positions on the southern, seaward side of the town. In another incident the SAS party covering the helicopter landing zone waited in concealment as three guerrillas came closer. They were only five

yards away when an SAS officer stood up and ordered
them to drop their weapons and surrender. They did so,
instantly. It was almost 10:30 before the most seriously
wounded—the medical orderly, Trooper Tobin, whose
jaw had been blown away, the obstinate and thrice-
wounded Fijian Trooper Ti, and the Omani gunner,
Walid Khamis—could be removed by helicopter. The
Fijian insisted on walking into the aircraft. By then,
Lance-Corporal H., the man who had held the mortar
between his legs, had moved from the Batthouse to the
gun-pit to aid the wounded in the closing stages of the
battle. By clearing Trooper Tobin's windpipe of blood, it
seemed that he had saved the man's life; but Tobin was
to die of his wounds later. The next group of wounded to
be flown out included some of the enemy who had been
taken to the Batthouse during the first lull in the battle.
By lunchtime it was clear that the position was under control again.

Kealy, whose judgement throughout the battle had
been impeccable, now decided to see what could be done
to save the original firqa patrol still in the mountains. He
took a group of men outside the wire and up to the Jabal
Ali area, which had been the first position to come under
attack that day. But by now there was no way of knowing whether the patrol had encountered the retreating
guerrilla force and if so, where. The firqa limped back
later in the day with four men dead and three wounded.

SAS casualties were two dead—Corporal Labalaba
and Trooper Tobin—and two seriously wounded; the
Gendarmes lost one man killed, one wounded; and the
Oman Artillery, one dead. The retreating guerrillas left
about thirty bodies and about ten wounded, taken prisoner, but their sources later admitted that the toll was
much higher. Factional feuds provoked by the defeat at
Mirbat caused further fatalities. Others died of their
wounds and these, added to the list of surviving wounded
and taken prisoner, left fewer than half of the guerrillas'
original élite force unscathed.

When the war ended four years later, one authority
concluded: "The rebel forces never recovered from this
defeat and were never able to deploy sufficient forces to
mount a similar attack elsewhere. But in Britain, the
battle received no publicity. Gallantry awards made pub-

lic four years later included a DSO for Kealy, a DCM for Trooper Tobin, a MM for Corporal B. and, posthumously, a Mention in Dispatches for Corporal Labalaba. In February 1979, Kealy, now a major, died of exposure while taking part in an SAS exercise in bitter conditions on the Brecon Beacons in Wales (see pages 232-237).

Mirbat was the high point of the SAS campaign in Oman. The guerrillas had lost some of their best men. Worse, they had lost credibility in a warrior society through defeat in open combat when the odds were in their favor. But the decisive effect of the Regiment on the war was more diffuse, more subtle than its skill at arms. By the time the war ended in 1976, the combined anti-guerrilla forces numbered about 15,000 men. The SAS commitment most of the time was a single squadron averaging about 80, and even this figure could vary by as many as 30 more or, more frequently, less. As one of those who had an important rôle in planning SAS operations in Oman argues, "It was not our numbers, but our ideas which made a big difference."

RUNNING THE FIRQA
The action at Mirbat was not the only one of its kind. One potent reason for the success of the SAS was that despite frequent disciplinary problems with the volatile firqas, the irregulars learned from experience that their British tutors would sacrifice their own lives rather than desert an ally in trouble. On 12 April 1974, Captain Simon Garthwaite was killed while trying to rescue a firqa pinned down by enemy fire. Garthwaite's magnetism was considerable: that his SAS soldiers used his Christian name is a measure of their respect for him. A friend who wrote his obituary recorded that Garthwaite was uneasy at formal mess dinners, but at home on the jebel. "Boots (no socks), shorts, a belt and his rifle were all that he carried. . . . He had an astonishing way with local soldiers. They were drawn to him and . . . whatever 'the Captain' said, they would gladly do; wherever 'the Captain' went, they would follow."

This does not mean that the firqa technique was an unalloyed success. There were furious debates within the SAS about the problems that resulted from paying some of the irregulars better salaries than the Sultan's regular soldiers, as well as supplying the firqas too generously with automatic rifles, ammunition and blankets. One lobby argued for a "lean-and-mean" style of management; the other believed that full bellies ensured loyalty. Certainly there was extravagance. At Mirbat during the first end-of-fast festival after Ramadan, the local firqa celebrated by firing 5,000 rounds—almost the entire garrison stock —into the air and hundreds of FN rifles disappeared.

There were also chronic problems of command, which depended crucially upon the relationship between the SAS team leader and his tribal second-in-command. According to one British veteran, every firqa experienced a mutiny of some sort at some time, and a few units were disbanded. These problems were least manifest when the SAS leader lived close to his firqa, like Garthwaite, but only one SAS soldier immersed himself so totally in native culture as to dress as a native and speak the language fluently. In general, SAS teams were with the firqa but not of them. They lived and ate apart, preserving their identity, even if the space between the two groups was a matter of yards.

Finally, there was a growing tendency among the irregulars to demand more and more supportive firepower from the regular army and air force before they would go into action, a process that cancelled out their natural advantages of stealth and surprise, and the guerrilla techniques they understood. At its best, a firqa backed by regular military forces worked with a speed and efficiency unique to Dhofar in recovering lost territory. In an unclassified lecture, the operational commander during the final, victorious phase of the campaign, Brigadier (now General) John Akehurst described how this happened:

"First, the firqa would select a base of their choice. Provided it offered good prospects for land access and drilled water we would mount a largely military operation, perhaps a whole battalion, to capture it. Military engineers would then bulldoze an access track and down the track would come a drill rig.

"Troops would then thin out to the minimum necessary to defend the base with firqa assistance. While the drill turned away, the Civil Aid Team set up a clinic, a shop (with Government rations which would be free at first but later sold, though at subsidized prices), a school and a mosque. Engineers would be building a distribution scheme for the water with water-points for humans and troughs for cattle and camels.

"All this probably took four weeks. Water is at a premium . . . and people throughout the tribal area would bring in their cattle . . . The civilians, of course, were in regular touch with the enemy, many of whom were their relations. When they came in for water and other Government munificence the firqa talked to them, first to gain Intelligence, but second, to tell them to let the enemy know that they should not interfere with the provision of these good things. The enemy themselves were totally dependent on civilian goodwill and therefore were forced not to interfere."

Firqa offensives did not always work so smoothly. In January 1975, the Liberation Front was being pressed back towards the border with South Yemen, with a growing intensity of conflict and increasing casualties on both sides. In a catacomb of limestone caves, almost invincibly protected by an ugly, dominating hill, the guerrillas had their main store of weapons and ammunition. It was a natural fortress, the conquest of which initially demanded speed, stealth and local knowledge. On SAS advice, a lightly-armed firqa unit was nominated for the task of spearheading a battalion assault. SAS climbers were on hand to assist in the final stages and, after the caves had been taken, the Regiment's demolition experts were to destroy them and their contents. But things did not work out that way. Before the firqa would cross the start line to begin the assault, they insisted upon a demonstration of supporting firepower from aircraft, artillery and armored cars, and demanded that this be repeated every few hundred yards during the advance. This orchestrated barrage advertised the beginning of the operation: not only was surprise lost, but the subsequent ponderous advance gave the guerrillas ample time to prepare an excellent defense.

During the next two days, under increasingly accurate enemy machine-gun, rocket and mortar fire, the assault ground to a halt. Akehurst recalled in his lecture how the situation deteriorated: "In an attempt to capture the caves the advance was ambushed by the enemy as it crossed open ground and the leading company lost 13

Above: David Stirling's men cleaning weapons, somewhere in the Western Desert circa 1942.

Below, left: An experiment in the Malayan jungle with tracker dogs. They were not much favored by the SAS, who preferred the greater silence of human trackers. Elephants, for use as jungle porters, were also a failure.

Below, right: Sergeant Hanna, his parachute canopy draped in the trees, joins the Regiment's return to the jungle.

Trooper Mulcahy, a casualty of tree jumping at the beginning of the Telok Anson swamp operation.

A classic way to travel in the jungle, by raft. For many veterans on their way to Oman, this was their last contact with the jungle.

"Squire" Perkins, as SAS "bush doctor," treats the inflamed eye of a villager in the South Arabian Federation (now the People's Democratic Republic of South Yemen) in the early 1960s.

What every well-dressed SAS soldier carries to meet a visting VIP in Aden.

Opposite, above: Double agent André Dennison (center, facing camera) and friends, Skyline Hotel near London Airport, 1975.

Above: Sharif Hussein, ruler of Beihan of the Yemeni border, whose "safe houses" were the base for clandestine guerrilla operations.

Left: Christmas Day briefing immediately before the attack on Jabal Akhdar, 1958.

Dhofar, circa 1972 in action.

SAS soldier (right) in Arab headdress, with pupil.

Above: Land Rover patrol in up-country Dhofar.

Below, left: Michael Reeves, GM, in Aden prior to his famous parachute rescue in Britian.

Below, right: Breaching an "unscalable" fence while testing new prison security, UK c. 1969.

The clock tower at the headquarters of 22 SAS Regiment, Hereford, inscribed with the names of those who did not "beat the clock."

killed and 22 wounded in less than an hour." The first to die, in a perfectly prepared ambush, was a British officer who was moving down an exposed forward slope with his company before attempting to cross a gully. This group was now hit by the full fury of well-sited machine-guns and mortars almost immediately above it. Attempts by back-up forces to save the now-isolated vanguard encountered more withering fire, and spectacular bravery was shown by individual officers and SAS troopers to recover the wounded. At dusk on the third day of the operation, the SAS Squadron moved forward to make withdrawal possible for the beleaguered company. Hitting back at rebel positions with accurate GPMG and rocket fire, they kept the enemy's heads down while the remnants of the advance guard fell back. (The SAS officer in charge of this rescue was awarded an MC and subsequently retired as a major, to freelance international security work.)

An operation originally intended to last 24 hours now ground on for three weeks, though without occupation of the caves by Government forces. What did happen, however, was that the approaches to the caves were denied to the rebels by constant fire from 76mm guns mounted on armored cars, and were nevèr again used as stores caves. According to one officer involved in the campaign, it was from that point on that the guerrillas began to lose to the Sultan's regular armed forces in straight military battles. Like Mirbat, it was a body-blow to the guerrillas' credibility.

One officer recruited by the Sultan from the original SAS force as a freelance, contract firqa leader, did adopt the tactics of the true counter-guerrilla. Working under the direction of another SAS veteran who was now in charge of Dhofar's military Intelligence, he lived for months on the edge of the Empty Quarter, dressed like his Dhofari warriors and indistinguishable from them. He dropped and collected agents over the border with South Yemen, the guerrillas' main supply base, and in 1972, decided to blow up an army fort at Sinau, 80 miles inside Yemeni territory. The operation was totally clandestine, so much so that if he had been taken prisoner he would have been disowned by the Sultan's hierarchy, most of whom, including the British Commander-in-Chief, had no knowledge of the operation.

With two Bedford trucks each carrying 500 pounds of
unstable gelignite, and 80 men, including a party of South
Yemeni exiles trained in Saudi Arabia, he arrived unimpeded at the fort, where the small garrison surrendered
without resistance. Little more than half an hour was
needed to plant the gelignite, still in its 50-pound boxes,
in each corner of the two-story stone fort, and to link
these with detonator cord to a five-minute safety fuse in
the courtyard. Having ensured that the engine of his escape vehicle was safely running, the British firqa leader
lit the fuse and got out. Just after dusk, a spectacular explosion mushroomed red and orange in the desert sky,
destroying not only the fort but also a government shop,
garages and a house. The object of such an operation was
to divert the resources of South Yemen's army from aid-
ing the guerrillas as these crossed into Dhofar farther
south, along the coastal plain. Although the Sultan of
Oman was impressed, his British military commanders
were horrified, however. Border crossings are a sensitive
political issue for Whitehall. The contract officer at the
center of this adventure transferred to other duties in
Dhofar soon afterwards, in charge of another firqa. His
direction of the Empty Quarter firqa was taken over by
an orthodox SAS team, and its cross-border operations
ceased.

THE UNEXPECTED VICTORY

The end of the war, when it came, was as improbable as
an Errol Flynn film. The final assault was to be launched
by helicopter at dawn on a day in October 1975. Its object was to seize high ground above a 2,000-foot-deep
wadi and elsewhere on mountains near the border with
South Yemen, while an armored car-bulldozer column
would advance simultaneously from the plain to control
the foothills. But, at the last moment, what was to have
been a simple diversion became the main pivot of the attack. The diversion was from an isolated, air-supplied
mountain-top position held by government troops at Sarfait. Such an attack was, predictably, a kamikaze maneuver and both sides knew it. The descent was by steps
down a series of cliffs, the first of which was an almost
sheer 600 feet. Government troops had tried to break out
once in 1972 and they had failed.

Nevertheless, on the night of 14 October the Muscat Regiment probed its way downhill to take the first plateau. There was no opposition. "We learned later," Akehurst has revealed, "that the enemy considered anything from Sarfait would only be a diversion and we believe they probably got confirmation of this from the firqa taking part. . . . In any event, they decided to do nothing.

"At about midday on the 15th, I sat with Ian Christie, the commanding officer of the Muscat Regiment and contemplated our unexpected success. I asked him what he thought he would need to carry on down to the sea. After some discussion he decided two more companies. In the next two minutes I threw seven months of planning and 40 pages of operation orders out of the metaphorical window."

The main attack went in from Sarfait the same night, and by morning the Government forces held a three-mile corridor to the sea, cutting the guerrillas' last supply line. From now on, the guerrillas' chief priority was to reach the safety of South Yemen. For many of them it was a long, pitiless march along waterless tracks north of the mountains they had controlled for five years. The war ended formally a few months later with a ceasefire between South Yemen and Oman.

The full story of how the fortunes of this war were swung from the near collapse of Government forces in 1970 to their outright victory by 1976 must await the memoirs of the operational commanders. Broadly, it is one of gradual penetration of Dhofari society, in which the firqas, trained and advised by the SAS, reoccupied the mountains using water wells as the ultimate currency of persuasion; and in which increasingly ambitious, orthodox military operations finally required thousands of Iranian and Jordanian, as well as Omani, soldiers to cut guerrilla supplies coming from South Yemen. This was accomplished by building a series of communication barriers, which employed barbed wire, booby-traps, mines and electronic ground sensors. Air and naval bombardment was used to soften up hostile areas before such operations took place, and everything that might aid the guerrillas, including cattle, was removed. The first of these barriers, the Hornbeam Line, covered 35 miles and took 12 months to build.

The closer Government forces came to the border with South Yemen, the more they came under attack from 130mm artillery fired from within that territory by regular forces. Government helicopters and strike planes were constantly menaced by some of Russia's latest anti-aircraft missiles supplied to the guerrillas. Contrary to even informed left-wing opinion in Britain, the war was not a totally one-sided affair. If it had been, it would not have lasted for ten years.

Was it all worth it? Contrary to press reports that the SAS suffered "scores of casualties," the Regiment in fact lost twelve dead during its six-year war. In the light of subsequent events in Iran and Afghanistan, and their impact on Western oil supplies, the strategic importance to British economic interests of winning the war can hardly be overstated. The victory also sustains in office—as Townsend, the Sultan's former economic adviser, points out—a régime in which trades unions are still outlawed and in which strikes, also illegal, "tend to be settled by the police or the army rather than by negotiation. . . . When the apparently infinite cornucopia of material benefits begins to falter, the Omani people may demand more say in their government."

Certainly the material well-being of the people of Dhofar is now incomparably better than it was in 1970, and the most petty restrictions on personal liberty have been removed. But what if the rebels had won? Townsend, a critic of many of the Sultan's policies from within the régime, does not conclude that life might have been better under a Communist government. The extremism and incompetence of the rebel movement, he believes, was such that it deserved to be defeated. "Victory for the Popular Front movement would have resulted in a harsh and negative extremism far worse than that of the Sultan, if the example of South Yemen is taken as a guide" is his conclusion. Townsend does not defend Qaboos's absolute monarchy. He asserts that the Sultan can only survive if he realizes that he is almost the last absolute ruler, and that the facts of history are against his survival. By assisting that survival at a critical juncture, the SAS helped to buy time for more peaceful evolution within Oman as well as serving the interests of the British, and other Western economies.

VI

The Irish Dimension, 1969-

WHEN THE PRIME MINISTER, HAROLD WILson, announced from Downing Street on 7 January 1976 that Special Air Service soldiers were being sent to Northern Ireland for "patrolling and surveillance" tasks in South Armagh, his statement was greeted by many journalists and politicians in the province with scepticism. Mr. Paddy Devlin of the Social Democratic and Labour Party, an amiable IRA veteran of the forties expressed a widely held opinion when he said: "It is only a cosmetic exercise. The SAS have always been here."

In a sense, Devlin was right. With its chameleon-like talent for blending into the local scenery, the Regiment had been a presence that permeated much of the security forces' activity, on and off ever since the breakdown of law and order in Northern Ireland in that fateful week of August 1969. In reality, what the Downing Street announcement signalled was a change of rôle from one of Intelligence gathering, control and analysis by a few selected SAS officers and NCOs sent to supplement the work of other Intelligence gatherers, to one of combat by the Regiment's four regular squadrons on rota. This participation was not sought by the Regiment, unlike the campaigns of Borneo, Aden and Oman where the SAS had lobbied Whitehall to ensure a rôle for itself. The Irish commitment was imposed by the Prime Minister without warning and without reference to the Ministry of Defence. Furthermore, formal commitment of the SAS as such also represented an extraordinary about-turn by the government of the day which, until then, had taken the view that the Regiment's presence would be a political liability. When the murder of a number of Loyalists brought Protestant indignation to boiling point, it was as a political device that the SAS was sent to Ulster, for the same reason that it had been excluded hitherto. The "bogeyman" image of the Regiment originally cultivated by the Republicans and their friends for propaganda purposes was now a positive advantage to Wilson in his efforts to reassure the Loyalists. Since the Republicans believed their own propaganda, this image would prove militarily useful.

Prior to 1976, the Regiment's Oman commitment (which ended, on paper at least, with the defeat of the Dhofar guerrillas in December 1975) had meant that there were assuredly not enough men to supply a squadron, more or less full time, to Northern Ireland. If such a commitment were accepted, then the precedents of postwar years implied that the SAS would take on a fighting rôle that could be expected to continue for some years. Obviously, the conclusion of the Dhofar war may have helped convince Mr. Wilson that the SAS was now available for another active campaign, though in fact the Regiment continued to have a commitment on the border between Oman and South Yemen for a considerable time after the formal end of hostilities in March 1976. By the time the Regiment was publicly dispatched to Ulster, it had missed the boat—or, as others would argue, the Regiment had not been allowed to catch the boat in the first place. Whatever the correct emphasis, the undercover war in Northern Ireland evolved new techniques which, for once, others—notably Brigadier (later General) Sir Frank Kitson—had developed during the years the SAS was elsewhere.

The Regiment's first foray into Northern Ireland occurred in 1969, soon after the breakdown of law and order. Men of D Squadron drained their glasses in bars near the Hereford base in response to the recall code, "Free Beer" before returning to barracks to pick up uniforms and Bergen rucksacks. (This code had to be changed after one irate parent, already angry about her son's drinking habits, construed it as yet another invitation to a bottle party: there was some doubt whether she would pass the message on.)

By now, the situation in the province was extraordinarily fragile. For twelve months, a growing dialectic of violence between civil rights demonstrators and the Royal Ulster Constabulary backed by part-time officers of the "B" Specials had convinced many Protestants that the civil war they had feared for fifty years was imminent. (They were wrong.) The Catholic communities, as well as some Government ministers in Dublin, feared that a carefully-prepared pogrom was about to occur. (They were also wrong.) In Belfast, the police commissioner sought the aid of troops from the local garrison. A company of the Queen's Regiment was moved to a local police headquarters, then moved out again on orders from London. The most dangerous miscalculation of all was made by the politicians on both sides of the Irish Sea, in the Protestant Government of Stormont and the London Government of Harold Wilson. Neither side could agree about the terms on which troops would reinforce the police, and the compromise that emerged from this deadly tug-o'-war created the worst of all possible worlds: the soldiers were to be supplied initially only under their common law power to make citizens' arrests. A legal precondition of this was that Stormont, the civil power, had to expend all its security forces, including the exclusively Protestant "B" Specials, in a final attempt to restore order. Implicitly, this policy required a complete breakdown of law and order and the demoralization of the RUC before troops would become involved. In the event, this is what happened in August 1969.

NIGHT OF THE ARMORED CARS

This latest Irish tragedy culminated in an horrific episode in which a group of police officers, already exhausted by three days' fighting in Derry, were ordered to take to the sensitive, Catholic Lower Falls area of Belfast in Shorland armored cars. The crews had not manned the vehicles before; they were unfamiliar with the Browning machine-gun mounted on the vehicles; and the guns had no night sights. The armored cars came under petrol bomb attack and, in the darkness, one crew opened fire with the powerful Brownings at short range on a block of

Catholic flats. The heavy-calibre bullets ripped through the building and killed eight-year-old Patrick Rooney as he sheltered in his bedroom. Later, the crew gave evidence to the Scarman Tribunal under codenames. In startling contrast to the treatment subsequently accorded to SAS soldiers in circumstances of equal apparent risk, the RUC men were not exposed to the threat of criminal proceedings. In the aftermath of this event, as well as a gun battle between the two communities in Belfast and the burning of Catholic homes, the Lower Falls became the city's first "no-go" area, surrounded by barricades.

Only now, as Ulster creaked on the brink of a real civil war, were British soldiers sent in to control the situation. Initially, they were greeted as saviors by Belfast's Catholics. But the Intelligence available to the incoming troops was scarce and inaccurate. At the time, the total resources devoted to military Intelligence in the province comprised one Intelligence Corps captain and one sergeant. And, as a Hampshire Regiment major wryly put it: "The Irish are long on 'intelligence' but short on information." Possibly as a result of this, a British general negotiated unwittingly with a leading Republican doubling as chairman of Belfast Citizens' Defence Committee in order to have the barricades removed.

One of the fears in the minds of those responsible for Ulster's security was that the traumatic events of August would at last precipitate a civil war. Troops were on stand-by in the Irish Republic to assist evacuation, and both communities were making efforts to smuggle arms into the province. The IRA, not yet divided between the predominantly left-wing, politically oriented "Officials" and the warlike, traditionalist "Provisionals," had contrived to produce only one Sten carbine and a few pistols to defend the Lower Falls. It also had some grenades which tended not to explode.

The men of D Squadron were more concerned with Protestant than Catholic guns at this time. During a tour lasting a few weeks, they paraded openly in SAS uniform and even laid a ceremonial wreath on the grave of the late Colonel Paddy Mayne near their Newtownards base. If the press did not notice their presence, it was because the main action was taking place in the cities of Belfast and Londonderry. The SAS, meanwhile, patrolled the

countryside between the Glens of Antrim and the Mourne
Mountains to establish whether the Protestant gun-
running operations of 1914—when the Ulster Volunteers
landed 3,500 rifles at Larne—might be repeated. The
Squadron searched incoming fishing vessels for the same
reason, but no arms were discovered. That clandestine
trade, by extremists of both communities, did not begin
in earnest until months later; by then, as a unit, the SAS
had found another and more familiar style of warfare in
Dhofar. However, if no SAS squadron as such was per-
manently committed to Ulster before 1976, selected individuals were to serve with security forces there.

The disbanding of the "B" Specials in 1969 greatly reduced the amount of street Intelligence flowing to the
Government, which in any case, as a matter of policy,
had chosen to adopt a passive rather than an offensive
Intelligence-gathering strategy. By the spring of 1971,
following the emergence of the hard-line Provisional IRA
and a bombing campaign averaging two explosions daily,
the authorities had become desperate to penetrate the terrorist network. The Army did so by adopting the
"counter-gang" tactics developed during Kenya's Mau
Mau campaign by Kitson. Ten proven IRA activists, including one who was a recently demobilized soldier of the
Royal Irish Rangers, were arrested and given the choice
between long terms of imprisonment or undercover work
for the British Army. They opted to join the British.
Commanded by a Parachute Regiment captain they were
known as the Special Detachment of the Military Reconnaissance Force (or more colloquially, as "Freds"). Their
guardians were ten volunteers for plain-clothes duty from
the British Army. The "Freds" lived in one half of a
semi-detached married quarter in the heavily-guarded
Holywood Barracks at Belfast, while their British guardians occupied the other half.

How would such men as the "Freds" be "turned
around" in this fashion? In his autobiographical account
of the Mau Mau campaign, Kitson suggests that "three
separate factors have to be brought into play in order to
make a man shift his allegiance. In the first place, he
must be given an incentive which is strong enough to
make him want to do so. This is the carrot. Then he must
be made to realise that failure will result in something

Northern Ireland

① South Armagh operations, 1976-77
② Dunloy: John Boyle incident, July 1978

Inset: The site of the border crossing by two SAS patrols on 6 May 1976. The scene of the Warrenpoint massacre of eighteen British soldiers in 1979 is nearby.
③ British Army checkpoint
④ Point at which SAS patrols crossed the border
⑤ Irish Police checkpoint where SAS patrols stopped

very unpleasant happening to him. This is the stick.
Thirdly he must be given a reasonable opportunity of
proving both to himself and his friends that there is nothing fundamentally dishonorable about his action. Some
people consider that the carrot and stick provide all that
is necessary, but I am sure that many people will refuse
the one and face the other, if by doing otherwise they lose
their self-respect. On the other hand few people will
choose the harder course if they think that both are
equally consistent with their ideals."

Initially, the task of the first MRFs was to drive round
Belfast's Republican districts to identify erstwhile comrades in the IRA who were then placed under surveillance or arrest. It was a lethal, complex and bewildering
game of cat-and-mouse and not many of the "Freds" survived to enjoy the freedom promised them after MRF
service. Some attempted to become double agents, and
one was murdered by the IRA after his messages were intercepted by the British and rewritten. Others made the
mistake of returning home to their Catholic ghettoes after
a decent interval, only to be interrogated under torture
by the IRA. Among British soldiers involved one was
prosecuted for attempted murder, and acquitted, after the
MRF team of which he was a member had hit four people
with shots from a Thompson submachine-gun in the Republican Andersonstown district of Belfast on 22 June
1972. The soldiers were dressed as civilians and were using
a traditional IRA weapon at the time. They believed they
had been shot at themselves, the accused soldier told the
court.

Surprisingly, perhaps, the SAS was not used for the
clandestine work of running the MRFs. There were two
reasons for this: first, the Dhofar commitment; and, second, political opposition in Belfast and London to the
"escalation" that an SAS presence was thought to represent.
But this did not inhibit local people from blaming the Regiment for any undercover military activity. In June 1973,
for instance, the Northern Ireland Civil Rights Association published advice about "What to do if the SAS shoot
you." It went on to refer to "SAS/MRF squads" and suggested: "Provided you are alive when the shooting stops,
pretend to be dead until the squad moves away, otherwise they might try to finish the job." More cheerfully,

one Irishman defined an SAS soldier as "someone able to speak six languages while disguised as a bottle of Guinness."

The pioneering work performed by the first MRFs did not satisfy the Protestant Government at Stormont. In August 1971, against military advice, the provincial Prime Minister, Mr. Brian Faulkner, persuaded London to introduce internment without trial. This was a political calamity, which alienated many hitherto uncommitted Catholics and exposed the poverty of the security forces' Intelligence system. Many of those rounded up had had nothing to do with the IRA for years, while volunteers who were currently active remained undetected by the security forces. Most of them, aware of what was in the wind, were not at home when the soldiers arrived. As the distinguished authority on terrorism, Richard Clutterbuck, has put it:

"The effect was disastrous. Of the 342 arrested on the first night a substantial proportion had no proven connection with the IRA and were quickly released. Of the remainder, 12 were interrogated 'in depth' which involved long periods of questioning, with interruption of sleep and a bread and water diet; they were kept standing against walls in 'search posture,' sometimes with pillow cases over their heads and background noise to stop them seeing the others who were being questioned.

"Though the amount of information obtained was considerable, this kind of ill-treatment aroused anger and criticism both inside and outside Northern Ireland. Interrogation is a slow business and requires much patience especially if, as in this case, some of those arrested resist violently. For comparison, in major operations in Malaya, it was customary to limit the number of suspects arrested for interrogation in depth to 20 or 25 per month. Arresting 342 in one night vastly exceeded the capacity for interrogation in Northern Ireland.

"The result was a rapid escalation of violence. . . . . While only 59 people in all had been killed in the two years from August 1969 to 9 August 1971, a further 231 were killed in the following six months. . . .

"British soldiers had carried out the arrests (though not the interrogation) and borne the brunt of attempting to control the violence afterwards. The British Government told Mr. Faulkner that they were no longer willing for British troops to be used under the direction of the Stormont Government, and that responsibility for security would have to be shifted direct to London. In March 1972 the Stormont parliament was prorogued and direct rule from Westminster was instituted. . . ."

A CEMENT FOR DISINTEGRATING
INTELLIGENCE

It was after this disaster that SAS soldiers, mostly officers and NCOs (who were, in some cases, Irishmen themselves), were posted as individuals to sensitive jobs in military Intelligence in Ulster. For convenience, some of them were attached to units already serving in the province. They were part of a much larger migration of Intelligence specialists of all kinds to Ulster over the next two years, which amounted to a counter-espionage "gold rush." As one Military Intelligence Officer put it later: "Anyone who wanted to make his name in Intelligence was trying to get to Belfast." Their world was like that of Gerald Seymour's novel about the underground war in Northern Ireland, *Harry's Game,* a world of petty but lethal jealousy and division among conflicting Intelligence agencies, a world of dirty tricks inaugurated by Military Intelligence Officers and their superiors, for which the SAS—by now not so much a military unit as a philosophical pantechnicon into which the Irish loaded all their suspicions—got the blame. To understand how this came about it is necessary to study the structure of military Intelligence in Ulster as it evolved between 1972 and 1974.

Attached to the Northern Ireland Office was an Intelligence supremo. His deputy, an assistant political secretary based elsewhere in the province was for a long time seconded from the Foreign and Commonwealth Office. He was, in truth, a senior officer of the Secret Intelligence Service, or MI6 (also DI6), which is traditionally concerned with espionage outside the United Kingdom. The reason for this appointment (which caused resentment in the Home Office, the department traditionally responsible for Ulster as well as domestic counter-espionage, or MI5) was that, on paper at least, confidential exchanges of security information with the security services of the Irish Republic were an external affair controlled by the For-

eign Office. The Secret Service was also keenly interested
in monitoring a growing Soviet and Arab terrorist attention to the Irish conflict. Yet another, more pragmatic
reason for the management of Intelligence in this way was
that Harold Wilson, as Prime Minister until June 1970
and from 1974 to 1976, trusted MI6 more than he trusted
MI5. The MI6 representative, through his boss in London, communicated with the Prime Minister with all the
influence this implies, while in Northern Ireland he had at
his disposal two "executive" arms. These were the first
plain-clothes MRFs and, separate from these, a Special
Military Intelligence Unit, also working in civilian disguise with the police Special Branch from the RUC headquarters at Knock, on the edge of Belfast. There was also
a traditional, if not explicit, link between MI6 and SAS
people derived from the clandestine operations of the
Second World War, Borneo, the Yemen campaign and
elsewhere. Key posts in Military Intelligence, including
the most senior jobs at Army Headquarters Northern Ireland and at brigade level, were occupied by a succession
of SAS officers, who returned to the SAS in Hereford or
London after a tour in Ulster.

Meanwhile, the Intelligence supremo attached to the
Northern Ireland Office an MI5 man, also had his private line to Downing Street, as did the Army by way of
the Defense Ministry. This spider's web suffered from grave
structural disadvantages. For a start, all these agencies
were jostling for control, offering conflicting analysis of
what was happening on the ground and not revealing their
thoughts to one another. The effect was sometimes to inhibit the Army while a fashionable intelligence scenario
was being tested. An equally irritating effect of this divided
counsel was that lines of command and responsibility within the rigid, hierarchical pyramids of the Army and RUC
command structures were blurred when, for instance, an
MI0 captain or Field Intelligence NCO (a "FINCO")
working with the Special Military Intelligence Unit had a
direct line to the MI6 Intelligence Chief at the army
headquarters and through him to Downing Street, over the
head of his local brigadier. Furthermore, because of the
intimately personal relationships between the Army's undercover agents and their informers, who were constantly
at risk, sources of information had to be kept within a

very small circle, away from orthodox Army Intelligence staff at brigade level, or the RUC Special Branch, or both. Loyalties were further divided by the MI6 practice of marking certain documents in a way that effectively excluded the Royal Ulster Constabulary. The RUC, knowing what was happening retaliated by withholding its best information and sources from the rest. To compound matters further, RUC Special Branch men and some of the Military Intelligence Officers working with them in the Special Military Intelligence Unit were running their own cross-border contacts with the Gardai Special Branch in the South, although these were ostensibly dealt with by the Foreign Office and MI6.

The confusion became total when the long-serving MI6 Intelligence Chief at Army HQ was moved to an overseas post and replaced by a less competent individual from MI5. It was after this change, according to two MIOs active in Ulster at the time, that ten informers working for the Army Intelligence network run by an SAS officer were assassinated by the IRA. An MIO known as "Major Fred," who repeatedly crossed the border in civilian disguise, bearded, wearing dirty jeans and carrying a false driving license issued in Dublin—in defiance of emphatic orders not to stray into the Republic—later described how the change affected his work. Hitherto, he had made his reports to MI6, but, following the departure of the MI6 representation, he explained: "I had no one to report to up at the top because I'd been told when I went up there by G1 Intelligence, this SAS major, "We're not working with MI5 because one of our lads has commited suicide. He had done four years here and handed over ten first class sources to MI5 who had just taken over, and within a week they'd all had a head job by the IRA, which means they've got a leak in their system. So under no circumstances give this information to the successors of the old Intelligence supremo. You must give this information to us, that is G1 Intelligence Army HQ, Northern Ireland.' "

The suicide mentioned by this officer and confirmed by another former MIO was not that of an SAS soldier but of a FINCO of the Intelligence Corps, who shot himself at the Army's look-out post in Flax Street Mill, Belfast. The former Intelligence officer explained how this could happen: "With an informer you get close, personally close. You know the man's family and you know the risks he takes to help us. To have a system which was incompetent because it was bureaucratic put people's lives at risk and made some of our own people crack up."

Before this bureaucratization, the MRF groups had enjoyed much success. The "Four Square Laundry," a creation of Army HQ at Lisburn, was a classic of modern Intelligence gathering. Until its cover was blown by an ex-IRA agent of the MRF, it was embarrassingly profitable, since no official channel existed through which the revenue it yielded could be spent. As time went by, however, the MRFs also suffered some disasters. As in Aden, two of these plain-clothes Army patrols shot at one another. In one such encounter at Belfast's Springfield Road, each believed the other was an IRA active service unit. And the circumstances in which a Protestant terrorist quartermaster was shot and wounded with a silenced Sterling submachine-gun raised, even among RUC men, the suspicion more loudly voiced by the IRA that some of the security forces were engaged on their own assassination campaign.

In 1974, in an effort to impose order on the Intelligence mess in Northern Ireland, more SAS officers were drafted in to control agents in the field. This had the advantage that, without any overt structural changes in Intelligence-gathering, there would be a cadre of people accustomed to working together who could act as a sort of cement to bond an organization that seemed, at times, to be falling apart. Many of their field agents were British soldiers not on the strength of the SAS but prepared to take extraordinary risks in impersonating the locals. Occasionally, as in the case of Captain Robert Nairac three years later, they were murdered when their bluff failed. (Nairac sustained his cover to the end. His killers thought he was a dangerous member of the left-wing Official IRA with which they had a long standing feud that was then reaching a climax.) Other field agents were genuine locals who were now serving, or ex-soldiers; a few more, like the first MRF "Freds," were IRA men who had been turned around.

Another effect of the Intelligence "gold rush" was the emergence of hybrid units whose exact function was never really clear. Some had only tenuous links, if any, with the SAS. An Army free-fall parachute display team, which became very popular at charitable fund-raising events through Northern Ireland, consisted of two former SAS men, one MRF soldier and a Military Intelligence Officer. The team, appropriately named "The Phantoms," never went armed. At Christmas 1974, one of its members parachuted into the grounds of a school at Crossmaglen, the IRA heartland of South Armagh, dressed as Santa Claus. He reasoned that not even the IRA would assassinate Santa.

THE "DOOMSDAY" PLAN

The year 1974 also saw the first excursion by an orthodox SAS squadron into Ulster, in spite of political resistance in London and Belfast to such a deployment at a time when negotiations with the IRA were going on in secret. During a raid on an IRA headquarters on 10 May in Belfast, the security forces had discovered documents including a "doomsday" contingency plan for counterattacks on Protestant areas if there were a repetition of August 1969 or worse. Army sources described the find as the most significant in five years of trouble. The plan, according to a British Intelligence source, was essentially defensive, but Harold Wilson, now back in office as Prime Minister, was influenced by an MI5 analysis of the IRA plan as an offensive one that imminently threatened a frightening escalation of the Ulster conflict. The reasons for this reflected the continuing rivalry between the two principal Intelligence agencies, MI5 and MI6, which, to do them justice, had never had to fight so closely on the same battlefield before and had, in Harold Wilson, a Prime Minister who was more than usually ambitious to "fine-tune" events around him.

At the time, the Foreign Office, through MI6, was seeking a political solution, which inevitably involved secret exchanges with the IRA among others. The IRA, then down on its luck both militarily and in other ways, participated in these talks, but the MI5 analysis was that the terrorists were merely playing for time. If the Army could be taken off their backs for a time, it was argued, they would regroup. (They did.) The seizure of the IRA "doomsday" document gave MI5 an ideal opportunity to discredit the hypothesis that the terrorists were serious about a political deal. Thus it was that the Prime Minister made a statement in the Commons to the effect that "the documents reveal a specific and calculated plan by the IRA, by means of ruthless and indiscriminate violence, to foment inter-sectarian hatred and a degree of chaos . . . to occupy and control certain pre-designated and densely populated areas in the city of Belfast and its suburbs . . . its intention would have been to carry out a scorched earth policy of burning the houses of ordinary people as it was compelled to withdraw. . . . An apparent IRA operation of potentially great danger has been brought to light." As a result, an immediate growth in the Army's plain-clothes MRF surveillance operations was sanctioned and ultimately, by March 1978, the Minister for Northern Ireland, Mr. Roy Mason, would announce that men from every unit in the province would be training for SAS-style undercover operations. But in 1974, as one of those involved put it: "We couldn't get the soldiers trained quickly enough because the orientation process took time. We had suitable men who had volunteered for twelve months undercover work in Ulster, but how could we make them look, talk and think like Irishmen? Two of them went to a Paisley meeting with unshaven chins and in scruffy clothes. Not surprisingly, in view of the Orangeman's emphasis on smart turn-out, they were shown the door. There was also embarrassment when two of these volunteers didn't know the words of a favorite Protestant hymn. I sang with them as loudly as I could, but they weren't even moving their lips and they stuck out like two sore thumbs.

"Eventually it was agreed at Prime Minister level that SAS soldiers should be sent to Northern Ireland, but not publicly. They were sent on the basis that, although they were members of the regiment, they were 'returned to unit' and immediately posted to plain clothes duties. They were filling a temporary gap until we had trained sufficient soldiers from other units. Meanwhile intensive training of other volunteers took place in the UK and Northern Ireland."

This peculiarly opaque period was attended by rumors of clandestine cross-border operations: if they ever occurred, they were contrary to the Regiment's insistence on staying within the law, if only because discovery of gross illegality would not be worth the political penalties involved. One example will suffice. On 8 November 1974, the Dublin-to-Belfast mail train was seized by armed men in the Republic and recklessly derailed near Portadown. The hijack was similar to IRA operations before and after this event. Yet, on the basis of hearsay, two former Army Intelligence officers were prepared to believe that the SAS had a hand in the derailment, the alleged purpose of which was to search Republican homes evacuated while the train was checked for explosives. As one ex-SAS soldier acidly observes, there were easier ways of accomplishing the same end. Yet the episode described is no more remarkable than a scheme entirely outside the ambit of the SAS, proposed to "Major Fred" by his MI6 Intelligence Chief. The proposal was to substitute a doctored, exploding .303-inch bullet for ammunition an IRA assassin was about to use to kill a policeman. The scheme, confirmed by two former colleagues of "Major Fred," was squashed by an Army brigadier. As Major Fred tells the story: "I went to the brigadier and said, 'Look, Sir, I have a bullet here which is the top round of a clip of .303 ammunition that's going to assassinate a policeman on Saturday morning and I suspect that when it's struck it's going to blow the assasin's head off.' The brigadier went absolutely mad with me and said, 'I'll have no dirty tricks in my area. This is bloody disgraceful. You call yourself an officer?' So I immediately put this bullet in my cupboard and forgot all about dirty tricks."

The SAS also had its critics among Army and police commanders, then and later, who felt that the introduction of the SAS somehow implied that they had failed. So when SAS soldiers failed to arrest a man in a Portadown pub after a fight, the news was greeted by the indigenous forces with a degree of schadenfreude. Soon afterwards, when two members of the Regiment were accused at Coleraine of bank robbery, the bad news spread more quickly. In a more general sense, it is not unfair to record that it was following the sharp expansion of undercover forces in 1974 that SAS veterans noticed a decline in the skill with which these forces operated. The decline is hard to quantify, and reflects subjective experience. Broadly speaking, it is said to result from a period of intensive recruitment into the SAS itself for counter-terrorism in Britain as well as elsewhere, during which (as ever) the veterans complain that standards dropped—increased bureaucracy surrounding clandestine reconnaissance coupled with official insistence that costs be reduced, and the general dilution of SAS reconnaissance techniques among men who had not passed the Regiment's stringent selection procedures.

The effect of cutting costs, for example, meant that the civilian cars used by MRF groups were resprayed less frequently. One officer, who was obliged to use an identical vehicle to trail an IRA suspect for five successive days in Belfast, was finally intercepted and shot in the head. An Intelligence officer responsible for the "Q" cars solemnly registered each bogus vehicle with a senior official of the Belfast licensing authority, who retained the registration books and recorded the correct fee of £25 per vehicle. Each time a car was re-numbered and re-painted the same laborious process was followed.

COMBAT IN SOUTH ARMAGH, 1976

Outside the cities meanwhile, long after the withdrawal of the SAS reinforcement group in 1974, one area of Northern Ireland that remained impervious to the successes of security forces elsewhere was the wild border country of South Armagh, centered on Crossmaglen. Never a natural part of the Protestant North, its inclusion in Northern Ireland was one of the more crass political errors of partition. The Irish Tricolor flies there as familiarly as the Union Flag in London. Throughout the troubles, the IRA has sustained a classic, rural guerrilla war in the area, hopping back and forth across the multitude of border roads to friendly territory in the Irish Republic. This is not to say that the Dublin Government (as Mr. Ian Paisley and other Protestant ultras allege) condones terrorism: the advantage to the IRA is that it does not recognize the border but the British and Irish security forces do, making hot pursuit in either direction, armed and in uniform, diplomatically impossible.

The IRA has had one other advantage in that area; skilled, professional military planning, which is attributed by British Security forces to a renegade ex-color sergeant of the Parachute Regiment. When Harold Wilson an-

nounced in January 1976—apparently to the surprise of
the Ministry of Defense—that the SAS was to be formally
committed to the area, the "score card" was: British
Army dead 49, IRA dead Nil. The peculiar advantage
the IRA enjoys in the area is that it is an Intelligence desert, a sparsely-populated place in which even local people usually know nothing about what "the Boys" are up to.
The Army's border casualties included three young members of the Royal Regiment of Fusiliers who were
surprised and shot dead in their observation post in November 1975. The only survivor, a lance-corporal, crawled
to safety and "played possum" while the IRA called on
the dying soldiers to surrender. They had been in the post
for just 36 hours. One theory in military Intelligence circles was that their position had been leaked, without ill
intent, by an undercover agent planted on the IRA, to
increase his credibility with the guerrillas.

There was another reason for urgency in bringing
South Armagh under control at that time. During the six
months before the SAS was publicly committed to Ulster,
21 civilians were murdered in the border area as part of
a tit-for-tat war of sectarian killing. During the week preceding the decision, ten Protestants were massacred in
one episode and five Roman Catholics in another. The
Wilson government dispatched the Duke of Wellington's
Regiment and 200 men of the Queen's Regiment as a response to this, but the Prime Minister concluded that this
would be insufficient to satisfy an outraged Protestant
community. Since the SAS was now assumed to be back
"on stream" with the end of the Dhofar campaign, he
chose to make the maximum psychological impact with an
announcement that they would now enter the Irish arena.

The initial advance party comprised only eleven men
of D Squadron who had returned from Oman only days
before. This fact rapidly came to the attention of the veteran defense correspondent Chapman Pincher, who described it as a mere "token presence." Wilson angrily
denounced the story as "a criminal misrepresentation of
the facts," but Pincher was not led manacled to the Old
Bailey or anywhere else. In spite of this propaganda mis-
hap, the value of SAS mystique did count for something.
The SAS, the IRA was led to believe, would wait in hiding for 36 days rather than 36 hours. In the ten months

after the Wilson announcement only two men, both off-duty members of the Ulster Defense Regiment, were murdered in South Armagh. SAS strength in the area was gradually augmented to something approaching a squadron—in this case, probably about 60 men—as it had been in Dhofar. By 1977, according to one informed source, the number was 160, or two squadrons. Their target, according to an SAS officer who later in England talked unwittingly to a journalist with long experience in Ulster, was the top echelon of ten Provisional IRA ("Pira") leaders in the area. In December 1976, less than a year after being committed to their combat rôle, the officer revealed: "We got four of them. The other six were chased away down South."

One of the first to go was Peter Joseph Cleary, an IRA staff officer and a scrap-metal dealer, arrested while visiting his fiancée's home 100 yards inside the border and taken to a nearby field to await a helicopter. The chosen landing zone was a short sprint away from the sanctuary of the border. According to the officer quoted above: "There were five of us. We radioed for a 'chopper'. . . . All of our men had to be used to hold up landing lights to let the machine down. Cleary was being held by just one chap. . . . He grabbed a soldier's rifle by the barrel and tried to pull it away. The soldier squeezed the trigger three times and got him in the chest."

Another man, Sean McKenna, was brought before the courts where he claimed that he had been hauled out of bed in the Irish Republic by three men in civilian clothes. The SAS commander concerned said that McKenna had stumbled, drunk, into an SAS patrol near the border. Two others on the SAS list were arrested in the Irish Republic as a result of tip-offs to the police there.

In January, 1977, just over a year after the Wilson announcement, the SAS scored a peculiarly satisfying victory. On 2 January, Lance-Corporal David Hinds of the Royal Highland Fusiliers was shot dead in an IRA ambush at Crossmaglen. A car in the vicinity was noticed by civilians and, when it reappeared, the security forces were tipped off. On 19 January, in the gathering darkness of a Sunday afternoon, an SAS patrol waited as a young man approached its position. The man wore a black hood. He also carried a bandolier of ammunition—which later

proved to be a strong buckshot used for deer hunting—
and a shotgun the barrel of which was sawn short. As one
of the patrol rose to challenge the man, he lifted the shotgun. The SAS trooper instantly fired several times. The
impact of the shots hurled the gunman backwards. Simultaneously, the soldier came under fire from one or two
other unseen gunmen using high-velocity Armalite rifles.
The shots, about twenty in all, missed their target as the
soldier ducked for cover. At the same time other members of the SAS patrol fired back 28 times, aiming at the
muzzle-flashes of the IRA weapons. Later, the soldiers
found a trail of blood in a dyke beside the road. The first
armed man they had shot turned out to be a twenty-year-
old building worker named Seamus Harvey. He lived
nearby at Drummakaval and was killed only 200 yards
from the site of the observation post ambush in which the
three British Fusiliers had been killed just before the SAS
arrived. Two of his wounds were caused by the IRA
Armalites.

The deterrent effect of such ambushes was dramatic.
While soldiers and RUC officers continued to be killed
regularly elsewhere in Northern Ireland after Harvey's
death, the IRA attacks in South Armagh diminished almost to vanishing point for a year. When they were resumed, at Forkhill, the first casualty was a local pig.

Soon, however, the SAS was to learn that "the Irish
dimension" presented them with problems not even their
previous campaigns, exotic though they were, had brought
to light. Having declared a war of liberation against the
British forces, the IRA was equally ready to claim the
protection of the law, whether in the Republic (whose
government it does not recognize) or in the North. Simultaneously, the SAS encountered covert hostility from elements in the police forces on both sides of the border,
although in theory all three were attempting to subdue a
common enemy. The first and most famous episode led to
the appearance of eight members of the Regiment (one a
Fijian) in a Dublin court, charged with, among other
things, the illegal possession of firearms with intent to endanger life. On conviction, the soldiers could have been
imprisoned for twenty years on this charge alone.

The episode began on the night of 5 May near Omeath
in County Louth, when a car containing a military plain-

clothes patrol was halted at a police road-block 600 yards south of the Ulster border. In spite of appeals to let the patrol return the way it had come, a police officer manning the road-block insisted on taking advice from his Dundalk superiors and thereafter the affair escalated. Two other SAS vehicles, searching for the one that was missing, ended up at that same point at 2:15 am and they also were detained. Weapons taken from them included Sterling submachine-guns, pump-action shotguns and automatic pistols. Army HQ Northern Ireland explained that the men had inadvertently crossed the border on an unmarked road as a result of a map-reading error. A *Sunday Times* journalist who went over the same ground concluded that the patrols had missed "a faded, but still visible, large yellow cross in the narrow road painted by the Army to warn troops that they were coming to the border"; that they had made a 180-degree compass error and had also missed two road signs at a cross-roads just before they arrived at the Gardai road-block.

The press, finding it incredible that two SAS patrols could make the same map-reading error, looked for a more plausible explanation and, they thought, found it. Nine terrorists had tunnelled out of the Maze Prison shortly before the SAS teams got lost. Further, a stolen car had taken six men from Forkhill in South Armagh and crossed the border earlier the same night. But this ingenious reconstruction, it was claimed by the Regiment after the trial, was wrong and ignored the simple, embarrassing truth that the whole episode was a foul-up," a comedy of errors which escalated out of control once an arresting officer in the Republic referred the matter to higher authority. Certainly this was the impression given during the Dublin trial by the police officer who arrested the SAS men. Asked what the soldiers had said at the moment of arrest, the officer coughed away his embarrassment, then quoted one of accused, Corporal Nicholson: "I was hoping to make it as a sergeant but after this fuck-up, there's no hope."

THE LAW V. POLITICAL RHETORIC

Legal limitations on a regiment accustomed to the freedom (as well as the perils) of the battlefield have emerged in Northern Ireland as well as across the border, in spite of the televised pronouncement of Mr. James Chichester-Clark, Stormont's penultimate Prime Minister, the morning after the first British soldier was shot dead in these latest troubles, in February 1971. "Northern Ireland," he declared, "is at war with the Irish Republican Army Provisionals." Prime Minister Harold Wilson echoed this sentiment in his House of Commons statement about the "doomsday" plan in May 1974: "We are not talking of a peace-time situation," he said. And, following the murder of Lord Mountbatten in August 1979, Prime Minister Margaret Thatcher voiced similar sentiments. The ordinary soldier might be forgiven for the belief that he was expected to react as though this were a war. In spite of the political rhetoric, the problem of adjusting a military campaign to the legal fiction that there is no war is one that has faced all soldiers in Northern Ireland. The SAS has encountered the problem in an acute form because of its rôle in capturing or fighting armed men in isolated ambushes laid by both sides, of which there are usually no witnesses except the combatants. The essence of the law governing the British soldier's conduct in Northern Ireland, as it has painfully evolved since the common-law arrangement of 1969, is that he may not shoot at an armed terrorist without risking criminal proceedings for murder unless he is in imminent danger, or can plausibly claim that he believed himself to be. This means that it might be illegal for a soldier to shoot at a gunman who has just killed one of his comrades, but who is now in the act of fleeing from the scene and threatening no imminent danger to the soldier in pursuit. The SAS has never been in the business of offering soft targets to an enemy, adopting Bismark's advice: "Only a fool learns from experience: I learn from the experience of others." It was inevitable that once the SAS was committed to combat in Northern Ireland, its philosophy would come into conflict with the legal niceties with which, for political reasons, that war is "deodorized." When it did happen, the circumstances were peculiarly tragic.

By now, internment without trial had been abandoned in favor of Diplock (juryless) courts at which legal proof of motive as well as fact was required, while the initiative for much military planning had passed from the Army to the police. A sophisticated enemy, less susceptible to the traditional SAS methods of winning "hearts-and-minds" evolved in Borneo and Dhofar, the IRA was not slow to cash in on the opportunities this unique legal environment offered. The only "heart-and-minds" initiative that would satisfy the IRA would provoke a Protestant uprising. Thus it was that the SAS became entrapped, with so much of British political history, in the Irish bog. The shooting of sixteen-year-old John Boyle should be seen as part of that history, rather than as a tale of military callousness.

On 10 July 1978, John Boyle, the son of a Roman Catholic farmer, took a break from his work in a hayfield at Dunloy, in an isolated part of County Antrim, and went to a deserted, overgrown graveyard nearby. John was an inquisitive lad. and there had been some discussion in his home about the possibility of an ancestral tombstone in the graveyard. What John found, in fact, was a blue plastic sack hidden under one of the gravestones. He told his elder brother, Hugh, about this find. Later the same day, their father, Cornelius, a careful and methodical man, heard about John's find. He checked it and telephoned Ballymoney police station, concerned that the cache might contain explosives that could endanger the lives of children he had seen near the graveyard. A detective constable said he would have the matter attended to. Later that day, this constable and three other RUC men checked the bag. It contained a detonator cap, cordtex fuse, what appeared to be gelignite bound with black tape and, in a separate fertilizer bag, what appeared to be a rifle. The cache also contained a revolver. They called in the Army.

At an Army base, a few miles away, Sergeant Allan Bohan, aged 28, an SAS soldier with twelve years' service, six of them in the Regiment, and his friend Corporal Ronald Temperley, aged 26, were watching a television program *The Waltons*, when they were summoned, with three of their comrades, to Ballymoney police station. Bohan later said that they were told that the weapons were probably to be used against a local Protestant march on 12 July, and it was expected that more than one armed man would return to collect them. It was now the evening of 10 July: clearly there was not much time to set up an ambush if this supposition were correct; no time, apparently, to check whether the illicit rifle was loaded. In spite of this, there were two briefings during which the soldiers were shown aerial photographs of the site and told who lived where in the area. According to Army and police witnesses, one of the detective constables present, the man who had received Cornelius Boyle's original telephone message, agreed to repeat an earlier warning to the family to stay away from the graveyard. Later, this detective constable denied giving such an undertaking though, in fact, he did telephone the Boyle family to reiterate the warning the following day, seven hours after the SAS ambush was set up.

The police officers involved went off duty at around 3 am, by which time Bohan and Temperley were concealed in the undergrowth twelve yards from the arms cache, while two of their colleagues were hidden in a farm building on the road opposite the path to the graveyard. The soldiers believed that the family had been warned to stay away. "We believed we would be up against three armed terrorists and our mission was to capture any person who came to recover the cache," Bohan said later in a statement. But it was clearly a matter of fine judgement, and perhaps split-second timing, if any terrorist collecting the arms were to be caught in the act, as the law required, yet simultaneously unable to threaten any soldier who had allowed him to arm himself. This may explain why, at the briefing, a "killing" as alternative to capture was mentioned during the planning of the operation. In Northern Ireland, as in Aden, a live captive was far more useful for intelligence-gathering than a dead terrorist.

The police warning to the Boyle family was given at 9:40 am, about ten minutes after young John had taken the family tractor out to the hayfield. For reasons about which learned counsel could only speculate later on, the boy returned to the graveyard to have another look at the arms store. There were two sources of evidence for what happened next. One was Sergeant Bohan, who opened fire on Boyle, killing him; the other was Ulster's Assistant State Pathologist, Dr. John Press. Bohan, from the outset, asserted that a man resembling a terrorist whose photograph he had seen walked straight up to the cache and extracted the rifle from it. "He stood up . . . turned bringing the weapon to bear on us and I thought our lives were in immediate danger. I fired and he fell and as soon as he fell I stopped. I fired not more than twice and probably once." As Bohan fired, so too did Temperley.

If this story were true, then clearly the first bullet to strike Boyle, who was facing Bohan, would have entered his body from the front. But it was contradicted by an autopsy report prepared by Dr. Press, who insisted that Boyle was hit by three bullets, one through the head and two through the body, all entering from the back. Not long after Press's postmortem, the contents of his report were leaked to journalists with predictable results. The journal *Time Out*, for example, reported: "Five high velocity bullets fired from less than four yards killed Boyle. All the rounds were fired from behind, the fatal bullet entering through the nape of the neck and blowing off the top of his head . . . the four men who murdered him were members of the Special Air Service." In the fullness of time, Bohan and Temperley were charged with murder and brought to trial, almost a year after Boyle's death. By then, an independent autopsy by the distinguished British pathologist, Professor J. M. C. Cameron, had cast doubt on Press's findings. Cameron concluded that Boyle was shot in the head from the front, and that his body was turned by the impact of this bullet so that the two subsequent shots hit him in the back. Even more telling was Cameron's discovery that the basic measurements of Boyle's body and the site of the bullet wounds according to Dr. Press were inaccurate. Having launched its case on the basis that Boyle was shot from the rear, the prosecution found it necessary, well after the case had begun, to float the theory that Bohan may have made a noise deliberately to induce Boyle to turn in Bohan's direction, "and then you shot him."

The Lord Chief Justice of Northern Ireland, Sir Robert Lowry, summing up the case described Dr. Press as "a most important" Crown witness, whose evidence was "a clear indication that the deceased was shot in the back and that the defence of self defence . . . could not possibly stand up." But defending counsel, Mr. Michael Lavery, had cross-examined Dr. Press "with such a wealth of convincing anatomical and scientific detail as to cast the gravest possible doubt on the reliability of his [Dr. Press's] principal conclusion."

"Put shortly, counsel achieved a position in which the witness [Dr. Press] admitted that the wound at the back of the head was for several reasons characteristic of an exit rather than an entrance wound . . . The argument as to the wounds on the deceased's back was more complex, but identified a number of unsatisfactory features of evidence such as wrong measurements, faulty relationship of various 'landmarks,' failure to record objective signs on the existence of which the witness [Dr. Press] later relied when pushed by counsel into a difficulty, and a number of facts which did not seem to support his essential hypothesis of the bullets having entered only at a slightly downwards inclination."

The defense, by contrast, "was suggesting a plunging effect which would indicate either firing from a considerable height (which was extremely unlikely) or (as defense counsel suggested) firing on the level into the body, the relevant part of which was almost parallel to the ground because (he suggested) the deceased, having been struck in the head, was falling as the two bullets of parallel height struck the trunk."

"I consider," the Judge continued, "that the most probable thing is that Soldier A [Bohan] shot the deceased in the head when the deceased's head was facing A, and slightly inclined to the left; that the deceased fell forward with his left shoulder coming under his body and towards the right; that while he was in that position two bullets from Soldier B's [Temperley's] rifle entered the deceased's back (which would cause them to make a downward track towards the fifth rib and lung) and that the deceased's body finished up roughly on its left hip and back. . . .

"To put it no higher, a responsible tribunal of fact is bound at least to assume in favour of the accused that something like this happened and that the deceased cannot have been shot from behind in the ordinary sense. . . ."

The result of the case satisfied no one and reflected the messy ambiguities of an undeclared war dressed up in the legal trappings of a civil police operation. Prosecution counsel had argued: "The security forces do not have a free hand to . . . claim the same immunity as if they were on the battlefield. . . . The Crown accepts that both accused looked at the short term advantage of eliminating a person whom they believed to be a terrorist in the knowledge that there was a rifle under the headstone and they could make it appear that the terrorist had armed himself." But the Lord Chief Justice (sitting, under the Diplock formula, as a jury) found the two soldiers not guilty of murder because "a collection of suspicious circumstances is not proof beyond reasonable doubt." Once the medical evidence (of Dr. Press) had to be discounted, the only way a defense plea of homicide in self-defense could be attacked was by not believing that the boy Boyle had pointed the rifle at the soldiers, and, said the Judge, "I am not infallible on a pure question of fact." At the same time, Sir Robert scourged Bohan as "an untrustworthy witness" who had gravely mishandled the operation because his team had shot an innocent boy, "whether or not he was holding the gun." If the soldiers believed Boyle was a terrorist, they had time to capture him. Furthermore, "if one accepts the defense case this was a badly planned and bungled exercise." For good measure, the judge rammed home the prosecution's message: "I do not intend to give any currency to the view that the army is above the general law in the use of weapons."

Following the case, the dead boy's father blamed both the SAS and the police for what had happened. The Republican Clubs and others attacked the acquittals as "absolutely outrageous." No one complained about those responsible for the original arms cache, though evidence had been given that the Armalite rifle picked up by John Boyle had been used in several murders and attempted murders in the two years preceding April 1978, and nitro-glycerine explosive from the cache had come from the Irish Republic.

The leak of the inaccurate postmortem report; the detective's denial of a pledge to reiterate a warning to the family; and an allegation that there was an SAS conspiracy to tamper with evidence after the shooting; all this did nothing to sweeten relations between the Regiment and the RUC (to which a soldier in Northern Ireland is answerable after any violent death in which he is involved).

Nor did another propaganda coup shortly before the trial began, alleging that a doctor's wife had been raped in Belfast by a lone, unidentified SAS man. Details of the rape undoubtedly emanated from police records, but the smear was sufficiently vague to make it impossible to get at the truth. It elicited an unprecedented statement from the Colonel Commandant of the SAS Regiment, Colonel B. M. F. Franks, "to rebut the ever-growing, ill-informed comment in the press and elsewhere about my regiment." No SAS soldiers were known to be in Belfast at the time, Franks said. A deafening silence followed the rebuttal. Whatever "evidence" there was for the smear was never deployed.

Yet the trial of Bohan and Temperley did serve one purpose. The details of Bohan's evidence threw much light on the way the soldiers there perceive their task, and the extent to which SAS ambushes are now orchestrated by a doctrine embodied in the Standing Operational Procedures (SOPs), which have evolved from hard experience in Ireland. Immediately after the Boyle shooting, Bohan—who had maintained radio silence hitherto —had snapped a terse message to his comrades posted just outside the cemetery: "Contact! Send QRF!" The word "contact" indicated that the first shots had been fired; the QRF, or Quick Reaction Force, on helicopter stand-by, was now summoned as a back-up force. Asked why this should be necessary, Bohan had referred to the case of "an OP (observation post) taken out by the IRA." This, of course, was the Drummakaval Hill episode in South Armagh after which the only survivor, a lance-corporal, had failed to use his radio until it was too late. Pressed about the tactics to be employed in arresting a terrorist suspect, and how to time his challenge, Bohan had repeatedly made the point: "We don't dictate the tactics to the terrorists. They dictate them to us." He was, he explained, concerned not only about Boyle but any other armed men who might be covering him. Yes, he had stood up out of cover as Boyle took up the Arma-lite, and perhaps, as counsel suggested, it was a crazy thing to do; but presenting oneself as a target was sometimes "the risk of being a soldier." In another reply, Bohan said laconically: "Tactics are like opinions: everyone has one." When counsel suggested that Bohan was in a "cool, calm and collected state of mind," as he fired at Boyle's head, Bohan replied: "I don't think anyone shooting from 12 yards at such a target would be cool and calm."

Immediately after the shooting he had again followed SOP in moving to the body, searching it, and then moving forward to clear his area. Stupidly, he agreed, he had emptied the arms cache on the same basis and, once the Quick Reaction Force had arrived, he again followed the procedure in returning to his base before the police appeared on the scene. Asked whether it was part of the SOP not to give his name to the police when they came to interview him, Bohan replied: "I believe that is part of an agreement between the Army and the police but I am not absolutely sure." (In fact, a soldier is required to give his name to the police.) And how did he feel when he discovered that John Boyle was not a terrorist? "His actions indicated to me he was a terrorist. . . . Nothing else. . . . I was told that the person who had been shot was not a terrorist but I didn't accept it. . . . I cannot regard any person who points a weapon at me as being a completely innocent person."

Such answers did little to reassure an uncomprehending and often hostile civilian population, which was disturbed by a mounting toll of people shot dead by the Army during the preceding months. Some were IRA bombers engaged in planting bombs. For once, Irish logic and legal doctrine were at one when *The Republican News* complained on 24 June 1978: "In the early hours of last Wednesday morning a three-man active service unit of the Irish Republican Army was surprised and trapped while on a bombing sabotage operation against Ballysillan Post Office Telecommunications Depot in Belfast. The unarmed volunteers having been surrounded by British soldiers and RUC men were summarily killed. Also shot were two passers-by, one fatally." The ambush party, as it happened, consisted of an SAS team accompanied by RUC men, and the operation brought bombings in Belfast to an abrupt halt for several months. If *The Republican News* was not impressed by the soldiers on this occasion, neither were the soldiers by the IRA appeal to a legal system that it does not recognize. But this is not to argue that the legal restraints are without effect both in controlling the soldiers and winning the unac-knowledged war in Northern Ireland. They are, in fact, a potent element in shaping perceptions, and SAS soldiers are carefully briefed about them—and the difference from earlier campaigns—before they operate in the prov-ince. Thus there is a school of thought within the Army which, relying on a counsel of perfection, argues that an SAS soldier who gets caught breaking the law deserves no special treatment. Yet, after the Boyle affair, it is not sur-prising that at least one SAS soldier, cynical about these unique ground rules, should explain: "Letting the opposi-tion shoot first is what we call the 'Irish Dimension.'"

What the Regiment has not been allowed to disclose, for security reasons, is the extent of its success in non-lethal activity in Ulster. Like the rest of the Army, its record of arms hauls and terrorist arrests without blood-shed in the province is one of its most impressive achieve-ments.

A few months after the Boyle case, in August, 1979, Lord Mountbatten was assassinated in a part of Ireland that he loved and where he felt secure. The same day, eighteen British soldiers were killed by IRA land mines near the spot where the SAS patrols had been arrested by the Irish police in May 1977. The new British Prime Minister, Mrs. Thatcher, visited Northern Ireland and returned, according to some press reports, appalled by the conflicting Intelligence assessments she received from the Army and the RUC. Soon afterward Sir Maurice Old-field, a retired head of MI6, was appointed as Intelli-gence supremo to co-ordinate the two services. Plus ça change. . . .

The campaign of terrorism and guerrilla warfare in Northern Ireland seems certain to continue until the men of violence are isolated from their host communities. But —unlike the Third World—Ireland is not a place where that isolation can be achieved by building protected vil-lages for non-combatants while converting large parts of the country elsewhere into "free-fire" zones. In this case, this author believes, isolation of terrorists has to be achieved politically, in men's minds, as well as militarily. That will only happen when the Catholic minority in Northern Ireland feels secure enough to support the se-curity forces. But, so long as influential Protestants such as Mr. Ian Paisley oppose power-sharing, and so long as influential Catholics in the Social Democratic and Labour Party cling to reunification, then a political consensus favorable to military activity against terrorism will not emerge. And without that consensus the security forces are often without sound Intelligence about the opposition, and are groping in the dark.

VII

War on Your Doorstep

O N 6 MAY, 1980, WHEN AN SAS COUNTER-
terrorist team abseiled from the roof of the Iranian
Embassy in London to halt the murders (then in progress) of twenty-one hostages, they had the sort of worldwide television audience that terrorist propagandists lust
after and sometimes—as in the Munich massacre of Israel's Olympic athletes—obtain. In this case, the high profile of SAS success in ending a six-day siege was of
incalculable help in propagating the unfashionable idea
that democracy could defend itself from terrorism if it
had to. As at Entebbe, Mogadishu and Assen, the propaganda of the deed reinforced the credibility of the rule of
law rather than the law of the jungle. This political mag-
nification factor was the only element missing from the
carefully rehearsed SAS scenario for Operation "Nim-
rod," as the rescue was officially named. But it was an
inevitable consequence of such a public success, and shattered the anonymity with which the SAS had masked itself for thirty years.

With the London hostages freed, the British promptly
suffered a rush of patriotism to the head. Crates of cham-
pagne were delivered to the Hereford base of 22 SAS
Regiment, which had supplied the rescue team, together
with invitations to accept the freedom of this or that bor-
ough (though Teheran was not among them). This well-
intentioned amiability was received by the SAS with a
degree of cynical amusement. Not only had the soldiers
been regarded for a long time as pariahs, but, as the
Regiment wryly observed, no one had noticed that only

187

four days before the Iranian Embassy was stormed, an
SAS troop commander, Captain Richard Westmacott, had
died in forcing the surrender of a group of terrorists besieged in a house in Belfast, Northern Ireland. Both
events ended with a display of white flags. That the London squad was personally fêted by the Prime Minister,
while Westmacott was cryptically described in a brief
Army statement as "serving in the Grenadier Guards, attached to HQ Northern Ireland," had much to do with
political expediency as well as with the conflicting priorities of psychological warfare.

The failure of the first US attempt, in April 1980, to
rescue its diplomats imprisoned illegally in Iran, the Soviet invasion of Afghanistan, even rising inflation and industrial disruption in Britain—all these things rendered
the subsequent seizure of the Iranian Embassy in London
a peculiarly grim event, seeming to rub home the belief
that democracy was impotent, and that "good guys"
tended to be losers. However, if the wider problems listed
above appeared to be beyond solution, the latest terrorist siege in London at least had the advantage that given
luck, daring and the right skills, it could be turned into a
media event that would make government more rather
than less credible. These grand considerations did not apply to the drab, familiar little war in Ulster.

There was another potent influence at work in shaping
events at the Iranian Embassy. This was the threat to
the lives of westerners in Iran if the siege continued as
well as the survival of the Iranian hostages in London,
where the terrorist objectives were to publicize the cause
of Arab nationalism and autonomy in the region of Iran
that contains the richest oilfields, and to force the release
of political prisoners in Iran. In Teheran, meanwhile, the
xenophobic Iranians were convinced that the London
siege was an Anglo-American plot to pressure Iran into
releasing the *American* prisoners, following the US failure
to rescue them by military means. In an increasingly fe-
brile atmosphere it was predictable that Islam's hack-
neyed "eye-for-eye" philosophy would assert itself. British
hostages would be taken, or, more dangerous still for
world peace, the existing US hostages (six months after
being imprisoned) would be put on trial. Events were certainly moving that way. According to that remarkably

alert London hostage, BBC sound recordist Sim Harris, the terrorist leader, "Own," constantly monitored Teheran Radio broadcasts. On the fourth day of the siege, Own told his captives that the latest Teheran broadcast had claimed that the Iranian hostages had smuggled a letter to Teheran. The alleged letter expressed the hostages' readiness to die for their brand of Islam. This was untrue, and of course all the hostages, including the Iranian hostages, knew it to be. So what purpose did this particular item of propaganda serve? Linked as it was to the suggestion that British police were preparing to storm the Embassy (at a time when the police were seeking to end the siege peacefully) it was, almost certainly, a crude psychological device to prepare the Iranian people for more "martyrs." In the tit-for-tat world of Islamic extremism, compensatory blood would then be expected to flow as surely as night succeeds day.

So the credibility of democratic government, the risk of armed conflict between the US and Iran, the well-being of westerners in Iran as well as the Iranian hostages in London—all were issues in what might have passed, otherwise, as just another terrorist incident in a troubled world.

The perceptions of the terrorists themselves, as they rode this tiger, were dangerously unrealistic. They had spent a month in London before the siege, enjoying the sort of social freedom denied to them in their country of origin, Iraq, including the delights of alcohol and a shopping spree for everything from children's toys to video equipment. Only one of their number, Own, spoke English, but even he needed the help of a Pakistani journalist during the siege to translate his most important pronouncements into plausible English. It seems that the terrorists had been misled by their political "godfathers" into believing that democratic London was a pushover for their commando operation. What they expected was a quick harvest of publicity, an element of diplomatic recognition (however transient) by Arab diplomats in London, and a free flight back to Baghdad to await the arrival of their air-freighted shopping. Armed with Soviet-made RGD-5 hand grenades (which they handled with frightening ineptitude, according to their captives), as well as automatic pistols and carbines, they were persuaded by their controllers that, since London was the ideal place for terrorist blackmail, the risk was minimal. They had not been briefed, as they might have been, on the basic lesson of previous hostage-taking episodes in the West—that the murder of a hostage usually removes any hope of bargaining with government. Once that occurs, then the terrorist has the choice, as Robert Mark once put it, of "going to a prison or to a mortuary."

PREDICTING EVENTS

The SAS anti-terrorist squad—more correctly, the Counter Revolutionary Warfare Team—had prepared for such a siege with rather more thoroughness than their opponents. For at least seven years, successive teams had trained relentlessly for just this situation. Each month, an elaborate exercise had been set up in which the scenario varied only in its location. The basic "storyline," or exercise plot, was always the same and eerily predicted circumstances as they developed in the Iranian Embassy:

1. Terrorists seize hostages and incarcerate themselves in a building, an aircraft, a railway train, a bus or aboard a ship.
2. The police negotiate in good faith, offering media coverage of terrorist demands as a bargaining chip, a substitute, or surrogate achievement for the terrorists' declared aims.
3. The terrorist demands are directed not at the British Government but a foreign one over which the British have little or no control.
4. The negotiations begin to crumble when terrorists threaten to kill a hostage, and shots are heard within the siege area. Later there are more shots and the contemptuous exposure to public view of the victim's body.
5. A timetable of executions is then announced by the terrorists, and the SAS assault follows.
6. As soon as the siege is over, police investigators and forensic scientists move into the terrorist stronghold to reconstruct exactly what has happened during the brief period of military control of the area. This change of command is made at the request of the police. (In the particular case of the Iranian Embassy siege, the request went to the Home Secretary, William Whitelaw, who submitted it for approval to the Prime Minister, Margaret Thatcher. Once approval was granted, the

Ministry of Defense was constitutionally in charge of the area. At the scene of the siege, meanwhile, the police officer in charge notified the SAS tactical commander that he was handing over control, and the decision was recorded in the police log of the incident.)

Afterwards, with control back in civilian hands, the police investigation includes pathological examination of the dead and ballistic analysis of the rounds fired and the weapons used. Thus, the SAS teams are aware throughout these dangerous operations of the legal implications of what they are doing and the possibility of legal action against themselves if they use more violence than can be justified by the phrase "minimum force." On siege-breaking exercises, the most testing and boring period for the soldiers is this time spent afterwards, waiting for the patient, careful police to "trawl" over the ground.

This degree of sophistication is the result of long and painstaking cultivation. The origins of SAS counter-terrorism in cities can be traced originally to the "Keeni-Meeni" period in Aden (described in pages 87 to 91). This experience gave credence to the notion that, if the enemy was disguised as a civilian, indistinguishable from the rest of the population, then the most effective means of matching the threat was for soldiers to be similarly disguised. Then, as now, the overwhelming priority was that the undercover soldier must be as near perfect as any human can be in the skilled use of firearms, to minimize the risk of causing innocent casualties. For a long time after Aden, however, the evolution of counter-revolutionary warfare (CRW) techniques as practiced by the SAS was the result of a series of historical accidents.

The Aden campaign ended in 1967, after which, until the Regiment went to war in Dhofar in 1970, it had no active campaign. The Commanding Officer of 22 SAS at that time therefore offered the services of his best marksmen to the British Government to train bodyguards for overseas heads of state who were thought to be at risk and whose removal would be contrary to British interests. "There were hundreds of them, as it turned out," one veteran of that period recalls, "and we went all over the world in their defense." It was a potent invisible export, which yielded Whitehall a rich harvest of goodwill as well as military Intelligence. In a few rare cases, for brief periods the SAS provided the bodyguard until local forces could be trained to take over. (One such case was Sultan Qaboos of Oman during the delicate days immediately after the palace coup that removed his father, Sultan Sa'id bin Taimur.) Simultaneously, in Hereford itself, a special house was constructed to train marksmen in the perilous skills involved in shooting would-be assassins or kidnappers in the close confines of a room, without hitting the VIP being guarded. The house is formally known as the Close Quarter Battle (CQB) House and, less formally, as "the Killing House." On their return to England, the six-man bodyguard training teams coached more bodyguards at Hereford, based on the practical lessons learned overseas, and formal courses in this work got under way. To maintain the momentum, a CRW Wing was created, commanded by a single officer whose task it was to keep international developments in his field under constant review. But in 1970–71, following the commitment of the Regiment to Dhofar, there was no longer a sufficient number of SAS soldiers available to act as the world's best bodyguards, and the Regiment's commitment to this work was drastically reduced. The CRW Wing, meanwhile, remained modestly in being.

What started to change this "caretaker" approach to CRW was the Munich massacre in September, 1972. Seven Palestinian terrorists seized the dormitory occupied by Israeli athletes during the Olympic Games, killing two athletes and taking nine as hostage. The Black September organization then demanded Israel's release of 200 imprisoned Palestinians. Israel refused to give way. The West German Government, however, agreed to a safe passage for the gunmen and their hostages out of the country; but then, at the airport, as the party was about to leave, German security forces fired on the terrorists. In the battle that followed, all the hostages, five terrorists and one police officer were killed. These grisly events were watched by a worldwide television audience estimated to be 500 millions, and the image of the West German Government was profoundly damaged. Western governments were alarmed by the implications of Munich. They noted that, through the magnifying glass of television, public opinion tended to blame governments rather than terrorists for the violent end to hostage-taking. Equally alarming, it was borne in upon most of them that no Western country had military people trained to the degree of sophistication necessary to defuse a massive psychological warfare threat of the sort mounted by a few well-trained "civilians," some of whom were already acquiring more operational experience of sieges than any security force. West Germany responded by creating the GSG-9 anti-terrorist squad under Ulrich Wegener (later to achieve fame with his two SAS advisers at Mogadishu). Other governments, including the French, took similar action, while in London the government turned to the SAS.

The Regiment was now given the resources it needed to create a small, permanent anti-terrorist team available at short notice to deal with hijacks and sieges—in short, any situation in which hostages had been seized for political reasons—anywhere in the United Kingdom. There was, and is, an orchestra of exotic equipment available for such missions, ranging from parabolic directional microphones to thermal imagers capable of identifying which flats in a given apartment block are occupied. But, at the end of the road, when all the cunning of "gee-whizz" technology had been exploited, the central problem of the siege is appallingly crude: to save hostage lives by killing, if necessary, the terrorists holding them. The SAS solution is to train its close-quarter marksmen to an extraordinary degree of skill, honing their reflexes in action as if they were tennis stars being groomed for the men's final at Wimbledon. The difference is that the tennis star may merely miss a singles title for the sake of a millimeter's inaccuracy, while the SAS soldier, obliged to fire a head shot at a terrorist holding his hostage against him as a shield, carries a graver responsibility.

Second in importance only to the skill of the men is the armament they carry. As Dobson and Payne have argued recently in *The Weapons of Terror*, such is the velocity of modern firearms that "the up-to-date bullets of law and order, when used without care, not only travel further [than required] but they strike in the cause of the terrorists they are seeking to overcome." In other words, excessive firepower will result in a propaganda victory for the terrorists, even if the security forces win the military engagement. And, since terrorism is primarily about shaping popular perceptions as part of its psychological warfare, the more important battleground is not the individual siege but the one fought in the pages of newspapers, on our television screens—and ultimately in our minds. For all these reasons, low velocity and accuracy are the desiderata of anti-terrorist weapons for use in cities. Reliability is equally important, since a weapon prone to stoppages is worse than useless. So what is required is a weapon that fires rapidly, precisely on target and at low velocity, hitting the intended target without penetrating one body and striking another. A dramatic illustration of this philosophy in action occurred when the joint SAS/GSG-9 team burst into the hijacked Lufthansa airliner at Mogadishu: every terrorist was wounded in the first quick burst of gunfire, but the ensuing battle continued for eight minutes. A woman terrorist was wounded nine times, and later survived after medical treatment in custody. Initially, the SAS/CRW team armed itself with the American Ingram submachine-gun, but on automatic fire it tended to spray bullets too liberally over the target area, with ominous implications for innocent hostages. Eventually, the Regiment chose the Heckler & Koch MP5. Experiments in West Germany, where the weapon is made, had led to the accidental discovery that a certain non-German bullet could yield unparalleled accuracy among such weapons, and stoppages caused by the new bullet were cured by redesigning the magazine, making it curved. The weapon was used in action by the SAS for the first time at the Iranian Embassy siege. The other firearms carried by the team include the thirteen-round Browning automatic pistol, a reserve weapon that lingers in the SAS armory partly as a result of the experience of an officer who found himself suspended from a tree in Malaya in parachute harness, weaponless, while an armed guerrilla prowled around immediately below him. The heaviest firearm used is the Remington shotgun, to blast the lock from a door to a room known to be occupied by terrorists. Also carried are plastic explosives and concussion grenades—"flash-bangs"—which are magnesium-based and have the shock effect of paralyzing the enemy during the vital first five seconds of an encounter. CS gas grenades can be used if surprise has failed to overcome an adversary. Both the "flash-bang" (an SAS invention) and CS carry with them the risk of causing an explosion or a fire or both. In an assault such as that which took place at the Iranian Embassy, team members wear protective gas-masks throughout the attack, so that if they use CS they will not need to waste time donning masks after the assault has started. Finally, the CRW team is equipped with a variety of specialized motor vehicles and aircraft, enabling it to travel with its equipment at short notice anywhere in Britain.

At the same time as this re-equipment was taking place, the Regiment expanded its CRW Wing to a permanent cadre, or cell, consisting of one officer and four instructors to be responsible for all aspects of training in hostage rescue, bodyguard work, Intelligence gathering about terrorist techniques, and so on. The CRW team, now about twenty men, drawn on rota from the four operational Sabre squadrons, was deployed in earnest for the first time in January 1975, when a civil airliner was hijacked at Manchester by an Iranian armed with a pistol which later proved to be a harmless replica. The whole affair turned into black comedy after the hijacker was persuaded that he had reached his desired destination (Paris) when in fact he was at Stansted Airport, Essex, where the SAS awaited him. The only casualty was a soldier bitten by a police dog as he left the aircraft. The hijacker, an Iranian, was sent to prison.

The next time the SAS were summoned to a siege, the mere knowledge of their presence was sufficient to induce the terrorists to surrender. In December 1975, a four-man "Active Service Unit" of the Provisional IRA was trapped by Metropolitan Police officers in a flat at Balcombe Street, Marylebone, where they held the occupants, a nervous middle-aged couple, hostage. Through the wonders of fibre optics, it was possible for a controller at Scotland Yard to monitor what was happening in the flat from minute to minute. The terrorists had a transistor radio and, when the BBC announced that the SAS were on the scene and standing by to take over the building, the terrorists surrendered. But the revelation that the soldiers were on the scene, successful though it was, also prompted speculation about who is in charge of such a situation: the police, or the military authorities The legal situation that has evolved to meet such a case is an effective British compromise.

In an exclusively criminal enterprise, such as the seizure of the Spaghetti House Restaurant in London in
September 1975, total operational control remains with
the local police chief, who has armed officers under his
control. However, if a siege is an exercise in terrorism—
that is, an attempt to coerce government for political reasons—then direction of the affair is in the hands of a government committee known as "COBRA" (for Cabinet Office Briefing Room). This is chaired by the Home
Secretary, and includes junior Defense and Foreign Affairs Ministers, with advisers representing the police, MI5
and the SAS. Thus, the Regiment has a direct channel to
the top of the decision-making pyramid as well as operational links on the scene with the police, who remain in
tactical control during the negotiating phase. This is as it
should be, since the SAS is stringently subject to the rule
of law, for which the police are responsible. The Army's
CRW teams are reminded of this by a litany of ground
rules, more elaborate even than the "Yellow Card" governing the rules of engagement for soldiers in Northern
Ireland. It travels with the team for display in their tactical operations room near the scene of the siege.

True, there might be some practical advantage in a more
organic arrangement through which, say, the SAS handled negotiations as well. But, as things stand, the CRW
team members know that they are on scene in exactly
the same way as military bomb-disposal squads might be
elsewhere, as Military Aid to the Civil Power. Politically,
they are not merely neutral, but "neutered" also. There is
another reason why the SAS—even in the view of the
Regiment itself—should not be in the "driving seat" at an
earlier stage of the siege. This is that the use of force,
albeit minimum force, is only one of several options open
to government in defusing the situation. The others range
from total surrender to terrorist demands, in the style
of the Austrian and past West German Governments (as
well as the British in the case of Leila Khaled), to a
measured response that permits say, a limited draught of
publicity but nothing else. Interestingly, there are cases,
still hypothetical in Britain though not elsewhere, where
government might advocate a violent solution to break a
siege, but where expert SAS advice might be that this
would be unwise—counter-productive, even. It cannot be

overstressed that the contemporary SAS is an acute instrument of psychological warfare, and is keenly aware of the political content and ramifications of the violence it can inflict. Most media men, for whom violence is an exotic and vicariously exciting beverage (along with group sex and drug addiction), usually fail to comprehend that the SAS does not share their perception of risk and violence. Like experienced drinkers, the SAS has learned the wisdom of avoiding intoxication, particularly if the party is attended by moralistic outsiders who are likely to accuse the Regiment of excessive violence, while using the excitement generated by that violence to improve newspaper circulation or television-viewing figures.

THE ROAD TO MOGADISHU

Different considerations apply when the CRW team goes into action outside the United Kingdom, where political control is in the hands of the host government. In October 1977, four Palestinian terrorists—two men, two women —joined 79 normal passengers on a Lufthansa flight from Majorca. The cursory baggage checks there enabled the terrorists to smuggle an assortment of weapons aboard the aircraft, which they then hijacked. The principal object of the operation was to force the West German Government to release the leaders of the notorious Baader-Meinhoff gang, a team of chic middle-class revolutionaries then in prison in Germany. For good measure, the hijackers threw in a demand for a £9-million ransom. The hijack occurred six weeks after the kidnap of Hans-Martin Schleyer, a powerful West German industrial baron; his release, like that of the Lufthansa hostages was conditional upon freedom for the Baader-Meinhoff team, and he was still imprisoned when the Lufthansa plane was seized.

Such was the crisis of credibility faced by the Bonn Government that much normal administration was being paralyzed by the need to manage the crisis. As so often before, government was in a "no-win" position: a surrender to terrorism would damage belief in goverment's ability to govern; a hard line, if it resulted in hostage deaths, would provoke a storm of protest from society's professional humanitarians. The terrorists knew they were on to a good thing, since, until that time, most captured terrorists had obtained freedom within one or two years as a result of such blackmail by their comrades outside. (The unfashionable Moluccans tended to be an exception to this rule.)

A wild aerial journey followed the Lufthansa hijack, around various places in the Middle East and the Horn of Africa. Soon after it began, a German minister travelled to London, accompanied by a member of the GSG-9 team, to seek British help and, in particular, liaison with the authorities of Dubai, where the hijacked aircraft was about to land. (A member of the United Arab Emirates, Dubai has close links with Britain.) Initially, the purpose of the Germans' visit was to ask Whitehall to use its good offices with the UAE ambassador in London to ensure diplomatic clearance for GSG-9 to go into action in Dubai. As a subsidiary objective, the GSG-9 representative thought that his SAS opposite number might have equipment that could be useful in breaking into the aircraft. The Germans had not appreciated that the SAS knows the Persian Gulf intimately and that, for example Dubai's élite presidential guard is trained and led by former SAS soldiers. During the London conversations, therefore, it became clear to everyone that an SAS liaison team on this operation would be a decided asset, and such a plan was instantly endorsed by the respective premiers, Callaghan and Schmidt. The two men selected for the job were Major Alastair Morrison, OBE, MC, a veteran SAS squadron commander, and Sergeant Barry Davies, BEM; with a specially crated collection of flash-bangs they left immediately for Dubai.

They arrived to discover that GSG-9's leader, Wegener, and two of his men were being kept "under escort" in the international airport's VIP lounge—in the politest possible way—while the hijacked airliner, with its hostages, stood on the scorching tarmac. Morrison and Davies sorted out this bureaucratic nonsense, and then set about training the Dubai Royal Guard in the basics of siege-breaking with a view to providing a back-up force for GSG-9, whose main force was then in a pursuit aircraft in Turkey. But, before this elaborate scheme could be put into operation, the Lufthansa airliner with its hostages flew on to Aden. Obstacles might have been placed on the Dubai runway to delay the hijacked aircraft's departure, but at that point the terrorists could threaten the hostages effectively while the security forces could not convincingly match that threat. In such a case, the golden rule is that government must be able to "put its money where its mouth is" if it is going to arrest, or even contain, terrorists, or pay for its failed bluff with hostage lives. So the Lufthansa plane, refuelled and replenished, took off, followed by another aircraft carrying Morrison, Davies, Wegener and his two aides. For a time, the hijacked airliner enjoyed sanctuary at Aden, while, for some hours, the Morrison-Wegener group flew in the vicinity seeking permission to land on the same airfield. But this was refused. Aden, now capital of the Marxist People's Democratic Republic of South Yemen, contained numerous East German and Soviet advisers, whose governments declined to put pressure on their Arabian client to assist GSG-9.

By now, Morrison and Davies had become de facto members of Wegener's team, and they stayed with him when the hunt moved from Aden to Mogadishu, in Somalia, where the German commander was joined by the main body of his force after a flight from Turkey. The whole rescue party got together just twelve hours before the rescue attempt. The rôle of the SAS men would be to throw the flash-bang grenades at the start of the operation if peaceful persuasion did not work. The Germans were in earnest about a peaceful solution: their pursuit aircraft carried the ranson—£9 millions in cash—in a large metal box. But at Aden, the hijacked airliner captain, Jurgen Schumann, was murdered by the terrorist leader, "Captain Mahmoud," after he suspected Schumann of secretly communicating with the security forces. The Lufthansa airliner flew on to Mogadishu, where Schumann's body was thrown from the plane. For many hours prior to that, it had lain on the floor of the aircraft, in full view of the terrified hostages.

From the moment the pilot's body was hurled onto the Mogadishu runway, there was no hope of a peaceful end to the siege and, five days after the SAS team joined Wegener, they threw their flash-bangs from each side of the aircraft to signal the assault. The attack plan, composed by the SAS team, was one in which fortune favored the bold. The assault team entered the aircraft through the emergency doors set above the wings on each side of the fuselage, kicking-in the doors as the flash-bangs exploded. Once inside, they had to tackle terrorist gunmen at the front and rear of the airliner. Aviation fuel as well as duty-free alcohol scattered by the terrorists inside the aircraft might have exploded, but it did not. During the eight-minute battle inside the aircraft, the terrorists rolled two hand grenades towards the assault team, but these exploded harmlessly beneath padded passenger seats. The hostages, strapped in their seats, were below the line of fire being exchanged between the terrorists and the raiders, and three of the four terrorists were killed. Later, their leader was identified as Zohair Akache, a professional assassin serving the Palestinian extremist Wadi Hadad. That he was operating on this occasion on behalf of the West German Baader-Meinhoff group was a vivid illustration of the organic nature of international terrorism in the seventies. Within hours of the Mogadishu battle, the terrorist leaders who had hoped to be set free as a result of the hijack—Andreas Baader, Gudrun Esslin and Jan-Carl Raspe—committed suicide in their cells. And, six days after the rescue, Schleyer, the kidnapped West German industrialist, was found shot dead in the trunk of a car.

Confirmation of the SAS involvement in the Mogadishu operation came immediately after the rescue from Prime Minister Callaghan, then in Bonn with Chancellor Schmidt. In front of television cameras, Callaghan told Schmidt: "It should have been Dubai." But even if the venue was changed, the event added new lustre to the SAS reputation, and it was good for Britain's relations with Europe. Within Germany, an agonizing political crisis had been resolved. And a secret agreement among West European governments to co-operate in the war against terrorism—made eighteen months before, at the time of the Moluccan siege at Assen, in Holland—was given operational reality for the first time.

INSIDE A TERRORIST'S MIND

The event was also to have momentous implications for the rôle of the SAS in future years. The quick-reaction CRW team was still little more than twenty strong and, in the light of the political crisis generated by expert terrorism within West Germany, the Callaghan Govern-

ment took the significant step of authorizing a substantial
increase in the British CRW force. From now on, each
SAS squadron was committed in turn to the CRW rôle
on rotation, between tours in Northern Ireland and training missions abroad. The implication of that decision was
that Britain was now a potential SAS operational zone in
a way not previously contemplated. The squadron dedicated to CRW would spend a prolonged period undergoing refresher training in the necessary techniques under
the guidance of the permanent CRW wing. During this
British tour—"the war on your doorstep," as one SAS
man called it—the CRW squadron would then work up to
the monthly siege-breaking exercise, usually in a new environment each time, followed by a prolonged de-briefing,
or "wash-up." At the end of the tour, the same squadron
would remain on stand-by and assist its successor squadron's retraining in the rôle. The wisdom of this decision
only became apparent two years later, when the scale of
the problem at the Iranian Embassy was within the compass of a squadron (about 80 men) but far beyond the
capabilities of the original team of twenty. Yet again, the
SAS had made one of its unique evolutions into a new
rôle to meet a need that others could not satisfy.

The period between Mogadishu and the Embassy siege
1977 to 1980, was one in which London became a battleground for various Middle East terrorist groups in conflict
with the Israelis and with one another, and during which
—in July 1978—Britain had to expel eleven Iraqi diplomats because of their involvement in terrorism. In Hereford, meanwhile, the increased emphasis on CRW was
accompanied by more funds and improved training facilities, which, as one veteran put it, "moved out of the
world of Heath Robinson in the late sixties, to superb
equipment in the late seventies." Details of those new
facilities are secret, and rightly so. In general terms, however, it may be said that they train the SAS teams to enter a terrorist stronghold by a variety of means and, once
inside, to distinguish instantly between terrorist and hostage (unless, as happened in the Iranian Embassy, some
of the terrorists neither fight nor surrender, but pretend
to be hostages). In the "Killing House" now furnished
with a television and pictures on its walls, dummies representing terrorists and hostages are moved from place to

place. The CRW team is divided into two specialist groups, the assault group, who enter the building, and the perimeter containment group, snipers who provide a cordon sanitaire around the scene. The assault group members have to be able to burst into a room in pairs and (as described on pages 248-250) instantly fire two pistol rounds or short, controlled bursts of automatic fire —the "double tap"—into each terrorist, aiming for the head, without causing injury to their fellow team members or the hostages. Each two-man team has its own room to deal with and each man has his own arc of fire so that, once one room is cleared and the next squad has followed through, the possibility of an "own gaol," or battle accident, is drastically reduced. The use of balaclava masks, first introduced in the Aden days for certain operations, assists the process of instant identification in action while in Britain; and it also ensures that any SAS soldier accused of murder (for, unlike the terrorist, he subjects himself to the rule of law) will go on trial without the encumbrance of a jury that has identified him from newspaper photographs. In an age when the camera is ubiquitous, and terrorist resources enjoy the sophistication of government backing in Iraq, South Yemen, Libya and Lebanon, the mask also assures the future anonymity of SAS soldiers. Over the years, the dissemination of CRW training throughout the Regiment means that most CRW men have been prepared for the sniper's rôle on the perimeter as well as the assault rôle, greatly enhancing the mutual comprehension of SAS team members. Such is the stability of the Regiment that the same small group will work together for years. Two of those who stormed the Iranian Embassy in London fought together at Mirbat in 1972, and one was decorated for his courage there. The SAS team at Mogadishu were among those who flew to the relief of Mirbat.

What the SAS does not attempt to do is to assume control of the negotiations with the terrorists. (There are, as have been explained, good constitutional reasons for this.) Negotiating the release of hostages has become a technique for specialists, which the SAS studies carefully, but is not best qualified to practice. The aim of such negotiations is to ensure the release of the hostages, alive, but not at any price. Thus, the terrorists have to discover, once the siege starts, how far their demands are "real" in the sense that there are some things no government could guarantee. Pressure on the Dutch Government by Moluccan extremists to arrange that part of another country—Indonesia—should be granted independence from Indonesia, over which Holland has no control, falls firmly into the category of total unreality. In practice, most terrorist sieges over the last decade have been aimed at securing the release of other terrorists from lawful imprisonment and, in general, it is a form of blackmail that has succeeded. At the other extreme from total surrender is the style adopted by the Israeli and French Governments, the full-frontal-assault technique, which affords the terrorists no scope for maneuver. This "gung-ho" approach to the siege problem carries with it the lamentable by-product of dead hostages, which is politically dangerous.

Both the New York Police (whose motto is "We bore them to death") and the Dutch security forces have pioneered the middle road of substitute, or surrogate achievement through the use of one subtle negotiator. His is the voice on the telephone, which, in a psychological sense, gets into bed with the terrorists, referring to the two sides—terrorists and negotiators—as "us," or "we," and the government and its security forces as "them" or "they," the outsiders. This Machiavelli gradually persuades the hostage-taker that if he kills any of his prisoners it will damage the terrorist cause. After all, the argument goes, the terrorist has commanded maximum media coverage of his grievance. Give it more time for the public to digest the lesson, Machiavelli continues, and meanwhile come out peacefully with clean hands to win respect by facing a bourgeois court. The argument is a seductive one for a terrorist who is trapped along with his hostages: it provides the terrorist with all the benefits of martyrdom without the unpalatable corollary of death, a bit like Mark Twain's description of attending his own funeral and being quite overcome with grief. But terrorists also read Mark Twain and much besides, and some of them have Ph.Ds. Even the comparatively rustic Iranian Embassy terrorists had apparently equipped themselves with tranquillizers to help sustain the stress they were about to face.

The clever ones now add to the pressure on democratic government by launching their assaults at election time, when government is peculiarly vulnerable to the pressures of public opinion, which in turn is influenced by the media. The Dutch Government, faced with such a siege during an election in 1977, discovered that to "play it long" in this way, became intolerable. The result, after days of negotiation, was a quick, brutal military solution using Air Force jets as well as Marine Commandos.

Yet another psychological factor is the so-called "Stockholm syndrome," by which is meant the emotional bond established between the hostage and his captor in joint opposition to the security forces. Such a bond is often created and, through various academic studies (usually American in origin), it has become a new orthodoxy that after a day or so the Stockholm syndrome will assure the survival of the hostages, provided the security forces do not precipitate a massacre by frightening the terrorists. But, as the murders of numerous European hostages in the Congo in the 1960s and the Iranian Embassy siege in London in 1980 demonstrated, the assumption underlying the Stockholm syndrome is a life-saver only if the terrorists share the same cultural values as the negotiators. Cultural assumptions about the sanctity of human life, and so on, are part of the fabric of Western, democratic and essentially Christian society. The SAS CRW training scenario does not rely on the essential good nature of the terrorist, though the Regiment accepts that—to put it at its meanest—public opinion will demand a convincing effort to end a siege peacefully before unleashing the soldiers. Still, it is worth noting that the training scenario described above assumes that a hostage will be murdered *after* prolonged negotiations, during which, if the academics are right, the Stockholm syndrome should have started to show results. Indeed, to judge from the treatment of the Iranian Embassy hostages by the SAS immediately after they were rescued—as Sim Harris put it, "thrown from one man to the next, no compassion, no thought of minor injuries"—and then tied up, also assumes, correctly as it proved, that some hostages will try to help their former captors.

Basically, the British style of negotiation appears to be a pragmatic blend of the Dutch and the Israeli styles:

to negotiate in good faith on issues that are negotiable, and to continue to negotiate merely to buy time once the murder of hostages begins. No doubt, in the light of events at the Iranian Embassy, the style will evolve still further. But, as that siege demonstrated, there is a limit to the extent to which even seven years' rehearsal can entirely remove the possibility of ill-luck and, therefore, disaster.

SEVEN YEARS AND ELEVEN MINUTES

The SAS assault on the besieged Iranian Embassy in London, which lasted a mere eleven minutes, began after the body of the Iranian press attaché, Abbas Lavasani, had been dumped on the steps of the Embassy at Princes Gate. Another hostage was to be murdered every thirty minutes, the terrorist leader Own announced, unless his demands for negotiations with three Arab ambassadors in London, as well as a guarantee of safe conduct out of Britain for the terrorists and their Iranian hostages were met. The police negotiators kept the discussions going, and successfully separated Own from the two British hostages (Police Constable Trevor Lock, taken prisoner in the first assault on the Embassy, and BBC man Sim Harris) as the SAS swung from the roof of the building on abseil ropes. Technically, this was an unusually hazardous operation if success, which the SAS defines as saving hostage lives, were to be achieved. The building had 50 rooms. There were now twenty hostages, fifteen of whom, all men, were in Room Ten, the telex room on the second floor overlooking the street. They had been moved there a few hours before, as tension increased and the terrorists prepared for an assault by the security forces. They were guarded by three terrorists, some of whom moved back and forth checking other rooms. Meanwhile, five women hostages, all members of the Embassy staff, were in the custody of one terrorist in Room Nine on the opposite side of the building, across a landing. Harris and Lock were near the telephone on the first floor landing, where they had been with Own as he negotiated with the police until seconds before the assault began. To complicate matters further, the only feasible assault route at the front, across a first floor balcony, was blocked by armor-plated glass which had to be blown in with an explosive charge.

It was of critical importance, to preserve a shrinking advantage of surprise following the murder of Lavasani, that the SAS assaults on both front and back of the building should be simultaneous.

In the event, this did not happen. At least four pairs of SAS men appeared on the Embassy roof to begin their descent on two ropes down the back of the building, while another team, armed with framed charges of plastic explosive to blow-in the front window, was stationed on an adjoining balcony. The first abseil team had started the descent when one of the pair swung against an upper storey window, smashing it with his boot. As this happened the terrorist leader, Own, put down the telephone and went to investigate. He was followed—perhaps stalked is a better word—by PC Lock, who had kept his full uniform, top coat and all, throughout the siege to conceal the fact that he was still carrying a .38 revolver. There was no question now of the abseil teams at the rear awaiting the sound of their comrades' explosions on the other side of the building before starting their own assault. It had to be done immediately.

The first pair dropped to the ground at the back at hair-raising speed, their descent recorded by an electronic camera smuggled into the area by Independent Television News. As they prepared to blast their way into the building, the second pair were already on the rear second-floor balcony, hacking at the window and hurling the first flash-bang grenade. But one of the third pair was trapped on the abseil rope, unable to move up or down. It is thought his problems resulted from the late discovery that insufficient rope was available and more had to be purchased in London. The new rope, although nylon, was of an inferior variety and overheated due to friction caused by the weights imposed upon it; it then ravelled into a knot, trapping one of the last men to use it. For the ground-floor team to set off their explosive charge now would certainly kill the man trapped immediately above it. They therefore followed the example of those above them, and hacked at the window instead, hurling flash-bangs as they entered.

Inside the building the terrorist leader, Own, was now taking aim at one of the SAS men coming through the back of the building when he was brought down in a rugby tackle by PC Lock. There was a violent struggle between Lock and Own, during which Lock drew the pistol he had been carrying for so long, but had sensibly not attempted to use. At this point, the SAS soldier intervened with the cry, "Trevor, leave off!" Own now rolled clear and pointed his weapon at Lock, at which point he was killed with a cool, precisely aimed burst of fire from the SAS man's submachine-gun. On the front of the building, meanwhile, two more SAS soldiers were busy hitching the big frame, with its explosive plastic charge, to the window. While one man set the ten-second fuse, the other covered him. The fuse activated, the second soldier gave a hand signal to his comrades below, and both men darted for cover to an adjoining balcony. Two minutes after the abseil team had started their attack, an impressive explosion destroyed the armor-plated glass. The SAS men stormed into the room through the smoke and up the stairs while the building was still shuddering under the blast. Harris, groping his way out through a front window towards the balcony, encountered an SAS man who snarled at him, "Get down!" He did so, and as the team swept past him in the wake of their own flash-bang grenades, Harris heard himself shouting; "Go on lads, get the bastards!"

To the smoke and debris from the explosions was now added the insidious, sickening reek of CS gas, as members of the CRW team outside fired a cartridge into a front room near the top of the building where a sixth terrorist was hiding. Heavy drape curtains broke into flame, and soon a fire had taken hold of the place. At the back of the building, still trapped on his abseil rope, a soldier in the third team was scorched each time his weight swung him close to the window. His only remedy was to kick the wall and swing clear of the flames. His comrades, spotting his predicament, cut the rope and dropped him unceremoniously to the ground. He collected himself, and followed the rest of the team into the building. There, coming face to face with an armed terrorist, he shot the man dead.

Among the two main groups of hostages, meanwhile, some strange things were happening. The terrorist in charge of the four women had thrown away his firearm and was hiding among his hostages when an SAS soldier found him. The women protested, "Don't hurt him: he's a nice boy." As the soldiers took him downstairs they searched his body for other weapons, and when he offered a flicker of resistance, he was hurled down the stairs before being dragged out of the building. The same pretense at surrender was adopted by the three terrorists in charge of Room Ten at the front. At the first sound of trouble, they started shooting their hostages, but abandoned this as the SAS men approached, and pretended to be hostages themselves. Although Room Ten was one of the first to be penetrated by the SAS—it was taken before all the terrorists elsewhere had been disabled—the terrorists shot dead assistant press attaché Samad-Zadeh and tried to kill the chargé d'affaires, Dr. Gholam-Ali Afrouz. First, he was shot in the face by one of the gunmen and wounded; then, as he lay with a cloth over the wound on his face, he was shot again in the legs. A third hostage escaped injury only through the simple good fortune of a 50-pence piece in his pocket, which stopped an assassin's bullet.

Seconds before the SAS team crashed into Room Ten, the gunmen threw away their weapons and began shouting in Farsi, "Tasleem!" ("We surrender!") before hurling themselves onto the floor where the hostages already lay. According to the only British hostage in that room, Mr. Ronald Morris, an embassy chauffeur, the terrorists did not give any signal that a soldier would recognize as one of surrender. No white flag was hoisted at this stage, and no one stood up to face a door or window with his hands in the air. No one sat with his hands on his head. "The terrorists just sort of wormed their way in among us," Mr. Morris recalled later. The soldiers had but one objective —the rescue of the hostages, alive. They were also prepared, after a recent spell of duty in Northern Ireland, for booby-traps. Possibly, in view of the terrorists' earlier claims to have the Embassy wired to an explosive charge, the whole building was a booby-trap laid by people who meant what they said when they spoke of embracing martyrdom. The only certain way of saving the hostages' lives, therefore, was to kill the terrorists unless it was unequivocally clear that they were identifying themselves for what they were and were very plainly surrendering. This was far from clear at the time, and the building was now on fire. The soldiers demanded: "Who are the terrorists?" When one of the hostages, apparently fearful that he might be mistaken for a gunman, pointed them out, the SAS team shot them as they half-sat, half-lay against a wall. As dead men, they would have no chance to blow up the building or attempt to "surrender" while carrying concealed grenades. The speed and urgency of the decision is of a kind faced by, say, a family motorist who is travelling at high speed, his wife and children in the car, when a tire blows out. He reacts instantly and takes no chances. Nor does the soldier on a military battleground, which is what the Embassy had now become.

Upstairs, the last terrorist was shot in the room in which he had locked himself. For some time, more shots echoed through the building as the SAS team blasted away locks to check other rooms. The fire had taken grip of the top of the building now, and the hostages, having been removed with expedition (if with some lack of diplomatic politeness), were bound and secured with straps on the lawn behind the Embassy. The women were still unwilling to identify their former captor—the only terrorist to survive—for what he was. This chore was performed by Sim Harris. Then, as he lay there, bound like the rest, Harris told another former hostage: "Think yourself lucky you have just been rescued by what must be one of the crack squads in the world." Later, in an interview with a BBC colleague, he ended his account: "Thank you, SAS, for saving my life."

This was a faint reflection of the emotional scenes that occurred immediately after the operation, in the SAS tactical headquarters near the Embassy. The wife of PC Lock, reunited with the husband she had so nearly lost, thanked the SAS soldiers who had saved him, again and again. Home Secretary William Whitelaw, who had advised the Prime Minister earlier in the day to sanction the use of the SAS, was also on the scene, his tears of joy and relief totally undisguised. The SAS were also relieved.

This was the first time they had fought a battle on Britain's own doorstep. If it had gone wrong, the political and public backwash could have been calamitous. In all the circumstances, one scorched soldier, and another whose thumb was severely mangled by a bullet wound, were a small price to pay for crowning seven years' preparation with such a success. It almost made the publicity tolerable.

At the end of that memorable day, someone at the tactical headquarters suggested that the party, which included the Prime Minister, should watch the television recording of the rescue. Everyone, including the Prime Minister, agreed that this was an excellent idea. In the darkened room, as the set came to life, there was a cheerful, impudent shout from one of the CRW team: "Sit down at the front and let the rest of us see it." Glowing with contentment, Mrs. Thatcher sat down, cross-legged, on the floor. It had been a good day for the SAS, and an even better day for Britain.

VIII

A Funny Thing Happened
on the Way to Everest

ONE EVENING IN 1968, THE BRITISH RAIL SIG-
nalman responsible for a stretch of track across the
Firth of Forth, including the Forth Bridge, noticed something odd about the Edinburgh-to-Aberdeen express. The
train was not particularly crowded, but three men appeared to be riding on top of it. The signalman took the
sensible course of stopping the express, but not before
one of the three had fallen from it, killing himself in the
process. Subsequent inquiries revealed that all three men
were volunteers in the Territorial SAS. They had become
bored with the journey and started speculating about the
possibility of climbing out of the train on one side, scaling
the roof, and re-entering the carriage by way of a window
on the other side. Their misplaced enthusiasm for this
impromptu initiative test resulted in a bet worth £1.10s.
and, after the inquest, some adverse publicity for the
Regiment.

It was, of course, a reckless little adventure, which shed
light on the lack of mature judgment of the lieutenant, sergeant and corporal involved. But it was also a reminder
that the man whose judgment is entirely mature will tend
not to gamble with either his money or his life: he will be
a pillar of society, but entirely useless if society, to its
surprise, requires the services of people who take risks. In
a society in which risk-taking is only vicariously respectable (within the evidently fictional world of James Bond),
the real climber, potholer, parachutist or hang-glider is regarded with suspicion. More numerous casualties in the

familiar and sedentary environment of motor accidents go almost unremarked, while the schoolteacher who seeks to take a party of children for a walk across calm hills is required to produce something called a Mountain Leadership Certificate.

Interestingly, it was a Labour government that recognized how, within the armed services, the calculated risk has value as military training as well as its own, intrinsic worth. In 1964, as part of the withdrawal of military forces from the Third World for concentration in NATO Europe, the Prime Minister, Harold Wilson suggested in a memorandum to his Minister of Defense, Denis Healey, that adventurous training be incorporated within the framework of official defense activity. This would enable service people on expeditions to enjoy the same pay and preferment as if they were on more routine duty elsewhere and, if hurt, to enjoy the same benefits that would follow a battle injury. Not surprisingly, SAS soldiers had not awaited the reassurance of Whitehall that Adventure was a Good Thing before finding out for themselves. The decision of one SAS officer, posted to Aden, to sail there in his own small boat was so routine as to raise only the most passing comment. After all, the same man had planned to ride home on a Lambretta motor scooter, until he was distracted by bitter fighting on Jabal Akhdar. (The journey home would have taken him from Malaya to Britain.)

The Regiment also pioneered high-altitude free-fall parachuting in Britain in the early 1960s. The military value of such techniques has yet to be proven beyond all reasonable doubt, but as an existential, life-enhancing experience it is the stuff that dreams are made of. No doubt there are smart intellectual explanations for such behavior, that the artificial creation of a risk, and its resolution, are a source of security for insecure people, in the same manner that detective stories resolve anxieties among the less adventurous. But this misses the point that, in the detective story, there are no loose ends, no maverick, unpredictable factors. A real adventure is full of them.

There is an apocryphal story concerning a group of SAS free fallers engaged in a night drop over Salisbury Plain . . . at least, that's where they thought they were. Uncharacteristically, their navigator placed them in the wrong spot as they left the aircraft at something over 20,000 feet. The leader, a small light gleaming from his helmet, went out first with the others following on each flank, rather like a flight of geese. The jump was technically perfect and the men landed in a compact group, but, as they foraged in the darkness, it became apparent that they were not where they should be. They decided to ask, and approached a modest, suburban bungalow. They marched up the front path, between rows of pansies, the leader in the van, his light still gleaming, and knocked on the door. It was answered by a slight, elderly woman wearing hair-curlers and a dressing-gown. "Good evening, Madam," the leader said, "Could you tell us where we are?" The woman's eyes darted along the line of strangely dressed figures. "Earth!" she said, and shut the door.

MID-AIR RESCUE
The basic and almost foolproof method of parachuting, used by armies since the 1930s and civilian novices still, is the use of webbing strap attached to a strong-point in the aircraft at one end and the parachute pack at the other. As the jumper leaves the aircraft, several yards of the strap—known as a "static line"—pay out until the pack is removed from the parachute, which then opens. Well, usually.

On 17 September 1967, at a civilian sport parachute center in the Midlands known as Halfpenny Green, 36-year-old Sergeant Michael Reeves of 22 SAS was enjoying a weekend's "fun jumping." He was also acting as jump master for a group of novices, a familiar enough task for an experienced man, involving leaning out of the machine on its final approach to the drop zone and shouting corrections to the pilot to bring it over the correct spot. Once there, Reeves gave the instruction "Cut." The pilot cut the engine to diminish slipstream, and Reeves told the novice to get out of the plane, ready to go. The man did so and, on Reeves's shouted order "Go!" he fell away. Only this time, instead of flying two seconds later beneath a normally-opened canopy 2,500 feet above the ground, he was spinning on the end of a static line. For some reason, this had not functioned as expected.

The aircraft flew on over an increasingly urban area.

Reeves leaned out of the plane again, and signalled to the alarmed pupil who, fortunately, remembered the emergency drill he had been taught and placed hands on helmet to indicate that he was conscious and aware. Reeves knew that, for the novice to survive, he would have to land under a normally-inflated parachute canopy; furthermore, that if the novice were to avoid descending onto a railway line, main road or factory roof, the landing must be back on the drop zone. He hurriedly consulted the pilot, and advised him to fly back over the drop zone and keep circling it until the problem was solved.

Reeves solved it by climbing down the static line, a knife in his own, free-fall parachute harness ready for the first stage of the rescue. Having reached his man, Reeves wrapped two legs and an arm around him, and signalled to the aircraft that all was well. They had climbed somewhat now, to give the two parachutists more height, and therefore more time, to accomplish a uniquely delicate operation. Having satisfied himself that they were back over the drop zone, Reeves sawed away at the static line, never releasing his fierce hold on the pupil's body. At last the line parted and they were falling, curling backwards as they did so. Reeves already had his hand on the man's chest-mounted reserve parachute. He grabbed the handle and pulled it away with ferocious urgency, then held on to the novice's body again. The white reserve canopy swirled past both of them and cracked open.

Both men might have landed safely under that one canopy, a similar model of which was to support an entire Cessna aircraft and its occupants in a near calamity a few years later. But the combined weight of the pair would certainly make for a hard landing. Furthermore, the way their bodies were linked would rule out an orthodox landing roll, with the consequent risk of a broken ankle, or a broken back, or worse. So, although they were now perilously near the ground, Reeves released his hold on the novice and hurtled away again into free fall. He allowed a few seconds to pass, creating adequate space between himself and the other man, before opening his own main parachute. This, of course, was a free-fall "rig," opened by the jumper by removal of the ripcord handle from the harness. Reeves's own canopy opened only a few seconds before he hit the ground. They were inside the official drop zone and Reeves did a neat, text-book landing roll. It was an exceptionally cool performance, requiring impeccable judgment, acknowledged through the award of a George Medal.

Between the recklessness of the Forth Bridge episode and the controlled courage of Halfpenny Green there is a spectrum of non-military adventurous stories involving SAS soldiers, which have become part of Regimental folklore. The Regiment tends not to be good at organized ball games: it shines in tests of endurance, illustrated by Warner's account of the feat of Trooper T. McLean in rowing alone across the Atlantic in 72 days.

"He landed," Warner recounts, "at Blacksod, County Mayo, on 27 July 1969. His diet on the voyage was sardines, curry and tea. McLean, who was appropriately named 'Moby' . . . and was 25 at the time of the 2,500-mile row, had been an orphan since the age of two, and, perhaps because of that, had developed a high standard of self-reliance. He certainly needed it, for the weather was stormy all the way and once he woke up in the night in mid-Atlantic to find the boat swamped and sinking; he had another very narrow escape when he ran onto rocks off the coast of Ireland and took 1½ hours to get off. As soon as he landed he sprinted 200 yards along the beach because he felt a bit stiff and wanted to get himself properly fit again." It is also likely that this was McLean's way of celebrating the fact that his feet were on dry soil once more.

What such episodes demonstrate is that a number of SAS soldiers would be exceptional people outside the military world as well as within it. Nothing could more completely lay the left-wing myth that they are really "café-society gangsters," whose heroism is really a carefully-manicured propaganda exercise shrouded in military security for the wrong reasons, than the Everest climb of 1976.

A CLIMBING MACHINE

The expedition was set up by the Army Mountaineering Association (AMA), a club open to all soldiers, including those of the Women's Royal Army Corps. The selectors were not SAS people. They chose the team on the basis

of climbing experience, age—no one younger than 25—
and temperamental suitability for teamwork in adverse
conditions. It was led by an ex-paratrooper, Lieutenant-
Colonel Tony Streather, as a joint-venture with the Royal
Nepalese Army backed up by a group of Sherpas. Interestingly, not only did two SAS NCOs emerge as the
summit team, but the four-man support party for that
team, which assisted in their subsequent rescue, included
another SAS soldier, while one of the expedition's two
doctors was a former SAS medical officer, a veteran of
Oman. Of the 27 British servicemen taking part in the
climb, only the Parachute Regiment, with four represen-
tatives, was as numerous. Since the Parachute Regiment
is still (in theory at least) three times numerically stronger
than the SAS, the relative contribution of the SAS to the
expedition was phenomenal.

The plan to climb Everest was conceived at an AMA
annual general meeting in October 1971, but it was to be
almost five years before the Government of Nepal was
prepared to allow the soldiers to make an ascent. During
that interval, the team made practice climbs in Britain, the
Alps and the Himalayas. In 1975, the soldiers made an
attempt on Nuptse, 25,850 feet and the lowest peak in
the Everest triangle, generally considered to be a more
difficult climb technically. The leading pair on that climb
were near the summit when they fell to their deaths and
subsequently, two more men were killed on a particularly
treacherous traverse. It was an unhappy beginning.

During both the rehearsals and the 200-mile walk-in
from Kathmandu to the Everest base camp, two men
emerged as clear starters for an attempt on the summit.
They were Sergeant John ("Brummie") Stokes, BEM,
and Corporal Michael ("Bronco") Lane, BEM. Stokes
had joined the SAS from the Royal Green Jackets and
Lane was an ex-gunner. They had climbed together for
ten years. Although not the most accomplished technical
rock-climbers in the party, their combined endurance
added up to what one of their companions later described
as "a climbing machine." Everest, in any case, is not a
mountain for the elegant, balletic rock-climber. It is a
monstrous, baleful challenge to human endurance.

In a book devoted to the expedition, *Soldiers on Everest,* the Scottish correspondent of *The Times,* Ronald

Faux, describes Stokes and Lane during a rehearsal climb in Wales, as follows: "Somewhere on that Welsh weekend, out in the frozen Carnedds and hammering themselves implacably through the bitter winter day, were Brummie and Bronco, two figures around whom quite a mythology had grown in my own mind. . . . Even casehardened paratroopers spoke of them with unqualified respect and although they were always regarded as a pair apart, one never somehow thought of one without the other; it was their self-sufficiency and unquestionable strength which made them the perfectly acceptable, a-political summit pair. . . . Regimental security overwhelmed them with Victorian reserve. At the sight of the camera they would slink away or regard the photographer with a cold stare. Was I going to cover the first conquest of Everest by anonymous men standing victoriously on the summit with their backs to the camera? There was no need to worry . . . An oxygen mask on top of three months' growth [of beard] and snow goggles are perhaps the most daunting disguise."

During the march-in, the Stokes-Lane team were invariably up and away before anyone else. Their occasional habit of sleeping in the open, as part of the hardening process, was not adopted by the rest of the team.

Climbing Everest requires sustained co-ordination by a team manager to keep a flow of food and oxygen moving up the mountain, with the obvious difficulty that the greater number of men required to put essential supplies where they are needed, the faster the consumption. Above 20,000 feet, even the fittest and strongest climber finds his legs crumbling beneath him and his mind disintegrating into a soporific nightmare. A gnawing cold that hacks away at the body's core heat makes sleep seem the only sensible thing, but it is the sleep of death. Even the most perfect human calculations, however, can be crushed with Olympian brutality by the mountain itself. Capricious changes of wind and temperature, and radical movements of the earth itself, creating and closing fissures, generate risks that cannot be calculated. One member of the expedition, an experienced Royal Marine climber, simply walked from his tent at Advance Base Camp (about 21,800 feet) into a deep crevasse on one of the "easiest" sections of the climb. Major Henry Day was dropped on the end of a rope into a hole as inhospitable as a deep freeze to recover, with considerable help from some Sherpas, the dying man. On another occasion a Sherpa was "projected into the air like a paper pellet from a ruler when a crevasse closed as he was crossing it on a ladder which sprang free."

The AMA route lay through the Khumbu Icefall, a place of avalanche and crevasse, and then by way of a series of camps hacked out of the snow to the South Col, a plateau 26,200 feet high, before ascending a massive ridge to the South Summit at 28,750 feet, and thence to the main summit itself, 29,028 feet above sea level. The first pitch, through the Icefall, was led by a party of eight, including the SAS team, on 27 March, and Camp I, 2,000 feet higher up, was established one week later. Already, the hazards were emerging. Pat Gunson, a REME captain and one of the best climbers in the party, found himself swinging 30 feet above an ice wall when a crevasse opened beneath him. Above Camp II (Advance Base Camp) at 21,800 feet, the going was exhausting, and the daunting task of leading was spread among the team. As one group worked itself out, it was brought down the mountain for more routine tasks, including the movement of more stores.

An early casualty on the higher slopes was a Gurkha corporal, who developed a prolapsed intestine, complicated by piles, at Camp III, 22,800 feet. An operation had to be performed on the spot, and this was handled by Philip Horniblow, the ex-SAS doctor, assisted by Stokes, a qualified medical orderly. Recounting this episode, Faux writes: "Philip's surgery, carried out in a tent at 23,000 feet, must surely rank as the highest operation ever performed, although as he admitted when he struggled into the open, hands dripping with unpleasantness, 'I'm not sure I'd get my fellowship with that one'."

Camp IV was established on April 29 after a remarkable feat of endurance by several of the team, including the expedition's organizing secretary, Major (later Lieutenant-Colonel) Jon Fleming of the Parachute Regiment and his partner, Captain Sir Crispin Agnew, of the Royal Highland Fusiliers. At about 23,500 feet, they moved the summit gear required by Stokes and Lane, as well as their own equipment, without oxygen, each man carrying a 50-pound load.

During the second week of May, two summit teams totaling four men, plus a small support group of six, reached the South Col and, on 14 May, with Lane and Stokes lightly laden and blazing the trail, the first summit pair with their support group of four, started climbing towards the site of Camp VI at 27,600 feet, the last one before the summit. It was a weary and difficult climb up the South East Ridge, over loose rock covered by powdered snow, a climb that forced even Fleming to pause between each step to breath oxygen. On the return to Camp V that day, Fleming writes that he could remember hardly anything of the final thirty minutes and "the final shallow slope up to the Camp site very nearly defeated me entirely." Waiting for him was the second assault team, Lieutenant John Scott (Parachute Regiment) and Pat Gunson; and a second pair in support, Captain Philip Neame (Parachute Regiment) and another SAS climber, Lance-Corporal Steve Johnson. Stokes and Lane were now on their own. All they required was 24 hours of calm weather to complete the climb.

Camp VI was about 1,400 feet from the summit and it was about 3 pm when the support team—consisting of a lieutenant-colonel, a brace of majors and a flying officer —withdrew, leaving the sergeant and the corporal to enjoy the privilege, as well as the hazards, of the last pitch. That night, however, a storm started blowing, which continued throughout the following day, and it was 36 hours after their arrival at this final launch-pad before Stokes and Lane were able to emerge from their tent. They were climbing, roped together, by 6:30 am and praying that the weather would not worsen again. If it did, the risk would be more than that of failure to reach the summit.

On the 55-degree approach to the South Summit they found, to their disgust, that the snow was not firm, but loose, powdery and resistant to swift movement. They had expected to reach this point after 90 minutes; the journey required six hours. At the South Summit, they paused and considered their position. It seemed sensible to turn back at 2 pm. The alternative might be to succeed with a late assault on the summit and failure to reach the sanctuary of Camp VI before dark. Neither man was seeking post-

humous recognition as an Everest climber. Before leaving
the South Summit they cached two half-full oxygen bottles to await their return. They now had just one full oxygen bottle each for the last 300 feet of climb, working with
increasing urgency to cut steps into the ridge before them.

Two o'clock arrived and they were not yet on the top
of Everest. In fact, they had still to overcome the last
technical obstacle before the summit, a 30-foot wall of
rock known as the Hillary Step. The account written by
Faux and Fleming describes how, "at the foot of a slight
chimney, the two men stopped for a 'Chinese parliament.' 'Do we go back?' inquired Bronco. 'No way,' replied Brummie.

"Bronco turned to the pitch and 45 minutes later both
men were on the final slope to the summit. Suddenly there
was nothing ahead, but a simple mound of snow like any
other mound of snow. It marked the summit of the world.
There was a quiet tumult of elation and satisfaction; they
had made it and the expedition had put them there. It
was a fine achievement; a few footprints to mark years of
planning, hope and grief for the five people who had died
in the attempt to put soldiers on the top of Everest, a few
footprints which would soon be wiped away by the wind
and which summed up the glorious inconsequentiality of
mountaineering."

The two soldiers paused just long enough to take photographs, and then began the return march. It was 3:10 pm
and they knew that their chances of reaching Camp VI
before nightfall were diminishing. The light seemed to be
fading long before they got back to the South Summit. On
the way, in an effort to speed the progress home, Stokes
removed his snow goggles. It was to prove an almost fatal
error. Furthermore, his temporarily enhanced vision revealed approaching cloud, and therefore worsening
weather. They were far beyond help here. Even if they
had carried a radio to link them with the rest of the team,
it would be practically useless because there was no helicopter in Nepal capable of reaching them at this altitude.

The point at which they had cached the oxygen bottles
on the South Summit was 1,000 feet above Camp VI. In
rapidly gathering gloom, and near exhaustion after 14
hours' climbing above 28,000 feet, they stumbled upon
the half-full bottles by the sheerest chance. Both men now

knew that they were not going to reach the tent that night. To make the attempt in the dark, in their condition, was the road to certain disaster. The alternative they now faced—a night in the open—offered the remotest hope of survival so long as the weather did not get too bad. . . . After all, it had been done successfully twice before, once by Doug Scott and Dougal Haston the year before, and in 1965 by an equally expert American team. But more, much more often, the gamble had failed. Stokes took the decision for them both. Removing his oxygen mask, he grunted through the ice hardening on his beard and face: "We'll have to stop here and dig in somewhere." Slowly and silently, like two drunken men, they staggered back and forth slowly clawing pawfuls of snow out of their survival hole. They were too tired for serious reflection that this was more likely their own grave they were digging in this benighted place. Like Scott during that final, doom-laden walk across Antarctica, they concentrated only on the job in hand . . . Stick-it . . . Stick-it . . . Stick-it. . . .

It is a profound mystery, even to the two men concerned, that they did not drift away that night into the long, endless sleep of death. The instant they huddled into the hole together they were engulfed by a mind-dragging cold. It seems almost certain that it was watchfulness for the other's welfare that kept each man alive. First one nodded towards oblivion, then the other, and each time it was the urgent pummelling of his companion that staved off unconsciousness.

ALIVE, BUT SNOW-BLIND

There was a moment that night when it seemed that Stokes was dying. His eyes no longer focused, and presently he lost his sight completely. According to Faux's account, Stokes's laconic description to his companion was to the effect that "some bastard's been sandpapering my eyeballs." To stay conscious in these conditions was bad enough if the eyes stayed open and aware, but eyes closed by snow-blindness—which was what was happening—monstrously reduced Stokes's ability to rouse himself from the temptation to let go, and lapse into deadly slumber. Lane fed his companion oxygen from his own bottle, and Stokes started to revive despite the fatigue and the onset of blindness. Miraculously, he produced from the depths of his layered clothing a piece of unpalatable looking fudge. They shared it and felt better, despite the numbness that had now seized fingers and toes.

At about 3 am the wind changed and started blowing directly into the snow-hole. They retaliated, blocking the entrance with rucksacks. Only two more hours to dawn, and they were in with a chance of survival after all. But they knew that they could no longer move without external help. The only place from which they could expect this was Camp V, on the South Col, about 2,500 feet below them. In bad or even merely mediocre conditions, that could be a full day's climbing away. In their hole, Stokes and Lane staved off the implications of that, and tried to conserve their energy and the rapidly dwindling oxygen supply. At least the sun was now shining on Everest. It was a cracking day for climbing, Lane assured his companion. Stokes was in no position to disagree. He was now entirely blind.

The alternative summit team, led by "Big John" Scott, found them at 9 am. Now began a perilous recovery operation, initially involving Scott and his climbing partner Gunson, as far as Camp VI. By 10 am, alerted through a radio message infinitely more optimistic than anyone had expected, the mountain was alive with activity. The imperative need now was to get Stokes and Lane back into an environment in which the insidious damage of frostbite and gangrene could be minimized.

From Camp V, on the South Col, the summit support party consisting of Johnson and Neame climbed urgently to assist the casualties down the steep, powder-snow gully that led from Camp VI. This accomplished, the next day the entire party set off downhill from the South Col, bound for Camp IV, at 1:15 pm, but it was a bitterly painful climb down. On one exposed traverse, those accompanying Stokes had to place his feet in the holds and they were travelling at only 100 yards an hour. The operation to bring them down to base camp, where a helicopter waited to fly him to hospital in Kathmandu, required four days. For the later stages of the journey off the mountain, he was on a McInnes stretcher, though he had to negotiate one ice-fall, painfully, on foot.

Both Lane and Stokes were to lose several toes as a result of their determination, and Lane also lost the terminal phalanges of his right hand. Both men learned to climb again in Wales in spite of these disabilities, and in 1979, Lane was awarded a Military Medal for his military work in Northern Ireland.

One incident, quoted by Faux, encapsulates better than anything the spirit of these men. On the way down, "Big John" Scott and "Bronco" Lane were met by Jon Fleming, the Parachute Regiment major who had been involved in the organization of the expedition from the beginning, and from whom the overall leadership had been whisked by the organizing committee at the last moment, after the Nuptse expedition. In the comfortable surroundings of the Army Staff College at Camberley, they had explained to Fleming that they saw him as "a potential summit man; to lead the summit assault, perhaps." At the foot of the Lhotse Face, just below Camp III, "Bronco" hugged Fleming. "Jon mate," he said, "we did this for you—to avenge last year." Last year had been the year of Nuptse, a year of tragedy for the Army climbers, and Nuptse had been the reason advanced by the committee when they changed the Everest leadership for the need to strengthen the team, as they saw it. But, as Lane saw it, Nuptse was not just a tragedy, it was also an unspoken contract.

IX

How to Select an Elite

IN THIS STUDY OF MILITARY ÉLITES, ROGER
Beaumont argues that such forces tend to suffer from
what he calls the "selection-destruction cycle." The most
able volunteers are selected for the most hazardous missions and suffer higher casualties than other units as a result. Governments, he believes, like such forces because
they reinforce belief in the myth of controllable, rationally
waged war. Moreover, in an age when the citizens' army
is being replaced by professional forces raised from volunteers, "one might ask if Western leadership outside the
neutral countries has not gotten into the habit of killing off
the flower of its youth rather than risking the political
feedback that might come from casualties suffered by the
generally raised forces. In Vietnam, even relatively few
losses toppled the Johnson Government. In a cynical vein,
in view of that experience, it seems that the best balance
of military forces in a society with anti-military values
and an elected government, would be the use of élite
forces and of conscripts and/or recruits from politically
impotent elements of the population."

The motivation and selection of SAS regulars is much
misunderstood in a society whose feelings about the military community are at best ambivalent. The anarchist
fringe, aware of the SAS's special rôle in counter-
revolutionary warfare, has a vested interest in purveying
a sinister image of the Regiment. Elsewhere, civilian incomprehension and suspicion are reinforced by the
secrecy surrounding SAS activities and by the minority-

mindedness of SAS men, which springs from their self-imposed isolation not only from the community at large, but also from the rest of the British Army. For psychological as well as security reasons, the Regiment has a feline appetite for walking alone, discouraging the interests of outsiders including even ex-members of the Regiment. Yet if Beaumont is right, the Regiment serves democratic society in a unique fashion by nominating itself as the élite military group willing to take risks that others, comfortable in their suburban semis, prefer to experience from the safety of a seat in the Odeon cinema (or, for that matter, the author's study). When hostages are seized in Balcombe Street or at Las Palmas to begin an enforced journey to Mogadishu, society needs such men as surely as it needs surgeons and public health officers.

THE REASON WHY

Why soldiers volunteer for SAS duty is as complex as the motivation of those who take part in such risk-sports as climbing and parachuting. The initial stimulus may be nothing more noble than adrenalin addiction. But for all dedicated risk sportsmen there is a learning curve: to overcome fear is to gain self-respect, self-possession and freedom unique in a secure, but increasingly claustrophobic, society bound by no doubt necessary rules. To win acceptance among a group who have found the same road to self-respect is to join a community and achieve an identity not attainable in the fragmented isolation of urban life, the world of the "electric light" people.

From time to time, SAS men are scrutinized by psychologists (one of whom was evacuated from Malaya some years ago in a state of collapse). The resulting conflict of cultures—the one expressing itself by action rather than talk, the other dedicated to intellectual abstractions —does not shed much light on why soldiers volunteer for such service except, perhaps, to destroy the myth that all SAS soldiers are incorrigibly immature personalities seeking to "prove" themselves. Most of those who are finally accepted are in their late twenties with several years' hard soldiering behind them. Good judgement in spite of stress and fatigue is one of the most important characteristics sought by the selectors, and that quality is rarely compatible with immaturity. The chimera of trying to catego-

rize the SAS soldier in the compartmental world of the
psychologist emerges from Peter Watson's exhaustive
study of such matters, *War on the Mind*. He reports:
"The psychologists [who test SAS recruits] look for those
who, on the tests, are: above average in intelligence; as-
sertive; happy-go-lucky; self-sufficient; not extremely
intro- or extraverted. They do *not* want people who are
emotionally stable; instead they want forthright individuals who are hard to fool and not dependent on orders.
The psychologists do acknowledge that occasionally, with
the SAS, there are problems of too many chiefs and not
enough Indians."

What finally links those who pass a rigorous selection
process is a dedication to soldiering as such. "We are a
bunch of misfits who happen to fit together" is how one
member of the Regiment puts it. In an anti-military culture it is an adequate working definition.

If there is a multiplicity of reasons why individuals volunteer for SAS selection, there is little doubt what the
Regiment is seeking. In 1955, Major Dare Newell drafted
a paper that still embodies the Regiment's basic philosophy. Newell explained: "Selection is designed rather to
find the individualist with a sense of self-discipline than
the man who is primarily a good member of a team. For
the self-desciplined individualist will always fit well into a
team when teamwork is required, but a man selected for
team work is by no means always suitable for work outside the team." Volunteers, Newell recorded, were
assessed for their reactions to loneliness, to unusual situations when tired, and their attitude to army life in general.
The last criterion, apparently banal, seeks to weed out
those who mistake the comradeship between officer and
man in the Regiment—in which Christian names, or
"Boss," are sometimes substituted for Sir—for a relaxa-
tion of discipline; to exclude also the tough who "is seldom at home on his own and without an audience . . .
soon loses interest."

The essential qualities needed for soldiers who were to
work for weeks and perhaps months in isolation were initiative; self-discipline; independence of mind; ability to
work unsupervised; stamina; patience and a sense of humor. What they represent cumulatively is a spiritual
toughness rather than a physical superiority over other

troops, and in that sense the pun that an SAS trooper is one of Nietzche's gentlemen is not far from the truth. Yet, as those who have served with the Regiment's fighting squadrons are aware, one of the paradoxes about SAS troopers is that they are not loners in the sense that, say an espionage agent must be: they cling to the tribal security of a small four-man patrol with total loyalty. Like all soldiers, they are essentially gregarious, but they function best in small, family-sized groups that do not swamp individuality. Because of the intimacy of SAS operations, the most important factor of initial selection is the subjective judgement of the Regiment's instructors as they observe the candidates. They are looking for people they could live with, basically compatible souls who are not rigid loners, manic teetotallers or fanatics of any kind. The comment, "I don't like him" is probably sufficient to ensure a candidate's failure even if he passes other criteria of selection.

PHASING SELECTION

The selection course for the full-time, regular 22 SAS Regiment, based at Hereford, is a prolonged and elaborate business, best understood if its outlines are first sketched in. It begins with ten days' fitness training and map-reading on the Brecon Beacons—let us call it Phase I—in which the volunteer is one of a group of about twenty men. This is followed by another ten days in which he is engaged in long cross-country marches in the same area, alone. This period—Phase II—culminates in a 40-mile endurance march to be completed within twenty hours, in which the soldier carries a 55-pound Bergen rucksack and a ten-pound rifle, and in which he may travel alone or with other volunteers, as he chooses. Phase II is known as Selection with a capital "S" because, when it is over, those who are not suitable and have not left the course voluntarily are returned to their units.

The survivors are then sent for fourteen weeks' continuation training: Phase III, during which they are still being tested for their suitability as SAS soldiers. Phase IV is the standard Army parachute course (low-level jumping employing static-line parachutes that open automatically as the jumper leaves the aircraft, a technique that has not changed much since the Second World War).

Finally, the candidate faces combat survival training (Phase V), including escape and interrogation methods. Some men are rejected on the final day of this exhaustive process. For the rest, a tiny proportion of the original volunteers, the hand-over of a new beret and cap-badge marks acceptance into the Regiment. In SAS jargon, the volunteer is now "badged," though recognition of this fact by his new comrades may well depend upon his performance on a live operation. (The Rhodesian SAS—still unofficially described as C Squadron—used operational experience as an integral part of its official selection system during the long guerrilla war in Zimbabwe-Rhodesia.)

The volunteer's induction is followed by Phase VI, specialist training in one of the Regiment's basic skills— Morse signalling, linguistics, field medical care, use of explosives, pistol shooting—combined with tactical assignment to one of four 16-man troops skilled in boat work, climbing, long-distance overland navigation in Land Rovers, or free-fall parachuting. By the time this "postgraduate" course is completed, the volunteer has been with the Regiment for almost two years and he is at last a trained SAS soldier.

His first tour with the Regiment is for a period of three years, after which, if he is still fit for service, he can remain for another three years, and so on. In a sense, therefore, only a tiny cadre of permanent staff are the true insiders. For everyone else, the ultimate disciplinary sanction is RTU—return to unit of origin.

Volunteers begin their phase of the prestige and agony of SAS service at a peak of fitness; for many of those who have been engaged with the operational "Sabre" squadrons, it ends with health impaired by exotic disease or physical injury, or shattered nerves. No one remains unchanged by the experience of SAS service.

THE "SICKENER" FACTOR

At the beginning of this selection process (until recent years) each cadre of volunteers was greeted by the Regiment's commanding officer at Hereford, or by his second-in-command, with a mordant welcome to the effect that "It's nice of you all to come along; I don't suppose most of you will be with us for more than a few days." In fact,

Phase I is now intended to achieve two things: to provide simple fitness training to ensure that potentially suitable people will not fail the course because they have not had time to get into sufficiently good physical shape and to induce the "passengers"—those seeking a break from the boredom of garrison duties in Germany and elsewhere— to drop out as quickly as possible. The first objective is accomplished by cross-country marches in which the distance covered, carrying pack and rifle, increases each day. The weight carried also increases from a basic 25-pounds. Until recently, this was clinically dispensed through an issue of numbered bricks from the SAS quartermaster's store; more recently, this policy has been changed so that the make-up weight comprises more useful items such as additional food or clothing. A veteran of the brick-carrying era recalls that his greatest moment of training was when he was ordered to return his bricks— which, in fact, simulate stocks of ammunition—to the store.

For some candidates, basic tuition in map and compass work must also be covered during this first phase. The SAS is dedicated to movement on foot across country, and good navigation is as important as sight itself. Since the only people permitted to join the SAS from civilian life must be members of the Regiment's voluntary, part-time Territorial squadrons, the majority of the candidates are already regular soldiers. Volunteers from the Guards and Parachute Regiment, who are numerous, require little tuition in basic navigation, but there is always a surprisingly high number of SAS men whose soldiering began in the various corps (Signals, Engineers, Transport, etc.) and who have to learn almost from scratch to read the contours of a hill rather than a road map. The end result is that the SAS contains quick learners with a bewildering assortment of individual skills. At this stage also, the candidate begins to learn something of the SAS approach to security. Map references should be memorized, never written. Even the map must be re-folded along its original seams so that it could not betray the soldier's ultimate destination to an enemy.

Disposing of "passengers" was traditionally accomplished by at least two exercises conducted during Phase I, coarsely described as "Sickener I" and "Sickener II." Sickener I, for example, has been known to include the

Mud Crawl, in which the volunteer is invited to immerse himself in a gully containing not only mud, but also a liberal quantity of rotting sheeps' entrails. There were other, less colorful, disincentives. At the end of a fifteen or twenty-mile march, the tired volunteers would arrive at a rendezvous only to see the lorries awaiting them drive away empty. Candidates would be told that it was necessary after all to march another ten miles. At that point, several more people would decide to drop out of the course. Those who stuck with it would find that the transport was waiting, after all, only two miles away. Another ploy, introduced during combat survival, was to order the candidate to carry the contents of his Bergen pack from the penultimate rendezvous to the final destination without the aid of the rucksack itself. "The sickener effect could be quite dramatic," one veteran recalls. "On my course we lost 40 volunteers out of 120 during the first weekend."

During the 1970s, however, the emphasis of basic selection has turned away from this approach towards a positive incentive to succeed. Even the word "sickener" has vanished from Regimental vocabulary. To some extent this change came about because of a growing need for SAS soldiers, as a result of events in Oman and Ulster, and the growth of urban terrorism in Britain. But it also reflected a change in the nature of British society itself. The young men who volunteered for SAS service after the late 1960s were no less fit or courageous than their predecessors, but they had grown up in an environment in which hardship and rejection were less familiar, and therefore more likely to demoralize. The SAS discovered that the generation of the 1970s had to be educated in the ways of adversity before it could begin to learn to cope with them. One of the architects of selection puts it like this: "We reached the conclusion that the soldiers coming forward did not have the same stamina as the wartime and immediate post-war soldiers. Those latter, the product of the lean pre-war and wartime years, were accustomed to a much harder form of life than those from a welfare state background. We decided, therefore, that our approach to the physical side of selection had to be adapted to the class of man available. This is not to suggest that 'little Tommy is not the man his father was,' but simply that Tommy has to be shown what his body can put up with if it has to. One of our greatest difficulties was to persuade the older NCOs and warrant officers that this was not a lowering of standards."

One basic rule is that the SAS volunteer is never more than an arm's reach from his rifle while in the field. One man who walked twenty yards to a lake to wash, leaving his rifle behind, received an instant sickener. "Do twenty press-ups," an instructor shouted at him. The man was about to begin when the instructor added: "No, not there . . . in the lake." After the victim had waded into the water and performed his task he was ordered to get up again and rejoin the group. "I can't," he replied desperately, "I can't get up. I'm stuck in the mud."

Among officers who volunteer for SAS selection, the sickener factor, though no longer known by that name, is still apparent. For a week before the beginning of the basic course, they are taken on long and tiring marches round the hills, then brought back to the Hereford base to be given Staff tasks—for example, calculate the amount of fuel and ordnance required to move a troop to a particular objective and demolish it, and produce a plan for the operation. The officer must then present his plan to a conference of veteran SAS troopers and NCOs, who will treat it with derision. "You must be joking!" "Where were you trained, the Boy Scouts?" are not responses young lieutenants have been taught to expect from other ranks. For some it is a punishing emotional experience. The officer's reaction to such criticisms will be carefully noted. Of one who failed the course it was recorded: "He is a good officer and a wonderful person, but he is not SAS material." The most insidious sickener is the inducement to give up the course without loss of face. Even before a man arrives at Hereford he is officially told that it is no disgrace not to be selected. The SAS itself is also genuinely concerned not to destroy the self-confidence of men it will reject, for they would be valuable soldiers in more orthodox units.

Phase II of selection begins in the early hours of the morning when the volunteer joins others in a routine muster parade and clambers into the three-ton lorry as usual. But this time, instead of starting the march with a group he is turned out alone at an isolated spot and given a map reference as his next rendezvous. If he is not very alert the lorry has departed before he has properly woken up. It is raining and he wonders whether he heard aright the six-figure number gabbled at him as the vehicle disappeared. Orthodox soldiering is essentially a gregarious, mutually-supportive activity, and this sudden isolation is a shock. He has yet to discover that to cover the route up to Pen-y-Fan and down again three times by different routes within the time set for the exercise, he will have to jog much of the way. In the rain, his Bergen gets heavier as it absorbs moisture.

The situation is one in which it is easy to brood upon the unfairness of the world. After getting lost once or twice, thereby adding to the distance to be covered, the volunteer arrives at the first rendezvous wet from the knees down after penetrating a bog, and soaked by his own sweat. The instructors sit drinking tea, apparently immersed in complacency. Until the seventies, it was normal for an instructor, with feigned solicitude, to say: "You look all-in, mate. Hop in the back of the truck and get your feet up." The wise volunteer knew that even to pause to consider the proposal was to invite rejection from the Regiment. To remove his pack at that moment was to ensure failure, even if his resolve weakened only for a matter of seconds. So, with a forced smile, he would reply: "Piss off. I've got better things to do," and continue his journey. Today, the solicitude is probably genuine and the volunteer, far from being seduced into abandoning the march, will be reminded: "Only another ten miles. You've come more than half way. Stick with it." Furthermore, the trucks waiting at the end of the march will not mischievously disappear. Not all rendezvous are simple check-points. At some of them the candidate will be required to perform an unexpected task, such as stripping and reassembling a weapon he has not seen before—the physically maladroit are a liability in a section fighting its way out of an ambush—or, perhaps, prove powers of observation by answering questions concerning a dam or railway line he has passed en route.

THE ENDURANCE MARCH
As the course continues, the volunteer finds that his judgment is becoming corroded by lack of sleep. Each

day begins at about 4 am and ends with a briefing at
10:30 pm or later for the next day's exercise. The effect
is cumulative over the whole 21 days, and it is at the end
of that period that the selectors subject him to the endurance march. One of those who passed the course recalls
that "it is a test of strength, stamina and sheer will power:
a real bastard. People worry about it and rightly so. Nothing that has gone before compares with this. Most people
who are fairly fit can keep going for eight or twelve hours.
This goes on for 20 or more. I took 21 hours which was
regarded as rather wet." By now, only the most determined
candidates remain on the course, but it is likely that at
least four to six more will be broken before the day is
out. The minimum distance to be covered over mountainous terrain is 40 miles in 20 hours. (Until recent years,
the target was 45 miles in 24 hours.) Allow for map-
reading errors, bad luck, bad weather and bad judgment,
and the distance may be considerably longer in fact.

The endurance march caused one fatality in 1979.
Three others—two of them Territorial volunteers—died
during preliminary marches over the next twelve months.
Before this, only three volunteers had died during the 23
years that the initial selection course had existed, and one
of those had suffered from a rare heart condition.
Through a tragic irony, the first victim of 1979 was not a
novice bidding for a place in the Regiment, but the hero
of Mirbat, six years before, Mike Kealy, now a major. In
the early hours of 1 February 1979, he joined 30 recruits
as they set off from Talybont Reservoir in conditions
made treacherous by darkness, snow and ice underfoot
and with visibility reduced to only a few yards by freez-
ing rain, sleet and snow. Even on a fine summer's day,
the 40-mile route would have been a formidable proposition for an experienced hill walker. That day, as events
were to demonstrate, it was virtually impossible.

Though the men moved off in two parties, each of
about fifteen, they were soon spread out across the hill
in smaller syndicates of two or three men. To be completely alone made it harder, slower and therefore colder
to walk on an accurate compass bearing in what one SAS
officer later described as "minimal visiblity." Two men,
after all, could take it in turns to act as markers for one
another if no other landmark were visible. A solo walker

The Brecon Beacons: Kealy's Last March

① Start of march   ④ RAF mobile radio transmitter
② Kealy   ⑤ SAS final base
③ SAS ground coordination HQ   ⑥ Point from which alarm raised

might be limited to the uncertain procedure of getting his "fix" on a patch of bare snow a few yards in front. A further hazard faced the solo walker. To move too slowly in such conditions carried with it the risk of increasing cold in a biting wind, and with it the insidious onset of exposure, which hacks away at good judgment long before it reduces bodily warmth to a dangerously low level.

Kealy chose the loner's way. To some extent this was inevitable: he was not part of that selection course, though he had twice participated in the shorter, twenty-mile marches during the preceding three weeks. Also, he was a comparatively senior officer, somewhat older than almost any other participant, and regarded by them with awe blended with the suspicion that he might be one of the selectors. But why should he participate at all? After all, he had been in the Regiment for years and had a record of rare distinction in Oman. A sergeant in charge of the course explained later: "He wanted to come on the endurance march to see if he could still do it in the time." Now 33, Kealy had been in administrative work after Service in Northern Ireland, and was returning to operational duties to command his own squadron. To an outsider, what may seem uncommonly like menopausal recklessness was, to him, common prudence. He had to be fit enough for the next operation in any climate, and the only way to be sure of that was to demonstrate it to himself.

Yet in other respects his judgment was questionable. He had made up the back-pack weight of his Bergen to 55-pounds with bricks, and was not equipped with the waterproof storm suit issued to the novices. Once on the hill in driving rain, his smock and trousers were quickly soaked, causing a rapid loss of body temperature. At the weigh-in proceding the march, his pack was overweight and a brick was removed. Others on the course made up the correct weight with additional clothing and food. They did not carry bricks. And, though Kealy had gloves in his rucksack, he chose not to wear them. One of the survivors of the exercise found it necessary to wear two pairs, and he was still driven off the prescribed route because of cold.

Initially, Kealy moved fast, passing the first man to leave, Trooper E. But, after an hour or so on top of the ridge, this trooper and four or five other candidates overtook him. By now, conditions were so bad that, despite their foul-weather suits, they decided to get off the ridge and into the shelter of the valley below. As they turned off the original route, Kealy shouted, "You're going the wrong way!" "In a sense, we were," Trooper E. later admitted. "The major just went on his own and that was the last we saw of him." By the time this group reached the shelter of a barn in the valley miles below and some hours later, one of their number was suffering from exposure.

Back-markers in the party later found Kealy staggering in the snow, and stayed with him when he finally slumped into a sitting position. But he threw away the gloves given to him by one man, and allowed a jacket placed over his shoulders to blow away, insisting that he

was "all right." Further offers of help made him so angry
that the two novices with him concluded that it was better to walk in front of Kealy and lead him off. He stumbled after them. Then they lost him completely in the
darkness. Wind filled in the tracks Kealy made in the
snow and after a fruitless search for him lasting well over
an hour, the cold drove the two novices down the hill
to shelter. At 9:30 am, less than seven hours after the
march had started, a captain and a corporal taking part
in the march spotted what they thought was a rock pro-
truding from the snow. As they got closer they saw that
it was Kealy. He was unconscious now, but a feeble pulse
could be detected in his neck. Hurriedly, the two men
dug a snow-hole and slid the unconscious officer into a
sleeping-bag. The corporal also entered the snow-hole
and remained with Kealy in an attempt, almost literally,
to breathe life back into him. The captain, meanwhile,
set off to raise the alarm. For the corporal, it was to prove
a long vigil.

By the time the alarm had been raised, several more
hours had passed. The first message to reach Brecon Police Station, inviting general police assistance, was timed
at 1:55 pm. The police contacted the Army only to be
told that it would be sufficient to put the local civilian
mountain rescue team on stand-by. Nevertheless, a police
inspector made his way by road through thick fog to the
SAS rescue HQ some miles away, only to be told, politely but firmly, that military authorities were organizing
the search. The Army did not wish to duplicate matters
by using police or civilians. In the event, it was 4:30 pm
the following day, 19 hours after Kealy had been found
unconscious, before his body was lifted off the hill by
helicopter. The corporal who had stayed with him, trying
unsuccessfully to transfer the heat of his own body to that
of the dying officer, survived the ordeal.

The SAS major in charge of the rescue, identified at a
subsequent inquest under the codename "Foxtrot," explained that when the alarm was raised about Kealy's
problem other soldiers were still missing. The exercise
was abandoned. Attempts by helicopter to reach the position where Kealy lay were defeated by bad visibility.
Foxtrot was concerned about the loss of not just one man,
however important, but possibly several. His first priority

was to account for missing men and to direct those still on the hill, including instructors at prearranged rendezvous, to come down. Furthermore, there were both Army and RAF mountain rescue teams at large. "I had advice from an experienced mountaineer," Foxtrot told the Coroner, "that it was unwise in those conditions to put too many men on the hill at the same time." The only oblique criticism of this strategy came from the Coroner, who asked whether it would not have been opportune to invoke assistance from the local civilian mountain rescue team, who knew the area well. Foxtrot's answer, in effect, was that he had not discarded this idea, but that it was overtaken by events in a complex situation.

It is highly likely that another factor at work was SAS determination to keep the problem "in the family" without external aid (but not for political reasons or because of misplaced "macho"). What makes the Regiment unique is its unswerving belief in self-reliance, in the soldier's ability as an individual to complete his task unaided, if necessary, in the frightening isolation of hostile territory in wartime. In such a culture, more readily comprehensible to a generation that experienced the Second World War than to those who have succeeded it, a commissioned officer enjoys no special privileges. Indeed, as an article by Major Dare Newell, OBE, in the SAS regimental journal, *Mars & Minerva*, once explained: "SAS operations require an officer, carrying the same kit as his men, to outshoot and outmarch them under most unpleasant conditions, without the company of other officers and those comforts that normally alleviate the officer's lot." Regimental philosophy would also have shaped attitudes about the weather conditions that night. It is an article of faith in the SAS that its soldiers will operate in any part of the world, in any climate, without pause for a period of acclimatization. As Watson's study reveals:

"At the end of 1972, a contingent of the Special Air Service . . . left its headquarters in Hereford bound for Malaya on a continuous 22-hour flight. Half a dozen psychologists had gone out before, armed with basic information about the men, collected in Hereford in the weeks prior to their journey.

"On arrival in Malaya . . . the men were continuously monitored doing various combat and support tasks. As a result of these tests the psychologists were able to come to two important conclusions. The details are classified, but in general the psychologists found that the men who performed best on the first couple of days after the flight were by no means the men who performed best later on. . . . Second, the psychologists found they were able to predict how well men would perform in a tropical climate on the basis of several psychological tests given in rural, and normally chilly, Hereford. The tests themselves are secret, but the results have now been put into effect in the selection of British SAS men who may have to serve abroad at short notice."

Subsequently, Watson concludes that the best way to organize military "fire brigades" would be to have specialist units that can travel and fight immediately for some days, to be withdrawn when the follow-up troops are ready to take over and "this may be the way the British Special Air Service operates." Certainly the notion of instant readiness to fight anywhere in the world is fundamental to SAS thinking. It is known, somewhat euphemistically, as "environmental training," and there seems little doubt that it was with this in mind that Foxtrot allowed the endurance march to proceed on the Brecon Beacons the day Kealy died.

Kealy's death, caused by exposure, disorientation and hypothermia, probably could have been prevented if he had observed basic survival drills. So, too, was the second death, that of an exceptionally fit corporal who was a candidate for selection. This man ignored, or overlooked, instructions to stay away from a short cut on the day's route—the summit of Pen-y-Fan—on an August day when 60mph gales were destroying the Fastnet Yacht Race. Like Kealy, he became soaked by driving rain, surfered exposure and died of hypothermia, although the still-air temperature in the valley was a tolerable, if chilly eight degrees Centigrade. The third death, in the autumn of 1979, was that of a Territorial volunteer taking part in a march on the Pennines during a week's selection course, who appears to have been swept away in the dark by a rain-swollen river. A common factor in all these cases is that the victims were regarded as being entirely capable of completing the course; all, however, could be said to have been over-confident of their ability to beat abnormal

conditions. The fourth death, in March 1980, again occurred in extremely cold conditions. The soldier concerned, a Territorial, collapsed and died soon after
passing through a check-point at which instructors felt the
bodies of all candidates for signs of abnormal cold. This
man appeared to be warm and was marching strongly.

Recruits who have completed the endurance march on
time and who pass the initial three-week selection course
for the regular SAS are gathered in a barrack room to discover that bad news rapidly succeeds the good. They are
being allowed to proceed to continuation training, they are
told, but only on sufferance, and it is by no means certain
that they will be finally accepted into the Regiment. There
is no cause for self-congratulation at having come this
far. With that deflating message, they are allowed to take
a long weekend's leave. It is not unusual for them to sleep
all the way home.

Initial selection lasts three weeks. Continuation training
—a refinement of selection—is an elaborate process
spread over nearly four months. Much of this time is
spent learning basic soldiering—fieldcraft, target reconnaissance, weapons-training from pistol to 81mm mortar,
ground-control of air and mortar fire—because such a high
proportion of those so far selected are not infantrymen.
The course also includes an introduction to the use of explosives for demolition and sabotage, with tuition in the
use of the standard SAS charge; four or five days devoted
to field first-aid training; a language ability test; a 1,000-
yard swim in shirt and trousers; and a variety of initiative
tests. There was a time when, on paper, these involved
planning a bank robbery or raid on some other local target in Hereford, but after one such plan was left in a restaurant, with embarrassing results, the practice ended.
Each short course ends with a test. "The object of such
tests," explains one former SAS soldier, "is to weed out
the total idiot who was fit enough and lucky enough to get
through initial selection."

Subsequently, as men specialize after acceptance into
the Regiment, they develop a high degree of expertise in
one of these techniques. The search for a quick learner,
which is what this part of selection is about, is a change of
emphasis from the Regiment's early post-war years, the
years of Malaya, when the accepted philosophy was:

"Head down, arse up and march from one end of the jungle to another until you find the enemy."

The first post-war SAS selection course in Britain was a simple one-week affair conducted in Snowdonia by Lieutenant-Colonel John Woodhouse, to check basic stamina and map-reading ability. During the course, he suffered an attack of malaria with the result, as he later recalled, that "my endurance was more severely tested than that of the recruits." In 1954, he submitted himself to selection, and passed.

COMBAT-SURVIVAL/INTERROGATION

One of the most testing and controversial elements of continuation training is a three-week, combat-survival course at Exmoor, in which candidates are stretched psychologically as well as physically. The point of such training is to prepare men to fight a guerrilla war behind enemy lines. Much of the course is run by a Joint Services Interrogation Unit staffed by SAS and other personnel. It is preceded by a special period of training at the Regiment's Hereford base. Both courses are a mixture of tuition in living off the land—identifying edible seaweed and fungus, learning trapping techniques to procure game or fish—followed by a realistic application of these lessons, in which the student spends several days and nights on the moor, being hunted by soldiers from other regiments. Cunning candidates have been known to pass some of this time comfortably as unofficial guests of people living on or near the moor.

The Exmoor course contains the usual "sickener" element. Devices include a variant of the numbered brick, a five-gallon jerry can of water to be carried over long distances. To eliminate the possibility of cheating, the water is dyed and the jerrycan checked by instructors.

At the Regiment's Hereford base and, subsequently, on the Exmoor course, SAS candidates are also subjected to interrogation of a kind that, to judge from the testimony of those who have passed the course, does not differ from the treatment about which terrorist suspects complained in Ulster in 1971, and which was studied by the Compton Commission. Already-exhausted soldiers have been subjected to physical hardship and sensory deprivation, including the use of a hood placed over the head for many hours, white noise and psychological torture. The object of these techniques is to force the combat-survival students to reveal the names of their regiments and details of the operations on which they are nominally engaged. Not all those participating are SAS candidates; Royal Marine Commandos and Parachute Regiment soldiers also take part. The difference is that for the SAS nominee to break is more than a chastening experience: it means he has failed to win a place in the Regiment. Those who fail at this stage are often the men who seemed best fitted to the physical rigors of the earlier selection process on the Brecon Beacons.

The experience of one successful candidate in recent years is that three periods of hooded interrogation occur during the two interrogation-resistance courses: a half-hour "nasty"; an eight-hour period and finally, during the Joint Services' Exmoor Course, one of 24 hours interrupted only for period of exposure to bright electric light while facing the interrogation itself. In one instance, hooded SAS candidates were hurled from the back of a stationary lorry by their over-enthusiastic captors, members of an infantry regiment, on to a concrete road as part of the pre-interrogation, softening-up process. One man suffered a broken arm as a result. A successful candidate on that course, who was still intact, recalls that he then spent eight hours sitting manacled in a puddle as a preliminary to questioning. During another period of interrogation, he was hooded and shackled to a strong-point in a room in which white noise and colored, flashing lights were used. After some time, guessing that he was alone, he contrived to remove the hood and regain a sense of reality. "I looked around and there were all these flashing lights," he said later. "It suddenly seemed ridiculous to me. But until then it was a bit unnerving. Some people get frantic in there. I think there is a limit to how long you can stand it. After 24 hours you begin to wonder if they are on your side. At the time, while it was happening, I was told that the 'treatment' would go on much longer and I was almost cracking." At Hereford, as both victim and interrogator, he took part in more refined psychological brutality during a preliminary combat-survival course run exclusively for the SAS. Candidates were tied to a wooden board and immersed in a pond for up to twenty seconds before being recovered to face the same questions: "What did you say your regiment was? What did you say you were doing?" One who survived this test later told his interrogators that he realized no one intended him to drown, but he did fear the possibility of a miscalculation, or that things would simply get out of hand.

An SAS interrogator with "a Machiavellian turn of mind" so arranged matters that hooded captives thought they were about to be attacked by "a perfectly lovable Labrador." In an adjoining room, meanwhile, they could hear a beating taking place followed by the sound of vomiting and running water. The victim of the beating was an old mattress; the groans and vomiting were simulated by the interrogation team. An even more elaborate charade involved the use of a railway truck in an old siding, part of a disused ordnance depot. "We had these guys handcuffed to the rails. By this time they were disoriented and tired. What they heard was a voice shouting from a distance, "Get those men off the line!" The other guards then went through a pantomine. "Bloody hell, there's a train coming. Get the keys!" The prisoners could feel the vibration of the truck approaching. As it got closer one of the guards shouted, "It's too late. Jump!" In fact, the wagon went past them quite harmlessly on an adjoining line into the siding. Among the prisoners, reactions differed. Some positioned their hands so that the wagon wheels would cut the shackles and set them free. Some got themselves into a position where they would have lost an arm. Others went berserk and ended up lying across the rails. But every one of them thought that this was a real emergency and that we had made a monumental cock-up."

The perception of another, older SAS veteran is that the account given above places undue emphasis on physical brutality. According to this source, the interrogation experts (who include at least one former captive of the Chinese) regard such brutality as counter-productive in breaking a prisoner's will. Furthermore, he adds, candidates are carefully briefed beforehand about what to expect from the interrogators. "My experience was that the Exmoor course emphasized psychological vulnerability," he said. In practice, in his case, this "psychological" approach meant his being left naked in the snow for several hours before interrogation by a panel which included a woman. The size of his penis, much reduced because of the cold, was the object of sarcastic comment. This veteran, a particularly hard man, added: "I wasn't always certain who was being trained: us or the interrogators. I think it was a bit of both, really." What is undoubtedly true is that, in action, the most successful SAS interrogators in Oman and elsewhere are those who have used guile and elaborate bluff to penetrate captives' defenses. Brutality, they believe, simply strengthens the will to resist.

Peter Watson's study concludes that neither sensory deprivation alone, used experimentally, nor simple physical brutality will break a victim during interrogation. He also points out that there is an inevitable difference in the climate of interrogation practiced by friendly forces, and the real thing. "So rar as controlled laboratory experiments are concerned, there can be little doubt that, by itself, SD is not as horrendous an experience as has been painted. But of course there is a large difference between the laboratory situation and SD when used as part of 'hostilities'." In the latter case "the captor-captive relationship is entirely different, the rôle of uncertainty and fear is magnified, and attempts to get people to talk will be far more assiduously pursued." Watson also finds that "the experience of captivity is far more disorienting than the experience of sensory deprivation, but together they are lethal. To counter them, soldiers have to have training in both. The world's armies are probably more aware of this distinction than non-military scientists."

The two combat-survival periods—the preliminary SAS course at Hereford and the Joint Services course at Exmoor—end with a solemn, all-ranks dinner representing tastes acquired during this time, including seaweed, frog, hedgehog and rat. On one occasion, following total failure to obtain sufficient hedgehog in the wild, rats were collected for the feast from an Army veterinary establishment. "What do you want these for, then?" the SAS messenger was asked when he arrived to pick them up. "To eat, of course," was the reply.

As well as resisting interrogation—or at least, coming to terms with the grim reality of it—combat-survival training also teaches escape and evasion. In winter exercises it is a long-standing military joke that the SAS man may be identified as the one who walks *backwards* across a patch of snow. The Joint Services Escape & Evasion course devotes a short time to lectures and demonstrations by police dog-handlers on eluding the dog by wading in water or through a farmyard where the scent will mingle with that of more pungent animals. SAS men are also taught how to kill a war dog, a skill some of the Regiment's soldiers used to remarkable effect during an exercise in friendly Denmark several years ago, to the outrage of the dog-handlers concerned.

The handful of men who complete the process of initial selection and continuation training—estimates of this number vary between five and seventeen out of every hundred—are welcomed into the Regiment by its commanding officer or second-in-command, and handed the beige SAS beret and cloth badge bearing the famous winged dagger.

FURTHER EDUCATION: HALO, ETC.

The new recruit is now ready for intensive specialist instruction. He can opt to serve in any one of four tactically different troops which make up each of the regular Regiment's four active-service Sabre squadrons. These are equipped for high-altitude free-fall parachuting; amphibious operations from small boats, canoes or even submarines, in ways similar to the Royal Marine Special Boat Section (though the ultimate purpose is different); mountaineering, including rock-climbing, ice and snow work; and overland missions by custom-built Land Rover. The last group, known as the Mobility Troop, traditionally functions in the desert and is trained to use sun compass, theodolite and astro-navigation. Many SAS soldiers, who would serve in Norway or Denmark in a European war, must also learn how to use cross-country skis and other techniques of winter warfare. One squadron regularly sends men for training in Northern Norway.

As practiced by the SAS, free-fall parachuting is more than usually hazardous and totally different from the basic static-line techniques used by the Army since the Second World War. A six-week HALO ("High-Altitude, Low-Opening") course of about forty descents in Britain, and at Pau in France, drastically introduces recruits to the art of free-fall stability, with an initial descent from 12,000 feet, or about sixty seconds of unimpeded fall, after only three days ground training. The basic task is theoretically simple: to remain stable in a face-to-earth, starfish posture, with the body's center of gravity at about solar-plexus level. This is achieved by arching the back and placing the limbs symmetrically so that air pressure on them is uniform. After leaving the aircraft, the jumper will accelerate for the first twelve seconds of fall—about 1,480 feet—to terminal velocity of 120 mph.

The danger of this "deep-end" method of training is that a novice can easily become unstable in the air by losing the symmetry of his position. If he starts an uncontrolled tumble at the moment when his parachute begins to open, there is a risk that it will snag on some part of his body, producing a "horse-shoe" malfunction, instead of deploying unimpeded from the launch-pad of his back. The civilian sport jumper, by comparison, makes a first free-fall of no more than three to five seconds before opening his parachute in conditions of perfect stability, well short of the radical air pressures presented by terminal velocity. What is more, an expert civilian will expect to perform all the maneuvers the sport involves—loops, turns, rolls, tracking—from about 7,000 feet, and it is unlikely that he will often leave the aircraft above 12,000 feet, which is the height at which the SAS novice begins his parachuting.

The HALO course progresses to train the soldier to jump from 25,000 feet or more, by day or night, using oxygen, carrying a rifle against his body and an inverted Bergen pack slung across the back of his thighs below his main parachute harness. Because he carries so much equipment—the load may be 110-pounds—the SAS soldier, burdened as he is, dare not attempt this maneuver preserve basic stability, is severely limited. For example, the unencumbered civilian normally opens his own parachute with his right hand, while the left hand and arm compensate for this loss of symmetry by reaching out directly in front of the helmet to "grab air." The SAS soldier, burdened as he is, dare not attempt this maneuver except as an emergency drill. For this reason, his parachute is equipped with an automatic opening device. The

risks of disaster escalate if, for any reason, the load being
carried shifts during free-fall. It was because his Bergen
shifted that an SAS Trooper, "Rip" Reddy, became the
first British soldier to die during an operational free-fall
descent in 1970. Because the load may vary on each
descent, the aerodynamic problem of one jump will also
differ from that of the last jump, or the next.

There are other peculiar hazards. As the exit height increases, so ice on goggles and chest-mounted altimeter becomes an acute problem. (So does the risk of frostbite.)
The SAS soldier, if he is not to jump blind, must learn to
rub the ice away with his gloved hands. Again, to preserve symmetry/stability he must use both hands simultaneously, at which point he will tilt head-down before recovering the basic starfish posture. And, because he jumps
as one of a group, the risk of mid-air collision is significant. For some exercises, the canopy opening height is
also reduced well below the usual 4,000 feet (at which
height the distinctive crack of canopy deployment is in-
audible on the ground). In Norway and elsewhere, the
soldier will travel into a valley in a 120 mph free-fall with
the walls of a mountain on each side of him. He must
also learn to stay with the group. To close a gap he will
have to maneuver across the sky in a tracking posture—
arms and legs in a delta position, posterior raised—so as
to make progress laterally as well as vertically.

Why use free-fall? Theoretically, it should enable a
small party of men to leave an aircraft well away from
their ultimate destination and to elude detection by radar.
The radar cross-section of a human descending at that
speed would resemble that of a bird, detectable only to
an unusually experienced radar operator in ideal conditions. Jump suits made from radar-absorbing material
further reduce the risk of detection. Behind a mountain
screen, as in Norway, it could be the perfect, silent way
to infiltrate a reconnaissance or sabotage party across enemy lines. So far, however, the handful of operational
free-fall descents made by the SAS, has not encouraged
anyone to believe that free-falling has many advantages
over the use of helicopters. Even the sound of helicopter
engines, it is claimed, can be minimized to a point where
it does not betray an operation. Meanwhile, free-fall par-

achuting, as well as being a tactical option, is also regarded by the Regiment as "a good character builder."

In its most dangerous form, free-falling into the sea is practiced by the boat-troops, specialists in diving and other maritime skills, who do not always use boats. In 1970, the Regimental journal, *Mars & Minerva*, described how "the boat-troop, in their rubber suits, flippers, containers and parachutes waited nervously by the door of the Argosy aircraft for the green light and their 'leap' into the sea. They all started as the voice of their favorite RAF parachute jumping instructor, Tommy Atkinson (who supervised the exits) rang in their ears: 'One more point, lads. At Suez, we had some casualties in the aircraft door whilst waiting to jump. So now, I have orders to simulate this sort of thing by practising just such an eventuality as you make this jump.' An amazed boat-troop looked goggle-eyed at Tommy as he made this statement, all frowning with concentration. 'What I propose to do,' continued Tommy, 'is to punch every third man in the ear as he leaps from the aircraft.' . . . The boat-troop parachutists descend lower and lower, swaying through the dusk on their parachutes towards the inky blackness of the sea. Good grief, it really is black! The boat-troop dropped into a large oil-slick and emerged like Kentucky Minstrels. There were some who thought that this might have been one of Tommy Atkinson's tricks. He was that convincing. . . ."

On one occasion, "the boat-troop Sergeant (a willing pupil of Atkinson) regarded the free-fall troop seriously as he briefed them for their annual swimming test in the cold, mid-winter Mediterranean Sea. 'If you have any worries,' he said, 'raise your fists above your head and shout. My boys are in the Gemini pick-up craft and they will be with you almost instantly. Incidentally, I should warn you about the basking sharks that occasionally appear in the Med at this time of the year. Mind you, a man has not been taken here for about seven years, but just keep your eyes open.' The free-fall troop had suddenly taken a new interest in their swimming. Some smiled in ridicule but nevertheless they all took a good look around as they jumped from the Gemini into the sea. Some five minutes had passed. All were swimming steadily towards the shore. Colin had drifted away from the others slightly, but was swimming well enough. Suddenly he felt a movement in the water close to him. With blurred vision, he peered under the water and sensed rather than saw the black shape flash past his legs; felt something sharp groping at his calf. His frantic cry of 'Shark!' and consequent action were all that the books had ever portrayed. He was practically standing on the water. The rest of the free-fall troop promptly developed that gregarious spirit and formed an instant, protective, hysterical cluster in the water. The black shape, and yes, a fin were seen by all. Frenzied shouts. Why the hell were the pick-up party so slow in reacting? They seemed to be doubled-up over their boats. . . . Then, as a note of hysteria crept into Colin's voice, Bob, the boat-troop's ace diver, emerged alongside him. In the Geminis, the boat-troop laughed and laughed. . . ."

SIGNALLERS AND SURGEONS
Within each troop (one officer and fifteen men), whatever its tactical rôle, every soldier has to acquire one or more of the specialist skills needed when the troop or its standard sub-unit, the four-man patrol, is functioning on the ground. Communication is of such importance that a gifted signaller will be particularly cherished by the Regiment. The SAS is one of the few elements of the British— or any other—armed forces still using high-speed Morse. Not only does this make for better security, but there are technical reasons why Morse can be more readily transmitted 1,000 miles across rough terrain than voice. The SAS basic signals course lasts three months. The need for a medical specialist well-versed in emergency first-aid and basic surgery, taught to SAS soldiers in this country and the United States, does not require a qualified doctor to satisfy it. If the situation is critical, a doctor will be flown or parachuted to the scene and the casualty will be evacuated. A good "bush doctor" will know whether such assistance is imperative. He will also weigh against that need the risk that the turbulence and noise inherent in a casualty evacuation may "blow" the security of a secret operation. The patrol "medic" is also valuable in dispensing simple medical care to civilians and their farm stock in a primitive environment as part of SAS policy to gain the co-operation of the indigenous population. For the

same reason, at least one man of the four needs an adequate command of the language of the war zone to which he is posted. Such courses are intensive and may be tailored specifically to SAS needs. They are held at the Royal Army Education Corps School of Language at Beaconsfield. For historic reasons, Malay and Arabic have been most regularly taught to SAS soldiers, but more recently European and Scandinavian languages and Russian have become equally important.

Certain fighting skills are also developed to an awesome level of ability. Among these, the use of the automatic pistol in close-quarter battle (CQB) is among the most impressive. The object of this six-week course, for which a minimum of 1,200 to 1,500 bullets per man is provided, is to teach the soldier to burst into a room ostensibly occupied by several armed men and to kill or disable all of them with aimed shots from a thirteen-round 9mm Browning. It is assumed that each target must be hit in the chest by two bullets from up to twenty yards. The technique developed by the SAS in its specially-constructed "CQB House" at Hereford, is to move continuously, rolling over and over on the ground if necessary, without pausing to fire accurately. Instant magazine changes and clearing jams in the pistol are also included in the repertoire. The ultimate effect of this training is deadly, as guerrillas and terrorists in Ireland, Aden and elsewhere have discovered. In a city or a crowded, hijacked aircraft, such training also minimizes the risk of innocent casualties that the enormous velocity of modern firearms makes all too probable.

The use of explosives is a basic tool of all SAS soldiers and forms part of the early continuation training. More advanced techniques taught to specialists in this field include the creation of booby-traps, knowledge of a wide variety of explosives and the use of sophisticated timing and trigger mechanisms.

The troop to which the SAS novice has now been assigned is part of a larger unit known as a squadron, of which 22 SAS, the regular regiment, has four. Each squadron consists of four troops plus a squadron commander (a major), a second-in-command, a sergeant-major, quartermaster and clerks—a total of 72 men and six officers. Theoretically, the novice is not basically pro-

250 INSIDE THE SAS

ficient until he has exercised with the whole squadron, though fighting actions involving an entire SAS squadron are rare.

At any one time, parts of the squadron may be dispersed all over the world in small "team jobs," either training friendly forces or on highly secret operations, often concerned with counter-terrorism in friendly states. But one complete squadron of 22 SAS is always on instant stand-by at Hereford, gear packed and a codeword, signalling an alert, memorized. Readiness is routinely tested, and men are extracted from their beds or their favorite pubs at unsocial hours. Some years ago the code was "Free Beer!" As it echoed through the Hereford bars many of their regular customers left: back at Bradbury Lines barracks they collected their Bergens and assembled. "This time it's for real, lads," they were told. "We're going to Ireland."

RESEARCH AND INTELLIGENCE

Also based at Hereford are other SAS groups, whose work is even more specialized. They include a separate signals squadron, an operations research group (evaluating new equipment and weapons), operational planning and Intelligence (colloquially known as "The Kremlin") and a training wing that runs selection courses and prepares men for counter-revolutionary warfare. Within this complex structure, a variety of exotic skills flourishes, ranging from "advanced lock neutralization" (safe-breaking) to expertise in foreign firearms.

The soldier who emerges from this extraordinary training—perhaps the most varied and intensive military education anywhere in the world—does not stand out in a crowd. He tends to be a European, of medium height—only members of G (for Guards) Squadron are taller than average—of lean, athletic build (greyhound rather than bulldog), somewhat hirsute, and distinctly wary in the presence of strangers. A minority of SAS soldiers grow a luxuriant, cavalry moustache verging on a parody of stage whiskers. The custom is a relic of the days of jungle warfare of the early fifties, when most men wore beards and —ordered to shave on their return to England—retained as much facial hair as Queen's Regulations permitted. The SAS trooper's background is probably working class, but he has learned to value such journals as *The Economist* as an aid to understanding the conflicts in which he might be involved at any time. (A junior Labour Minister, having been introduced, at his request, to a "typical trooper," later accused his Hereford hosts of substituting an officer in disguise. The suspicion was unjustified.)

Within the SAS family, where the trooper's weaknesses as well as his strengths are public knowledge, he shares a ribald humor that mocks everything and almost everyone. It is a world in which the sonorous Regimental motto "Who Dares Wins" is transmuted into the plaintive question, "Who cares who wins?"

A prolonged period of active service with the SAS involves great stress. The Regiment is well aware of this and, not wishing to waste valuable human resources, defies Beaumont's "selection-destruction cycle" by regularly posting troops from tough operational jobs to less exacting posts in training at home or abroad, to operational research and elsewhere, where the latest experience of active duty can be fed back to those preparing for such work. Over a period of years, therefore, service with the Regiment is a sort of roundabout, from training to operations and back again. But in career terms, what is the cumulative effect?

PAY AND PREFERMENT

In an age when counter-revolutionary warfare has become the most common form of armed combat, expertise in internal security in all its manifestations is a marketable commodity in and out of the British armed forces. In the short run, however, the soldier who volunteers for SAS duty does not always help his orthodox military career. The effect on non-commissioned ranks can be particularly detrimental. A Guards sergeant earning, say £5,000 per annum basic will be reduced, like all other ranks, to Trooper (the equivalent of private soldier) on acceptance into the SAS. During his first year of SAS service, he will continue to receive the same pay as he had before joining the Regiment; after that, like the rest of his comrades, he will be paid as a corporal, about £3,650 basic per annum. However good a soldier he is, he may never achieve the same rank he had while serving with his parent unit, because 22 SAS, with a total strength of about 750, is not large enough to offer such preferment. Most volunteers treat the problem as another, permanent manifestation of the sickener factor, as well as a symbol of their commitment to soldiering for its own sake, and of their esprit de corps.

Young officers, by contrast, improve their position marginally by winning their SAS spurs. Most who come in as troop commanders are junior or senior lieutenants. As SAS troop commanders they are promoted to captain. Thereafter, it is not unusual for them to engage in a series of cross-postings between the SAS and their former regiments, with no loss of promotion. But the higher they reach up the ladder outside the SAS, the more difficult it becomes to return to the Regiment with the same rank. There are, for instance, about 200 brigadiers in the Army as a whole, but only one who commands the SAS Group (regulars and TA volunteers) based in London. At least one senior officer, Colonel David Smiley, is on record that he declined command of the three SAS regiments and left the Army in 1961 because, as General Bob Laycock, SAS Colonel Commandant at that time, explained to him: "I know how you feel, David, but in fact the War Office simply isn't willing to pay a brigadier."

There is also in the higher echelons of the British Army a traditional scepticism about "funnies." Their élitism, independence, apparent informality, and special rôle out of mainstream operations in large-scale warfare, all make them a caste apart. This factor can act as an intangible blocking mechanism to officers' later promotion. Some, because they are supremely expert soldiers, do return to former regiments, such as the Green Jackets, to command a battalion with the rank of lieutenant-colonel after, say, a period at the Camberley Staff College. But many others find orthodox soldiering too tame and restrictive after a life of dangerous freedom with the SAS. Some of the best men, having become majors, quit the British forces altogether after SAS duty, to seek their fortunes as soldiers, or in some similarly risky occupation, elsewhere. The process was lucidly described by one officer who did this some years ago. "One of the hardest things to assimilate, when you first join, is the dedication of the average Trooper. He is in the SAS for love, not money, nearly always sacrificing what he could attain materially elsewhere. . . . A troop is the most idealistic institution you can imagine. The troop comes before anything. . . .

"The Achilles heel of the SAS is administration. Soldiers come to the Regiment, often at great self-sacrifice, and serve it well. Operationally, they are well taken care of, but self-advancement and career planning leaves a lot to be desired. . . . Officer recruitment is an aspect of regimental life which needs drastic revision. . . . Perhaps the very excellence and freedom enjoyed with the SAS has caused many Regular officers to leave the Army at the end of their SAS tour, unable to face life in a battalion or regiment again.

"I could not have lived a more full life than the one I have been lucky enough to experience for the last four years. Britain, I feel, does not fully appreciate what a superb weapon she possesses in her armoury. If wise, she will look after it well."

There are signs that this advice has been heeded at last. An SAS tour is now regarded as a bonus point in the promotion race. Following the election of the Thatcher Government in 1979, the new Minister of Defence, Mr. Francis Pym, decreed that operational SAS officers would not be required invariably to pass the Camberley Staff College entrance examination (an essential step if a professional soldier is to rise above the rank of major). This unique dispensation recognizes that a professional fighter does not have the same opportunity for study as his less mobile colleagues, particularly those in garrison regiments. It also reflects changing attitudes to counter-revolutionary warfare as such. After a decade of urban terrorism in Europe, "funnies" are no longer odd men out. They may be said to have come in from the cold.

Appendix A
SAS Casualties, 1950-80

To stay alive, in SAS parlance, is to "beat the Clock." This derives from the tradition of carving on the Regiment's memorial clock at Hereford (a collapsible, portable structure) the names of those killed in training or in action. The clock was erected soon after the Regiment occupied its Hereford base in 1980. Each year, the list of those who did not beat the clock grows longer.

MALAYA

Tpr. T. A. Brown	1950	
Pte. G. A. Fisher	1950	
Tpr. J. A. O'Leary	1951	
Sgt. O. H. Ernst, Rhodesian SAS	1951	
Cpl. J. B. Davies, Rhodesian SAS	1951	
Tpr. F. G. Boylan	1951	
WO2 W. F. Garrett	1951	
Cpl. V. E. Visague, Rhodesian SAS	1952	
Tpr. A. Fergus	1952	
Major E. C. R. Barker, B.E.M.	1953	
Tpr. J. A. S. Morgan	1953	
Tpr. E. Duckworth	1953	
Lt. P. B. S. Cartwright	1953	
Tpr. B. Watson	1953	
2/Lt. F. M. Donnelly-Wood	1953	
Lt. (QM) F. S. Tulk	1953	
Cpl. K. Bancroft	1953	
Tpr. F. W. Wilkins	1953	
Cpl. P. G. R. Eakin	1953	
Lt. J. L. C. Fotheringham	1953	
Lt. G. J. Goulding	1954	
L. Cpl. C. W. Bond	1954	
Tpr. B. Powell	1954	
Tpr. A. E. Howell	1954	
Tpr. A. R. Thomas, New Zealand SAS	1956	
Tpr. W. R. J. Marselle	1956	
Lt. A. G. H. Dean	1957	
Cpl. A. G. Buchanan, New Zealand SAS	1957	
Tpr. R. Hindmarsh	1968	

MALAYSIA
Tpr. N. P. Ollis   1969

WEST MALAYSIA
L. Cpl. R. Greenwood 1967

OMAN (JABAL AKHDAR)
Cpl. D. Swindells,
 M.M.   1958
Tpr. W. Carter   1959
Tpr. A. G. Bembridge   1959

BORNEO
Maj. H. A. I. Thompson,
 M.C.   1963
Maj. R. H. D. Norman,
 M.B.E., M.C.   1963
Cpl. M. P. Murphy   1963
Tpr. A. Condon   1964
Sgt. B. Bexton   1964
Tpr. W. E. White   1964
Pte. G. H. Hartley   1964

BRUNEI
Sgt. E. Pickard   1973

SOUTH ARABIA
Capt. R. C. Edwards   1964
Tpr. J. N. Warburton   1964
Tpr. J. Hollingsworth 1966
Tpr. M. R. Lambert   1966
Tpr. G. F. F. Iles   1967
L. Cpl. A. G. Brown   1967

ETHIOPIA
Cpl. I. A. Macleod   1968

OMAN (MUSANDAM)
L. Cpl. P. Reddy   1970

OMAN (DHOFAR)
Capt. I. E. Jones   1971
Sgt. J. S. M. Moores   1971
Tpr. C. Loid   1971
L. Cpl. D. R.
 Ramsden   1972
Tpr. M. J. Martin   1972
Cpl. T. Labalaba,
 B.E.M.   1972
Tpr. T. P. A. Tobin   1972
L. Cpl. A. Kent   1974
Capt. S. Garthwaite   1974
Tpr. C. Hennessy   1975
L. Cpl. K. Small   1975
Sgt. A. E. Gallagher   1975

FRANCE
Maj. R. M. Pirie   1972
Sgt. S. H. Johnson   1978
Cpl. F. M. Benson   1978

NORTHERN IRELAND
S. Sgt. D. J. Naden   1978
Capt. H. R. West-
 macott   1980

UK
Cpl. K. Norry   1962
Cpl. R. Richardson   1965
Tpr. P. C. O'Toole   1965
Tpr. J. Hooker   1965
L. Cpl. J. R. Anderson 1967
L. Cpl. A. C. Lonney   1968
WO1 E. T. Nugent   1968
Cpl. R. N. Adie   1968
Tpr. C. P. Martin   1968
WO2 J. E. Daubney   1974
Maj. M. J. A. Kealy,
 D.S.O.   1979

Appendix B
An Idea Spreads:
The Overseas Regiments

THE IDEA THAT DAVID STIRLING HAD IN the 1940s has succeeded because it is inherently a good one. The SAS structure works because it embodies a flexibility unique among today's increasingly complex and bureaucratic armed forces, as well as a capacity for change in a world where soldiers and politicians alike are seeking quick, cost-effective solutions to military problems for which there are no precedents.

In post-war years, the Regiment has found itself in a sellers' market. Soldiers of 22 SAS served in at least 26 foreign countries during the year 1978/79, and many of these men were employed as training teams for other people's armies. Its three most durable offspring, so far, are the SAS regiments of Zimbabwe-Rhodesia, New Zealand and Australia. Each has acquired experience not shared by the others, but the lessons learned by each tend, within a short time, to be picked up by the others in that organic way peculiar to the SAS family.

Links with US Special Forces (the Green Berets) are of long-standing. In 1962, Major-General William P. Yarborough, the Green Berets' supremo, was made an honorary member of the SAS Regiment, in recognition of the help received by the SAS in its US training in 1962. (Only one other man, General Sir Walter Walker, has been so honored.) The two-way traffic continued in 1977, when a new US rescue force, the Delta Force, was formed under the command of Colonel Charles Beckwith. Beckwith, a Green Beret officer who had served on secondment with the SAS in Malaya, brought his new team to Hereford for basic training. By an historical irony—no fault of Beckwith or his team—he was obliged to call off an attempt to rescue American diplomatic hostages in Iran only weeks before the SAS rescued Iranian diplomat-hostages in London.

RHODESIANS IN MALAYA

The first of the overseas SAS regiments was the Rhodesian, founded during the days of Brigadier Michael Calvert's desperate recruiting campaign for the Malayan Emergency. Calvert flew from Malaya to Salisbury and toured Rhodesia in 1950, addressing meetings in his efforts to find men. From the 1,000 volunteers who came forward was created C Squadron of the Malayan Scouts (SAS). Their first commander was Peter Walls, then a major and subsequently the "supremo" of all Rhodesia's armed forces. The military contribution of C Squadron to the Malayan campaign was not significant. Partly, this was because many of the volunteers were soldiers who had not experienced bush warfare in their own country, unlike their successors who fought the guerrilla war. The unit was peculiarly prone to jungle ailments, particularly scrub typhus, and at any one time a significant percentage of C Squadron was unfit to fight as a result. Two men were killed in action in Malaya. The main contribution of this formative period, in the view of one squadron veteran, was "the ultimate injection into the Rhodesian Army of officers and men who were thinking along SAS lines."

After its return from Malaya, the Squadron was reorganized, and in 1961 it was based in Ndola, Northern Rhodesia (later Zambia) as part of the forces of the Federation of Rhodesia and Nyasaland, with a total strength of 250 officers and men. One of those attached to it at this time was John Peters, who achieved fame as commander of Five Commando in the Congo soon afterward. C Squadron was itself deployed on the border with the Congo during the civil war in that country, notably when tension rose following the death in a Congolese air crash of the UN Secretary-General, Dag Hammarskjöld.

It was also during this period that the men of C Squadron became the first airborne troops in Rhodesia, and on

30 October 1961 a newly-formed Parachute Training
School at New Sarum, Salisbury, started basic training.
To begin with, the Squadron used standard X-type static
line parachutes and jumped from Rhodesian Air Force
Dakotas. These parachutes had a tendency to oscillate in
the prevailing air conditions, which in addition made for
heavier landings than would occur in Europe. By 1970,
the SAS had turned over to larger American-designed T
10 canopies, while a small cadre of soldiers would use
more advanced, steerable parachutes for a high altitude
"stand-off" approach, totally silently under cover of darkness, to the most sensitive targets.

The pioneering days of the early 1960s saw the unit's
first operational parachute deployment into Rhodesia's
eastern districts, to pursue dissidents who carried on a
campaign of arson against the area's pine and gumtree
plantations. The Squadron also trained in Aden with 22
SAS from Britain.

The collapse of the Federation of Rhodesia and Nyasaland in 1963 led to considerable dilution of the Rhodesian SAS capability. With the reduction of the manpower
and economic base provided by the Federation, the
armed forces were also cut. In the ensuing struggle for
survival, there was much jostling among senior military
people naturally concerned about their own careers, the
overall effect of which was not helpful to C Squadron. As
morale in the unit declined, so many of the more experienced soldiers accepted "golden handshakes" then being
offered in exchange for unemployment, to start a new life
in Rhodesia, South Africa or Britain. Others, including
Peters, joined the Congolese mercenary force then commanded by Mike Hoare. Only a small cadre of officers
and men remained to preserve the core of what would ultimately emerge as a reconstructed C Squadron. This was
commanded by Major Dudley Coventry, who had led the
Parachute Regiment Squadron of the Malayan Scouts
(SAS) during the Malayan campaign, with Captain Peter
Rich as his deputy. They had a few subalterns and about
two dozen men. During the following year, as the constitutional conflict with Britain accelerated, the Rhodesian
SAS cast its net wide in search for suitable recruits. A
former second-in-command of the Regiment, Major Mike
Graham, recalls: "We ended up as a fairly cosmopolitan

crew: Rhodesian, South African, British, American, French, German, Greek and Portuguese. For a short time we even had a lad from Finland whose only English was the phrase, 'Fetch my umbrella,' which was not much use in the Zambesi Valley in the dry season."

UDI AND AFTER

The reaction to Ian Smith's Unilateral Declaration of Independence in 1964 and the constitutional crisis that followed between Britain and Rhodesia seems to have provoked no conflict of loyalty in the minds of Rhodesian SAS soldiers. British public opinion over the issue was so divided (and so cunningly "massaged" in Britain by the last Rhodesian High Commissioner and his team) that it seemed plausible to hope that there would be no military action against the Salisbury government by Britain. Good relations established with the RAF crews of a Javelin squadron flown to Lusaka soon after UDI also reassured the Rhodesians. There was no British military action against the Rhodesians, so whatever doubts might have existed in both the British and Rhodesian armed forces about making war on kith-and-kin were never put to the test. Nevertheless, the Rhodesians (including the SAS) were prepared for a fight. Standing orders, issued about what they should do in event of an airborne attack, included details of defensive positions to be occupied near Rhodesian Light Infantry barracks in the country, contingency plans for the removal of ammunition from a central ordnance depot and the mounting of a guard on the Kariba Dam. In anticipation of a water-borne attack by either British or African troops across Lake Kariba or the Victoria Falls Bridge, defensive positions including anti-tank weapons were dug-in and, in Salisbury, key positions were guarded against any attempted assault by British parachute troops.

By the late sixties, the Rhodesians were beginning to experience the first serious terrorist infiltration from other countries, including Mozambique, then still a Portuguese colony. Salisbury's reaction was to try to emulate the methods adopted in Malaya, and undertake a program of military aid to the civil power, but the Africans proved impervious to a European oriented hearts-and-minds scheme. When this failed, the SAS had to increase in size

and recruit soldiers peculiarly suited to bush warfare. The
men in question were young—some still in their teens—
and exceptionally fit, as well as being sharp eyed, superlative trackers. They were known as "junglies" because of
their love of the bush. After protracted operational periods in that environment, some of them would spend their
leave hunting on game ranches. The risks of such a life
were, as Mike Graham recounts, manifold. They included
(in addition to the human enemy) elephant, rhinoceros,
lion, leopard, hyena, crocodile, electric-barbel fish, mosquito, tsetse fly, snake, scorpion and other pests. In their
turn, the SAS nomads were also predators, for game provided food. One anecdote illustrates this environment.
According to Graham: "A young trooper, after admiring
a large herd of elephant on a river bed, ran into a very
large cow accompanied by her new calf. The elephant
flipped away the soldier's FN rifle and in almost the same
motion, beat him to the ground with her trunk. She then
stood astride him and kicked him with all four feet in turn
for some time. Not content with that, she then knelt
down and pushed a tusk through the man's chest and
and lifted him into the air. The soldier, still conscious,
grasped the elephant's second tusk in order to take the
weight off his injured chest. At this, the elephant threw
him to the ground, kicked him a couple of times and ran
off after her calf." The soldier was evacuated by helicopter and light aircraft to Salisbury, where he received immediate surgery. Ten days later, with 76 stitches in his
chest, he was discharged to the Regiment's drinking club,
"The Winged Stagger." He returned to duty after another
six weeks, having spent his convalescence qualifying as an
Outward Bound School instructor in rock-climbing. But
other encounters by the SAS with the occupants of what
was still, in theory at least, a wildlife reserve caused some
distress to conservationists including National Parks officials. Like others in Rhodesia, they started to describe
the unit as "C Squadron, Rhodesian Special Air Sa-
faris."

Although they loved the bush, the "junglies" regarded
the early stages of SAS soldiering as less than satisfactory.
The rôle primarily allocated to C Squadron at the beginning of the war was exclusively that of reconnaissance.
One veteran explains: "There was nothing more frustrat-

ing than watching the bandits from hiding, knowing that the information we would pass about them was going to units less combative and effective than we were." This was, in effect, the Borneo strategy without the benefit of a Gurkha step-up party to do the killing. The tactical lessons acquired at that time were to be of great value when the Squadron began its own offensive operations.

ACROSS THE BORDER

It was inevitable that in such a vast area the Regiment's rôle would change from one of reconnaissance to that of a quick-reaction fire-force, responding to attacks that had already happened or begun. Air mobility, particularly through static-line, low-level parachuting from the vintage Dakotas into the bush to begin hot pursuit, was the chosen response. Simultaneously, the Squadron was also learning to work across the border. The guerrilla war had taken firm hold not only on Rhodesian soil but also that of Mozambique and Angola, both of them Portuguese colonies until 1975. Indeed, the Angolan war had started long before, in 1961. It was to improve Rhodesia's own security, as well as to enlarge their operational experience, that some men of C Squadron fought in Angola alongside Portuguese security authorities in 1967. From the early 1970s, there was also a long series of joint operations in Mozambique. The Rhodesian Air Force provided air reconnaissance of the Portuguese operational zone, after which small tracking units from C Squadron were placed by helicopter in an area where the guerrillas were training or operating. If the target merited the trouble, Rhodesian Hunter strike aircraft would also be employed. Guerrilla camps were destroyed and the Portuguese would promptly celebrate the creation of a guerrilla-free "white" zone as the enemy slipped back to the sanctuary of Zambia. The SAS would then move to the next promising area. While they were thus engaged, the guerrillas would start infiltrating back to the zone that was officially cleared. One of the most dramatic operations in this series resulted in two helicopters each depositing four SAS soldiers inside a camp occupied by 300 anti-Portuguese Frelimo guerrillas. Instead of the customary SAS skirmish with a defensive Frelimo rearguard, the error generated "a fairly exciting punch-up."

After Portugal's withdrawal from her African colonies in 1975, the bush war in Rhodesia intensified. As a result, the SAS was obliged to recruit younger, less experienced soldiers, including men "who were in many cases no more than teenagers," as Graham puts it. "We placed enormous responsibility on their shoulders and they did things that one would normally expect of seasoned veterans. But it would be wrong to expect the self-discipline we wanted to be evident in every single aspect of these young soldiers' lives. So back in camp, discipline was tight. We dressed correctly, marched properly and generally let Rhodesia know we were as professional on the base as on operations. Instead of joining a mad scramble for élitism, we quietly stuck to the rules. Along with the Rhodesian Light Infantry, which had the same attitude, we eventually got the lion's share of operations without indulging in histrionics or having a General deposited on us through every weekend." When the rules were broken, "our misdemeanours were skilfully disguised as somebody else's problem."

In the peculiar, highly-pressurised circumstances of a country at war, Rhodesia evolved an intensive form of selection, which proved, according to a former member of the British 21 SAS who survived it, highly effective. The volunteers began in a camp near Salisbury with a period of harassment lasting between 36 and 48 hours. The men had to swim, play football, and run, always carrying bricks. No sleep was permitted. This "sickener" period deterred a predictably large number of volunteers. It was immediately followed by the equivalent of Hereford's endurance march. Each man carried a 40-pound pack plus rifle, over a twenty-mile course in a hilly area south of Salisbury, in daytime temperatures exceeding 80 degrees Fahrenheit. A series of similar marches followed during the next two weeks, involving accurate map and compass reading and the completion of the route in a time that demanded much of it to be covered at jogging speed.

Even after nominal acceptance, the volunteer was not "badged" until he had participated in one or more live operations, during which his performance was carefully evaluated. Operational experience, in turn, was only acquired after a period of continuation training, which included Scuba diving and canoeing, to equip members of

C Squadron for the many water-borne Commando operations assigned to the SAS. There was also, inevitably, a static-line parachute course. By 1971, the Parachute Training School had recorded 12,000 descents, at which point the Squadron started operational free-fall training. This course, in which four out of ten operational Rhodesian SAS soldiers were trained, normally lasted six weeks and built up each man's experience, if the weather was good, to around 50 jumps from a maximum altitude of 12,000 feet. This included night descents with equipment and was, effectively, the C Squadron equivalent of the British "HALO" course. One of those concerned with this program told the author that operational free-fall had been invaluable in placing small teams into enemy territory for reconnaissance or limited offensive tasks, and as pathfinder groups for larger numbers of men who were dropped by more orthodox static-line parachutes. Most operational free-fall descents were nocturnal. The total number of descents of both types, by the time of the Lancaster House constitutional conference, was around 45,000.

As the war intensified, so the SAS specialized in launching surprise attacks against guerrilla bases both inside Rhodesia and across the border in Zambia and Mozambique. One man who took part in some of the raids concluded that they had two objectives: first, to inflict the maximum number of casualties on the guerrillas; second, to seize arms, documents and a few prisoners for interrogation. The arms, including Kalashnikov AK–47 rifles, RPG missiles and various anti-aircraft weapons, were taken for use by the Rhodesian forces rather than as propaganda souvenirs.

In a typical cross-border operation after Portugal had withdrawn from her colonies, the troopers parachuted from a mere 450 feet above ground from Dakotas in a dawn assault, only to notice on the ground below "the enemy, hundreds of black dots like ants, running clear of the perimeter of soldiers dropping around their camp." These airborne raids were often preceded by Canberra bombing and Hunter missile bombardment, which destroyed the camps but also removed any hope of surprising the occupants. The number of kills increased when free-fall parties led the way in the dark, and were already positioned as ambush "stop groups" as the main assault began. As an alternative, the SAS were sometimes dropped miles away from their target and advanced to it on foot, in encircling groups in the dark. But this approach, while it preserved surprise, might require several night marches, and was not practicable as an approach to bases deep inside Mozambique or Zambia.

TO WAR BY BOAT

Such raids did not always proceed according to plan. An attempt to destroy a base in Zambia after an approach by boat across Lake Kariba came to nothing when the assault team failed to find the target and simultaneously lost radio contact (which was by voice on high frequency rather than Morse) with its base. After two tense days and nights, the party re-established contact and was recovered by boat. This was just as well, according to one participant, who discovered that the initial radio exchanges had been intercepted by the Zambian Army, which then evacuated the target camp and waited in ambush for the SAS.

But other water-borne operations were more elaborate, and successful. Graham told the author that the Zambesi River and Lakes Caborra-Bassa, as well as Kariba, were all used as routes into enemy territory. "Apart from the fairly standard equipment of Klepper canoes and Zodiac inflatables, we sometimes employed much larger 'mother ships' equipped with radar and armed with Russian 12.7mm light anti-aircraft weapons which we acquired from people no longer capable of operating them." Overland assaults by vehicle were also tried. "We even built two specialized cross-country armoured vehicles based on German military Unimog chassis and fitted with 20mm Hispano cannons taken from inoperable Air Force Vampire jets. We claim no spectacular success with these because a guerrilla war in Rhodesia was very different from the North African desert in the Second World War."

The operations that appear to have succeeded best were those more in the post-war tradition of the British SAS regiment, comprising parties of between two and eight men moving on foot and at night to mine roads and bridges routinely used by the guerrillas, to sabotage communications and ambush convoys before the patrol melted back into the bush. In this context, the Rhodesian SAS in the seventies was in a similar position to the British regiment in South Arabia in the sixties, acting as counterguerrillas on one side of the border and guerrillas on the other. Much of the work on both sides was still close reconnaissance by four-man teams, which remained in concealment by day, keeping watch from a distance, and moving close enough to the target by night to obtain detailed information with the help of night-vision equipment. Some teams succeeded in remaining on station doing this stealthy work for weeks at a time, constantly feeding data back to Salisbury without detection. Yet the results of attacks on guerrilla bases that followed these arduous preparations were, as one of those involved observes, sometimes just a matter of luck. "We sometimes hit the jackpot and returned elated. On other occasions we found that only a 'caretaker' group was in camp when we hit it, the real prize having flown the nest between the time of our reconnaissance and the assault. . . . It's the sort of thing which happens to all soldiers, some of the time."

Because of the very small numbers of men available to the SAS, planning and organization were peculiarly important in Rhodesia, and elaborate care was taken to reduce the risk of error. Until the formation of Combined Operations Headquarters ("Comops") in the mid-1970s, SAS soldiers were "Army" troops exclusively administered by the headquarters of the brigade in whose area they were based, but for operational matters the Squadron had to report to the Army commander in Salisbury. Linked with this arrangement was a close liaison with the Rhodesian Central Intelligence Organization and the police Special Branch, both of which briefed the SAS on reconnaissance and sabotage missions.

LESSONS FROM ENTEBBE

After the creation of "Comops," all lines of command and planning led directly to the military supremo, Peter Walls. Mike Graham's experience was that this made it easier for the SAS to obtain air support, air-photographic reconnaissance and other forms of Intelligence. This development was soon followed, in July 1976, by the Israeli commando raid on Entebbe to rescue more than 100 hostages held by Palestinian and German terrorist hijackers. The Rhodesians studied film of the raid at a time when they were themselves planning an ambitious attack on Chimoio Camp in Mozambique. (That attack was ultimately launched in January 1978, and caused 1,500 casualties among supporters of Robert Mugabe.) An essential ingredient for such a raid, the Rhodesians concluded, was an airborne command post equipped with superlative communications, flying high enough to avoid all but the most sophisticated surface-to-air-missiles. As Graham puts it: "We had seen on the movies how the Israelis used a command Boeing 707, but since Air Rhodesia had only three Boeings we had to lower our sights a bit and ended up with an Air Force VIP Dakota equipped with an incredible range of radio sets and teleprinters and festooned with an incredible array of antennae. It worked excellently and General Peter Walls himself operated from the aircraft many times."

The SAS's own Intelligence section also evolved to a sophisticated level. "In addition to the map and airphotographic coverage of any target area, we had a team of seconded cartographers—specialists of great artistic talent—who made extremely lifelike models of the ground to be covered. Our routine in such cases was to start with a 'think evil' session, initially with some of our own officers. We would then bring in the Air Force and go through the same routine. Eventually we were doing expert presentations to the War Cabinet." ("Think-evil" was jargon for anticipating the worst, and for devising the greatest possible damage to the enemy.) "The final stage was always a briefing to the men from the same model, without disclosing our plan. We outlined the task and set them various problems relating to the operation and placed the men in syndicates to find solutions. Then they came back and we listened to their opinions. Usually, the plan that emerged from the consensus of these sometimes heated discussions was the one we had already chosen, though with occasional modifications suggested by ordinary troopers. By the time we had rehearsed and given formal orders, again by reference to the models, every individual was thoroughly familiar with the task, so familiar that when the unexpected happened—as it usually did—

the men were able to figure that out for themselves and react intelligently to changed circumstances. . . ."

Throughout 1977 and 1978, the strength of what was still officially known in Salisbury as "C Squadron" gradually increased and edged back towards the 250 officers and men it had had in 1961. This development coincided with a general reorganization within the Rodesian Army and, as a result, C Squadron was renamed the "Rhodesian Special Air Service Regiment." "Troops" became "squadrons," and "sections" became "troops." Interestingly, it was the veterans who were least pleased by this change in title: after enjoying for 27 years the intimate comradeship embodied in the name "C Squadron," some of them were less sure about the increased anonymity implicit in a full regiment. With the inauguration of black majority rule, many of the longest serving Rhodesian SAS soldiers returned to Britain or went to South Africa, some to join the armed forces there. Others soldiered on, uncertain what future, if any, the recently renamed regiment would have after Lancaster House and the confusion of the election campaign that followed it.

There was one other contribution to the Salisbury Government's war effort by the SAS that is worth recording. This is the birth of the Selous Scouts, a useful military unit, which finally ran out of control and was disbanded. Because of the SAS experience in infiltration techniques required, it became almost routine for senior subalterns to act as Military Intelligence Officers during their period away from the SAS engaged in staff training. Other, more senior officers, were also seconded for special Intelligence duties with the Special Branch and the Rhodesian Central Intelligence Organization. One of these was Mike Graham, who, with Brigadier John Hickman and a Special Branch officer, recruited black soldiers, policemen and rehabilitated guerrillas for the risky game of penetrating enemy camps by bluff. They were sometimes joined by a few whites whose knowledge of African languages gave them an even chance in the more hazardous rôle of disguising themselves as Africans. The groups thus formed bore a close, but coincidental resemblance to the multi-racial "counter gangs" organized by Kitson during the Mau Mau campaign in Kenya during the 1950s. Through these cadres, and as a "shop window" for disguising more clandestine activities, there also developed a highly-specialized tracking element which could pursue enemy raiding parties to their bases accurately and without detection. What emerged was the Selous Scouts, one of whose members described to the author how the trackers, black and white, operated: "We would follow a spoor only so long as the sun was on the slant, between the hours of 6 am and 10 am and from 3 pm until dusk. That way we could read the spoor as if it was a guidebook: the crushed grass, the traces of human urine, and so on. Sometimes we laid the ambush ourselves but more frequently we left that to others, having infiltrated the camp itself."

When the Scouts was formally created, Graham was offered the post of second-in-command but preferred the atmosphere of the exclusively-white SAS, with its emphasis on professional soldiering and careful character selection. He was made a Member of the Legion of Merit (Rhodesia's equivalent of the MBE) for his pioneering work in the formation of the Scouts. Command of the Selous Scouts went to Colonel Ronald Reid-Daly, a former Malayan Scout and a contemporary of General Walls in that unit.

THE KIWI SQUADRON

The New Zealand Special Air Service Squadron was formed in 1954 to operate with 22 SAS, as New Zealand's contribution to the British Commonwealth Strategic Reserve in South East Asia. Although New Zealand had had no airborne units as such during the Second World War, it was not entirely without experience and knowledge of such operations. A number of New Zealanders had served with the Long Range Desert Group after it had become parachute-trained. Others had joined the British Parachute Regiment and the original Special Air Service Regiment.

Applications were invited from civilians early in 1955, and a total of 800 were received. The Squadron required men of zeal and high morale who were physically tough and who possessed a high standard of discipline. It was made clear that volunteers must be prepared to undergo parachute training and, in addition to normal parachuting, to parachute into jungle or any other obstacles as was found necessary from time to time. Also, volunteers must be prepared to live for long periods in the jungle, to operate in small parties and participate in operations demanding self-reliance and leadership.

By imposing strict selection standards, the applicants were reduced to 138, and these, together with 40 selected officers and non-commissioned officers who had volunteered from the regular Army, marched into Waiouru Camp to commence training on 7 June 1955. The Squadron establishment, which had been fixed at 133, allowed considerable margin for final selection, which was carried out during training. A total of 49 men were rejected during this period. Of the force that survived, about one-third were Maoris. Major F. Rennie, MBE, New Zealand Regiment, a regular officer commanding the new unit, was given complete freedom to select regular officers and non-commissioned officers.

The Squadron trained at Waiouru under the direction of its squadron commander. Emphasis was placed on developing physical and emotional endurance, skill-at-arms, minor tactical drills and the preparation for parachute training, which would take place in Malaya. The new unit also adopted the maroon beret of British Airborne Forces, then still in use among 22 SAS in Malaya, as well as the Regimental winged dagger badge and its motto, "Who Dares Wins."

Between 20 November and 10 December 1955, the Squadron flew to Malaya to come under the command of 22 SAS. It began immediate parachute training at Changi, Singapore. In addition to the eight descents required for basic military training, the Squadron's members also made on average a further six jumps, three from S-55 helicopters, as part of their continuation training. Two men who had been sent with the Squadron to Malaya without the screening of selection in New Zealand failed their parachute courses and one, who refused to jump, was sent back to New Zealand. Parallel with these jump courses, the Squadron was receiving instruction in jungle warfare during a three-week course in rugged, mountainous terrain in Perak, about 160 miles north of Kuala Lumpur. This initial jungle training was conducted by officers and NCOs of 22 SAS, assisted by an advance party of New Zealanders who had completed the course themselves only a short time before. The process of selecting and training the New Zealanders had taken more than six months, and the Squadron's subsequent performance in the jungle was to demonstrate the value of this cautious and coherent approach to the formation of such a unit.

By the time the Squadron became operational, the SAS had evolved a technique of identifying the enemy in a given area as specific targets. These were usually the terrorists' "Special Liberation Army" organizations, controlling the aborigines. Having been allocated its target group of terrorists, an SAS squadron would then move deep into the jungle, make contact with the aborigines, and persuade them to move to new quarters such as a fortified jungle fort. It was an axiom of such operations that the confidence of the aborigines was not entirely won over until the terrorists who had controlled them were eliminated. On average, each operation now lasted thirteen weeks, with resupply by air during that time, and this was regarded as the minimum necessary to become familiar with the operational area as well as to influence the aborigines. The New Zealand Squadron's first operation lasted only five weeks, in fact, and it was carried out in Pahang. The target was the remnant of an independent Communist platoon, which had been responsible several years earlier for the murder of a senior diplomat. The operation was planned as a "reconnaissance in force" to "shake down" the Squadron as a cohesive fighting machine. The experience, although useful, led to no contact with the terrorist targets.

AH MING'S DOWNFALL

This operation was followed by two long operations, each of thirteen weeks' duration, in the Fort Brooke area on the Perak-Kelantan border. The main target was a terrorist ASAL organization of approximately eleven, which had controlled the aborigines for a number of years. The terrorist organization was led by Ah Ming, who had dominated the area and the aborigines since the Emergency commenced. During the two operations in this area, eight terrorists, including Ah Ming and his second-in-command, were killed and two terrorists were wounded. An aborigine terrorist was also captured. The Squadron had two casualties, one of them a leading scout who died of wounds after being hit in ambush. During these operations, the Squadron re-grouped a total of approximately 1,200 aborigines into two main areas.

The last three long operations were carried out in the mountainous area of Negri Sembilan. The target was a group of 24, consisting of the Communist State Secretary with a party of VIPs, and two armed workforces each under a District Committee member. The terrorist operations in the area were controlled by Li-Hak-Chi who had achieved considerable success against the security forces. The mountainous area was approximately 400 square miles and bounded by roads; it was particularly rugged and provided excellent hides for the terrorist groups. As a result of the Squadron's operations in the area, eight terrorists were killed including Li-Hak-Chi. Two were wounded and nine surrendered.

The original New Zealand SAS Squadron organization consisted of four troops and a squadron headquarters, but after six months' operation it was realized that the size of each troop could be reduced to create a new fifth troop. The Squadron also "donated" approximately twenty officers and men to the British Special Air Service Regiment as its contribution to that headquarters, and a proportion were also left at the base in squadron administrative appointments. Never at any time did the Squadron deploy more than 90 personnel in the jungle operations. In all, troops spent seventeen months of the 24½ months in the jungle on operations during the tour in Malaya.

The following statistics give a fair idea of the Squadron's impact on the Malayan campaign in which 26 terrorists were killed for the loss of one SAS soldier:

Contacts (Squadron fired first)	10
Incidents (Terrorists fired first)	4
Kills	15
(+ 1 killed by artillery fire in support of the Squadron on Squadron information)	
Surrenders	9
Captures	1
Total eliminations as a result of operations	26

(+ 4 wounded)

Own casualties (died of wounds)	2

The following decorations were awarded to Squadron personnel:

Military Cross	2
British Empire Medal	1
Mention in Dispatches	4
Negri Sembilan Conspicuous Gallantry Medal	2
Negri Sembilan Distinguished Conduct Medal	3

Between operations, opportunity was taken to carry out continuation parachute training and to practice small-party raiding techniques, usually against Royal Air Force airfields in Malaya and Singapore. One large-scale raid with the entire Squadron taking part was carried out against the Kuala Lumpa Royal Air Force airfield.

In addition, members of the Squadron were detailed from time to time as members of a parachute rescue team that was on continuous stand-by to jump into aircraft crash sites in the jungle. One large-scale rescue operation was commanded by a Squadron officer. Also, some Squadron personnel carried out a limited parachute operation against a terrorist target by jumping into an unprepared jungle landing zone. Personnel practiced this technique during parachute training, but, because of the hazards involved, it was only undertaken during active operations.

In November/December 1957, the Squadron returned by air to New Zealand and was disbanded, but, when the New Zealand Regular Brigade Group was created in August the following year, the Special Air Service Squadron was included in its permanent order of battle, and was resurrected six months later under the command of Captain J. A. Mace, a member of the original unit. The standard of the selection process imposed then, and maintained since, was such that on average only 25 per cent of those volunteering for SAS duty are accepted. The Squadron also included a nucleus of the Malayan veterans. Parachute training for the new squadron took place in Australia, with continuation training of all kinds being carried out in New Zealand. In 1961, a Territorial element was included to augment the regular squadron should the need ever arise. The reactivated squadron was tasked to function in South East Asia to perform classic SAS rôles, including long-range, small-party offensive operations behind enemy lines against troops, materials and communications, as well as routine medium reconnaissance on foot or in wheeled and tracked vehicles.

In May, 1962, a detachment of 30 men from the NZSAS Squadron, commanded by Major M. N. Velvin, was sent to Thailand, a fellow member of the South East Asia Treaty Organization, when a deteriorating situation on its northern border (where China, Laos and Burma meet) raised fears of a new guerrilla war. Based at Korat, the detachment assisted US Special Forces in training Thai soldiers and border police in counter-revolutionary warfare.

An official report records that "the Kiwis" unorthodox methods posed problems for the Thai troops during training. New Zealand soldiers acting as "enemy" arrived in an area where Thai troops were defending a village. The New Zealanders set up a road block some distance away. When a truck appeared, carrying the Thais' prepared lunches, the "insurgents" captured it and drove unchallenged into the village. Recognizing the truck, the Thai soldiers knocked off for lunch and were "mown down" by a burst of concentrated—fortunately blank—fire from the vehicle as it sped through the village and out the other side. About five miles further on, the Kiwis stopped for lunch, having set an ambush party to frustrate any Thai recovery attempts. It was several hours before the baffled Thai troops could contact the American directing staff to transmit an appeal to the New Zealanders to return the food.

When the crisis had passed, the Squadron was withdrawn from Thailand in September 1962, having received high praise from the Americans. General James L. Richardson, commander of Joint Task Force 116, said that the Kiwi SAS was a remarkable fighting unit. "If the position in Thailand became worse again, I would be pleased to have you alongside us," he said. One of Richardson's special forces sergeants commented: "They're the best people I've met. I'm really sorry to see them go."

A year later, the New Zealand Army commemorated the centenary of two of its most famous indigenous guerrilla forces—Major Gustavus von Tempsky's Forest Rangers and Major Harry Atkinson's Taranaki Bush Rangers—by renaming the Squadron the 1st Ranger

Squadron, NZSAS. The Forest Rangers in particular had adopted guerrilla tactics and deep penetration patrols in pursuit of Maori war parties during the nineteenth century Maori Wars. An official statement explained: "The new name is more descriptive of the Squadron's rôle as an Intelligence unit trained to fight with its own or captured weapons, to live off the country for long periods and to operate by parachute, vehicle, small boat or on foot in order to move fast and stealthily through enemy territory."

It was not long before the SAS Rangers were in action again in the region. Following a request from the Government of Malaysia, a detachment of 40 men of 1st Ranger Squadron, New Zealand Special Air Service, left home in February 1965 to join the Commonwealth force in Malaysian Borneo. No. 1 Detachment, commanded by Major W. J. Meldrum, was located at Kuching, operating in the West Brigade area and sharing facilities with 22 SAS. After seven months, it was replaced by No. 2 Detachment, under Major R. S. Dearing, initially at Kuching and subsequently with 22 SAS Headquarters at Labuan. This detachment also participated in combined operations with the Special Boat Section of the Royal Marines. In February 1966, No. 3 Detachment succeeded No. 2 Detachment; commanded by Major D. Ogilvy it was based at Labuan, operating, like its predecessor, in the Central and East Brigade areas. The Rangers' final tour was by No. 4 Detachment, under Major D. W. S. Moloney, from June 1966 until November, when it was withdrawn to West Malaysia. Throughout the period of Confrontation, a small team of instructors from the Regiment was attached to the Jungle Warfare School at Kota Tinggi, on the Malay Peninsula, as specialists in the art of tracking.

In November 1968 it was decided to augment the New Zealand commitment to South Vietnam by sending an SAS troop to the country. The unit was known as 4 Troop, NZSAS. Based at Nui Dat, it operated in Phuoc Tuy Province, the tactical area covered by the 1st Australian Task Force. It was attached, not surprisingly, to the Australian Special Air Service Squadron and maintained its high reputation as a superlative tracking, jungle reconnaissance and Intelligence-gathering group. Operationally it received close support from helicopters of the

Royal Australian Air Force. The troop returned to New Zealand in February 1971.

AUSSIES IN VIETNAM

The Australian Special Air Service was raised in July 1957 at Campbell Barracks, Swanbourne, in Western Australia, at a time when the Malayan campaign was all but over. It had a modest beginning as an independent 1st SAS Company, but ample scope—which it used—for expansion within armed forces that hitherto contained no special forces element. In the years since its foundation, the Australian SAS has acquired a monopoly of all commando operations, including those which in Britain would be performed by the Royal Marines and in the US by the Marine Corps. In 1960, the SAS Company became part of the Royal Australian Regiment. It was a brief, but useful, marriage which ended when the Commonwealth forces in Borneo urgently needed an increasing number of SAS soldiers. As a result, the Company was augmented to become the Australian Special Air Service Regiment, retaining the sand-colored beret of its British counterpart as well as the Regimental badge and wings. The date chosen for this expansion was 4 September 1964, anniversary of Australia's first combined land, sea and airborne operation in New Guinea in 1943.

During the four years preceding this expansion, the SAS Company had participated in exercises in Thailand, New Guinea (where Australia still has a military presence) and Okinawa, as well as in Australia itself. After expansion, the Regiment initially comprised a Headquarters, a Base squadron, 1 SAS Squadron, 2 SAS Squadron and a dedicated element of 151 Signals Squadron. A third Sabre squadron was formed in 1966.

The Regiment's first operational tour was by 1 SAS Squadron in Brunei in 1965; subsequently, 2 SAS Squadron saw service in the Kuching area of Borneo. Even fifteen years later, little is said about that period and, if official statements are to be believed, the Australian SAS took no part in the cross-border operations against Indonesia that were undertaken by the Gurkha regiments as well as British and New Zealand SAS soldiers.

Almost simultaneously with its participation in the Borneo campaign, the Australian SAS began operations in

Vietnam, where the three squadrons served in rotation from 1966 until 1971. Most of this service was in Phuoc Tuy province, south-east of Saigon. There the Regiment often suffered the galling experience of identifying, through carefully-concealed reconnaissance patrols, large numbers of Vietcong guerrillas, only to lose the quarry in the slow, ponderous follow-up operation by regular American and Vietnamese forces. It was also sometimes difficult for the SAS to adjust its traditionally stealthy jungle tactics to the "Prince Rupert," cowboy approach of helicopter-borne squadrons of US cavalry, as well as the high-profile, high-technology techniques generally adopted throughout much of the war by the more orthodox US forces.

The Australian SAS now consists of a Headquarters, two Sabre squadrons (1 and 3), a Base squadron, Support Squadron and 152 Signals Squadron. Selection is as stringent as in similar regiments elsewhere. According to Philip Warner, "The Australian SAS Regiment has a 'Recondo' (Reconnaissance/Commando) course in which those chosen to take part endure hunger, thirst, exhaustion and occasional physical danger for three weeks, with an average of only three or four hours of sleep a night. At one point in the course you may reach the coast in time to receive sea transport but if you do not make it you have the mortification of seeing the transport out at sea while you have to face further gruelling journeys because you have missed it."

Continuation training follows the pattern familiar elsewhere, with a greater emphasis (in the absence of an Australian Marine Corps) on the maritime environment, including diving techniques employed by the Royal Marine Special Boat Section and the US Navy Seal team, with which the Australians run exchange postings. This illustrates one of the characteristics of the Australian regiment, which is its function as a clearing-house of information about special forces operations in much of the western world. While the Vietnam war was being fought, for example, Australian SAS instructors at the Jungle Warfare School in Malaya were relaying to British troops the lessons of that war, in particular the booby-traps—including lorry springs adapted as devices to impale a man against a tree—that the Vietcong had developed.

Another example concerns the development of SAS weapons. In Malaya the British SAS pioneered the use of the shotgun as a modern fighting weapon, a lesson they learned from the terrorists. In 1952, a British study of the jungle war revealed that up to 75 yards' range the likelihood of hitting a fleeting target in the jungle was greater with a shotgun than any other weapon. The Vietnamese experience, years later, revealed that despite the tons of bombs dropped from high-flying B–52s, about 70 per cent of casualties inflicted on the Vietcong and North Vietnamese forces were caused by infantry weapons. It was an Australian who studied the work of his own SAS regiment in Victnam and Borneo, Duncan J. Gordon, who followed the logic of contemporary jungle warfare by designing a convertible automatic shotgun able to fire belt-fed ammunition (like an orthodox machine-gun) or carbine-style ammunition carried in a box magazine.

The paradox of this ingenious and expert force is that its home base is remote from any obvious scene of conflict. How, therefore, does the Australian SAS justify its existence? It can do so by reference to two potential hazards to the country's security. One is the external problem of western security generally, in such sensitive areas as the Arabian Gulf. Australia depends on the infrastructure of economic activity in Europe and the US, so its defense interests are ultimately indivisible from those of its allies. At times of international crisis, such as the Soviet invasion of Afghanistan, the SAS is a valuable political instrument through which to express that reality as a military fact.

Somewhat more controversial, but equally important to Australia's military planners, is the potential need to defend a vast continent with a small, professional army. Although it is never socially admitted, and rarely acknowledged privately, Australia still has reason to fear that in an increasingly overcrowded world, its empty space and rich natural resources may make it a target for expansion by any one of several of its neighbors to the north. If Australia were faced, some day, with hostile landings at several widely separated points around its enormous coastline, then only the SAS possesses the mobility and the experience to generate training teams capable of leading local citizens' armies raised from the civilian population, leaving the regular forces to react in force to the area where the enemy attack is concentrated. This theory, expounded by some Australian SAS veterans, is one of the most novel in the canon of SAS military lore.

Bibliography

BOOKS

Banks, J. *The Wages of War.* Leo Cooper, London: 1977.

Barthrop, M. *Crater to the Creggan: The Royal Anglian Regiment, 1964–74.* Leo Cooper, London: 1976.

Barzilay, D. *The British Army in Ulster,* Vols. 2 and 3. Century Services, Belfast, 1973, 1978; Beekman Publications, New York: 1976.

Beaumont, R. A. *Military Elites: Special Fighting Units in the Modern World.* Robert Hale, London, 1976; Bobbs-Merrill, Indianapolis: 1974.

Blaxland, G. *The Regiments Depart: The British Army, 1945–70.* William Kimber, London: 1971.

Burchett, W. and Roebuck, D. *The Whores of War.* Penguin, London and New York: 1977.

Clutterbuck, R. *Guerrillas and Terrorists.* Faber and Faber, London: 1977.

Colvin, I. *The Rise and Fall of Moise Tshombe.* Leslie Frewin, London: 1968.

Cowles, V. *The Phantom Major.* Collins, London: 1958; Harper Row, New York: 1958.

Darby, P. *British Defence Policy East of Suez, 1947-1968.* Oxford University Press, Oxford and New York: 1973.

Dempster, C. and Tomkins, D. *Fire Power.* Corgi, London: 1978.

Devlin, P. *The Fall of the Northern Ireland Executive.* Paddy Devlin, Belfast: 1975.

Dillon, M. and Lehane, D. *Political Murder in Northern Ireland.* Penguin, London and New York: 1973.

Dobson, C. and Payne, R. *The Weapons of Terror: international terrorism at work.* Macmillan, London: 1979.

279

Farran, R. *Winged Dagger*. Collins, London: 1948.

Fleming, J. and Faux, R. *Soldiers on Everest*. H.M.S.O., London: 1977.

Greenwood, C. *Police Tactics in Armed Operations*. Arms and Armour Press, London: 1980.

Halliday, F. *Arabia Without Sultans*. Penguin, London and New York: 1974, 1975.

—— *Armed Struggle in Arabia: Counter Insurgency in Oman*. The Gulf Committee, 1976.

Harper, S. *Last Sunset*. Collins, London: 1978.

Hart, Sir Basil H. Liddell. *The Sword and the Pen: A Collection of the World's Greatest Military Writings*. Cassell, London: 1978; T. Y. Crowell, New York: 1976.

Hoare, M. *Congo Mercenary*. Robert Hale, London: 1967; Walker and Co., New York: 1967.

James, H. D. and Sheil-Small, D. *A Pride of Gurkhas*. Leo Cooper, London: 1975.

Kitson, F. *Bunch of Five*. Faber and Faber, London: 1977.

Maclean, F. *Eastern Approaches*. Jonathan Cape, London: 1949; US title: *Escape to Adventure*. Little Brown, Boston: 1950.

Mockler, A. *Mercenaries*. Macdonald, London: 1970.

Paget, J. *Last Post: Aden 1964–67*. Faber and Faber, London: 1969; Faber and Faber, Salem: 1969.

Pocock, T. *Fighting General—The Public and Private Campaigns of General Sir Walter Walker*. Collins, London: 1973.

Seale, P. and McConville, M. *The Hilton Assignment*. Temple Smith, London: 1973; Praeger, New York: 1973.

Smiley, D. and Kemp, P. *Arabian Assignment*. Leo Cooper, London: 1975.

Smith, E. D. *East of Katmandu* (7th Duke of Edinburgh's Own Gurkha Rifles). Leo Cooper, London: 1976.

Stirling, D. "The Special Air Service" (from *The World History of Paratroopers* by Pierre Sergent) Soc. de Prod. Litteraire, Paris: 1974.

Sunday Times Insight Team *Ulster*.

Swearengen, T. F. *The World's Fighting Shotguns*. Arms and Armour Press, London: 1979; T.B.N. Enterprise, Alexandria: 1978.

Taber, R. *The War of the Flea:* A Study of Guerrilla Warfare, Theory and Practice. Paladin, London: 1970; Citadel Press, Secaucus: 1970.

Ten Years of Terrorism: Collected views. Royal United Services Institute, London: 1979; Crane Russak, New York: 1979.

Townsend, J. *Oman: The Making of the Modern State*. Croom Helm, London: 1977; St. Martin's Press, New York: 1977.

Walker, General Sir Walter. *The Bear at the Back Door.* Foreign Affairs Publishing Co., London: 1978.

Warner, P. *The Special Air Service.* William Kimber, London: 1971.

Watson, P. *War on the Mind: The Military Uses and Abuses of Psychology.* Hutchinson, London: 1978; Basic Books, New York: 1978.

Young, D. *Four Five: 45 Commando, Royal Marines, 1943–71.* Leo Cooper, London: 1972.

PERIODICALS

Daily Express, 13 January 1976; *Daily Mail,* 17 September 1977; *Daily Mirror,* 19 December 1977; *The Daily Telegraph,* 4 February 1970; *The Guardian,* 11 December 1976 and 3 August 1979; *Mars & Minerva* (Journal of the SAS Regiment); *The Republican News,* 24 June 1978; *Sunday Dispatch* (series), September 1959; *Sunday People,* 6 August 1967; *The Sunday Times,* 18 January 1970, 9 May 1976, 10 July 1977, 17 July 1977 and 27 November 1977; *The Times,* 9 April 1959; *Time Out,* 21-27 July 1978 and 8-14 December 1978; *Wire* (The Journal of the Royal Corps of Signals).

Index

incident at Long Jawi, 54; cross-border reconnaissance missions into Indonesia ("Claret"), 57-63; Lillico Patrol, 63-65; Radfan operations, 72-74, 91-92; Edwards Patrol, 78-87; urban counter-terrorist activities in Aden, 87-91; campaigns in Oman, 119-156; Jabal Akhdar ("Green Mountain") campaign, 120-131; Dhofar campaign, 132-156; Operation "Storm," 136, 137; Battle of Mirbat, 140-150; Firqa technique, 150-154, 155; begin operations in Northern Ireland, 158; become part of military intelligence in Ulster, 165; first orthodox SAS squadron used in Ulster, 169; in South Armagh, 172-176; the John Boyle incident, 178-185; establishment of Counter Revolutionary Warfare Team, 192; anti-terrorist weapons, 193-195, 201-202; at Balcombe Street siege, 195; at Mogadishu airline hijack, 197-200; anti-terrorist tactics, 201-204; at Iranian Embassy siege in London, 13, 187, 205-210; assault on Everest by members of Regiment, 216-223; selection process, 227-232, 239-244; specialist training, 244-251; composition of Regiment, 249-250; pay and preferment, 251-252; casualties, 254-255; links with US Special Forces, 256-257; Regimental journal (Mars & Minerva), 56, 63, 237, 247; Mobility Troop, 244; Sabre squadrons, 41, 195, 228, 244; Special Boat Eervice, 8; Territorials and Reserves, 23, 25, 39, 98, 102, 110, 117, 282; Squadrons: A, 23, 25, 26, 41, 49, 51, 72, 74, 87, 93, 98, 128; B, 23, 26, 41, 54, 71, 87, 111, 140, 148; C, see Rhodesian SAS; D, 36, 38, 41, 53, 63, 74, 87, 123, 127, 128, 158, 160, 173; G, 55, 148, 250

Special Air Service Regiment, New Zealand, 34, 55, 268-275

Special Air Service Regiment (C Squadron), Rhodesian, 23, 26, 34, 41, 103, 112, 115, 228, 257-268

Special Forces Club, 2

Special Military Intelligence Unit, 165, 166, 167

Special Operations Executive (SOE), 17, 22, 23, 98, 99

Springfield Road, Belfast, 168

Stansted Airport, 195

Stirling, Colonel David: on military ability and philosophy of the SAS, 2, 3, 4; career, 4,5; approaches Auchinlek with plan for strategic raids, 6; captured in Tunisia, 7; rôle of SAS envisaged by him, 15; mercenary activities of, 97, 101, 106, 107, 108, 109; mentioned, 16, 23, 34, 113, 115, 128, 256

Stirling, William, 8

"Stockholm syndrome," 204

Stokes, Sergeant John ("Brummie"), 4, 216, 217, 218, 219, 220, 221, 222, 223

"Storm," Operation, 33, 136